IN MY OWN TIME

Inside Irish Politics and Society

IN MY OWN TIME

Inside Irish Politics and Society

JAMES DOWNEY

Gill & Macmillan

Gill & Macmillan Ltd
Hume Avenue, Park West, Dublin 12
with associated companies throughout the world
www.gillmacmillan.ie

© James Downey 2009
978 07171 4636 9

Index compiled by Helen Litton
Typography design by Make Communication
Print origination by O'K Graphic Design, Dublin
Printed and bound in Great Britain by the MPG Books Group

This book is typeset in 12/14.5 pt Minion.

The paper used in this book comes from the wood pulp
of managed forests. For every tree felled, at least one
tree is planted, thereby renewing natural resources.

A CIP catalogue record for this book is available from
the British Library.

5 4 3 2

CONTENTS

PREFACE

ardinal John Carmel Heenan entitled his autobiography *Not the Whole Truth.* The ill-fated Marshal Petain said that people wrote their memoirs solely to disparage their enemies. George Orwell thought that memoirists could not avoid boosting themselves beyond their merits.

They were all at least partly right. Nobody can tell the whole truth; it is hard enough not to distort what one knows. Disparagement of one's enemies, with or without malice, comes with the territory. Boosting yourself is wholly unavoidable, when you are your own central character, and false modesty is worse than exaggerating your merits and achievements. Novelists have it easier, as the great A.J. Liebling observed.

Over the several years during which I made tentative and erratic plans for this book, I kept these points firmly in mind. I was concerned most of all with accuracy and fairness. It baffles me that so many people can describe so sloppily and inaccurately events they have witnessed and personalities they have known intimately, and risk confusing cause and effect with their hopeless grasp of chronology. That is not to say that I can vouch that my own work is free of errors, and I greatly regret that I have made very few attempts to keep a diary, and these sporadically and unhelpfully. Everybody should keep a diary. I am still blessed, in old age, with a good memory, but it sometimes fails me on precise dates and I have had a lot of difficulty in checking certain facts, because those who could enlighten me have died and there is no documentary evidence—at any rate, none available to myself.

Originally I planned this work for posthumous publication, partly for fear of the cruel Irish libel laws. From time to time, many friends urged me to publish in my lifetime, and as soon as possible. I have in a drawer hundreds of pages of notes and attempts at whole chapters, most of which, in the event, I have drawn on very little. At last, in 2007, my liver gave me a serious reminder of mortality. These things concentrate minds. In the end, I wrote the entire book, starting at the beginning, in the nine months from September 2007 to the end of May 2008. I completed the revision in February 2009.

Its shape is unusual. It begins with family history, my childhood and youth, and a description of life in the most impoverished part of Ireland in the postwar period, which was also a period of mass emigration, social breakdown and despair. It moves on to my career in journalism, inevitably at most length and with most emphasis in respect of my quarter-century with the *Irish Times* and how it ended. So far, so good, chronologically speaking. But intermingled with the account of my own life is an account of the political developments. Here I sometimes agree with, and sometimes challenge, the conventional wisdom. My views are based on exceptional knowledge of the characters and events. I have known, often intimately, almost all the main Irish players North and South, and quite a few in Britain and farther afield; and I hope I can claim the interest of readers who want an honest, objective and, so far as possible, impartial view of them. Those who have no wish to read the family history or the descriptions of ways of life now dead and gone can skip, if they like, to the politics and journalism. But I think it worth recording where an author came from and what influences, familial or environmental, made him; and I hope that younger readers especially will find interest and perhaps profit in my descriptions of life in Leitrim and Dublin in a society so different from the one in which they have themselves grown up.

I thank most sincerely all those who have helped me, by encouragement, by refreshing my memory, and by pointing out to me incidents which made me reconsider my own recollections of particular events. I owe a special debt of gratitude to my wife Moira and my daughters Rachel and Vanessa, whose intense interest in my work—and whose frequent and occasionally excessive praise—have helped to sustain me through tougher times. Catriona Crowe and Andrew Whittaker made invaluable comments on the present work. Don Lavery set me right on the truth of a couple of intriguing stories. I must also thank Mike Burns, Seán Donlon, Vinny Doyle, Seán Duignan, Pat Foley, Dermot Gallagher, Colm Hefferon, Peggy Hefferon, John Horgan, John McColgan, David McKittrick, Seamus Martin, Mary Maher, P.J. Mara, Conor O'Clery, Pat O'Hara, Gerry O'Regan, Arthur Reynolds and Michael Wolsey—and apologise to anyone whose name has been inadvertently omitted. Finally, I cannot praise sufficiently the insight and professionalism of Fergal Tobin, prince of publishers, and his team at Gill & Macmillan.

In my concluding chapter here, I say how much I have enjoyed writing over the decades. I cannot say the same for this book. It has been dreadfully hard work, the hardest of my long life, and writing it has forced me to recall and contemplate many painful memories. But Dr Samuel Johnson said that what is written without pain is usually read without much pleasure. I hope it gives my readers pleasure.

James Downey
2009

| 1933: DROMAHAIR

Aunt Mary, my father's sister, was a lady of wit and grace, and of a cheerful and optimistic disposition, spoiled only by a conviction that we had all been deprived of our inheritance.

Our branch of the not very numerous Downey clan were long settled in the King's County, now Offaly, where they owned a substantial estate in the early and middle nineteenth century. It would be nice to fancy that they were old Catholic gentry who had somehow managed to hold on to their property throughout a century of oppressive Penal Laws, when Catholics were forbidden to own land, but of that there is not one chance in ten thousand. Most likely they had risen in the world by means of trade and taken out a mortgage to buy their estate after 1793, when a measure passed by the semi-independent Irish parliament, 'Grattan's Parliament', permitted Catholics to own land freehold.

From time to time I have heard at least three different accounts of how Aunt Mary's ancestors and mine lost possession of the property. She held that it should have passed to her grandfather and from him to her father, as the eldest sons of eldest sons, and dropped hints of a wicked uncle. My father thought it much more probable that the owner in whatever generation bequeathed it to a younger son on the sensible grounds of competence. At any rate, my grandfather John Downey had to start again at the bottom. He worked as a labourer before joining the Royal Irish Constabulary (RIC) and serving as a sergeant in the remote hill village of Coolaney in County Sligo.

Aunt Mary took pride in her grand connections and kept among her mementoes a photograph of a British general, her father's cousin. This must have been Lieutenant General Sir Edward Bulfin, one of the better staff officers (there were few enough of these) in the first world war. My father professed a disdain for any such sentimentality.

John Downey married late in life. His wife, very much younger, was

Annie Goodwin from Grangegeeth, near Slane in County Meath. Her father, John Goodwin, was a prosperous farmer whose forebears had held their land, albeit as tenants, for centuries. Their tenancy, and a public house licence, supposedly dated back at least as far as the Battle of the Boyne, fought nearby on 1 July 1690. According to the family folklore, they could hear the guns booming but carried on making the hay.

John Goodwin, like many of his relatives and neighbours, was a devoted follower of Charles Stewart Parnell, who represented Meath in the British House of Commons, where he led the Irish parliamentary party: blindly devoted indeed, to the point where he refused to believe the stories of his hero's affair with Katharine O'Shea, whose disclosure brought about Parnell's downfall. My grandmother as a young girl overheard a conversation between her father and one of his farm workers. He opened a newspaper and said: 'We're done for, Dominic. He's married her!' In other words, he had not been convinced even by the successful divorce action brought by Katharine O'Shea's husband, and only the marriage proved to him that he had been wrong.

In private matters, though, John Goodwin was no romantic, but hard-headed and hard-fisted. He was angered by his daughter's desire to marry a poor man. He retaliated by withholding her dowry, an action which gave Aunt Mary better grounds for resentment than any legend about what had occurred on the Downey side of the family. His behaviour was cruel but not uncommon in that society.

In later years he made a lot of money. Legend had it that some of it, in the form of gold coins, was buried under the floorboards in his house. But when his grand-nephew Gerry McGuinness, who inherited the place, had the house rebuilt, he found nothing. Doubtless the coins, if they existed, had been transformed into bank accounts and shares.

Dowry or no dowry, Annie was happy in Coolaney; happy, too, in Drogheda where the family lived when her husband retired from the RIC. They lived in Trinity Street, in a delightful little house, stuffed with the furniture of an earlier age, with an elevated back garden which afforded a view across the River Boyne to the fields beyond. My father claimed to have recollections of childhood poverty, but that is odd: my grandfather had an RIC pension and an income from working as a bookkeeper. The answer must have been improvidence on my grandfather's part, a characteristic presumably inherited from the man who lost the land and passed on to my father and myself.

There were four children of the marriage: Mary, the only girl, and three boys. Gerard became a Revenue official in Dublin. He died young, leaving six children and a wife pregnant with a seventh. Michael spent most of his life as a parish priest in Australia. The youngest, my father Patrick, went to the De La Salle teacher training college in Waterford. There followed a sequence of events which he never explained and which remained a mystery to me.

He must have been a brilliant student. In his final examinations, he came first in the country in both Irish and English. Yet instead of finding a job in Dublin or some other substantial population centre he chose to bury himself away in a tiny, though very pretty, village in Leitrim, in a region looked on by his siblings and cousins as a place where 'the children have no shoes.' His first school, Kilcoosey, was not even in the village but in the countryside four miles away. He lodged in a small farmhouse which lacked almost all the creature comforts to which he had been accustomed in Drogheda. He called the village and the neighbourhood a 'magical' place, but delight in the magic hardly compensated for the more satisfying career he might have had, the want of company at his own intellectual level, or the frustration he must have felt from knowing that very few of his pupils, no matter how bright, had any prospect of a career suited to their talents.

Soon after his arrival he did meet someone who was his equal in intellect—James McGowan, principal of the national school in Dromahair and my maternal grandfather. It is one of the regrets of my life that I never knew him, for he died before I was born. He was a powerful and colourful character, endlessly engaged in a variety of controversies and confrontations with other figures of authority from the parish priest and the Church of Ireland rector to the British government. He was the secretary of the local co-operative (the co-operative movement, organised by Sir Horace Plunkett, was then a force in the land) and for one year, 1909, president of the Irish National Teachers' Organisation. In that capacity he travelled to Westminster to meet the Chancellor of the Exchequer, David Lloyd George. Closer to home, he wrote letters to the teachers' journal, arrogant and dismissive in tone as when he told his brethren that in matters of the governance of Ireland the Viceroy did not matter, the Chief Secretary ruled. (That was not entirely accurate, since some viceroys did interfere in politics, but they would hardly have concerned themselves with matters like teachers' pay.) After independence, although his sympathies lay with the Cumann na nGaedheal government, he denounced the agriculture minister as 'the minister for grass' and stood for the Dáil, unsuccessfully, as an independent candidate.

He commanded tremendous respect in the neighbourhood and was frequently consulted on business and legal matters, there being no solicitor in the village. During the first world war, when farm prices skyrocketed, he advised farmers who had got hold of some real cash income for the first time in their lives to buy British war bonds instead of keeping the money in the bank. 'Ah! Master,' one man replied, 'the banks are safe.' They would have been far from safe if Britain had lost the war.

He was fearless and endlessly combative. Unusually, the Catholic church in the village was not built until 1891. Before that, Mass was said in private houses. The congregation sometimes spilled out into the street. Legend has it that on one occasion a land agent called La Touche tried to make a way through the crowd in his carriage. McGowan confronted him, berating him for disturbing a religious service. When La Touche lifted his whip, McGowan told him that if he used it, it would be the last blow he ever struck.

Another land agent, Wilton Vaugh, brought a Rhinelander, Josef Jeiter, to build a hotel in the village. Under his ownership and that of his sons Frank and Paul, it became famous as the Abbey Hotel, long a haunt of anglers. When the first world war broke out, feeling in the locality was high in favour of John Redmond, the nationalist leader who committed his volunteer force to fighting for the British in France. Again according to legend, some idiots decided that they should lynch Jeiter as a German spy and went so far as to fetch a rope for the purpose. McGowan appeared on the scene and denounced them as 'poor unfortunate fools', whereupon they slunk away. Jeiter was interned by the British authorities as an 'enemy alien' in Sligo Prison, where, alas, he soon died.

James McGowan's confrontations by no means ended there. There were sensational incidents during the civil war, engendered by the activities of his daughter Florence and his son Joe. Contrary to the general family feeling and the overwhelming view of the neighbourhood, both of them took the anti-Treaty or 'republican' side. Joe was captured by Free State forces, imprisoned and sentenced to death, but survived thanks to the amnesty granted at the end of the civil war. Florence carried despatches for the republicans. She had a relationship—I have no idea of its length or how far it went—with a local IRA chief, Ned Bofin. Towards the end of the conflict Bofin and his men established themselves in the Arigna Mountains, south of Dromahair. One night two of them came down to the village, overpowered the Free State guards on the McGowan house, and abducted Florence. She went willingly, but not before her father descended the stairs in his nightshirt and denounced the abductors. She and the raiders then forded the River Bonet below the village and made their way to a small Church of Ireland rectory, Killenumery. The rector gave them shelter and spent most of the night arguing politics with them.

She returned home within weeks. By then Bofin and his men must have accepted that their cause was lost and Bofin must have been planning to escape to England.

In my childhood I heard partial versions of this story from my grandmother. Eventually I got a full account from a Leitrim county registrar, Shane Flynn. So this part of the tale at least is fact, not folklore.

Joe McGowan's brother Charles was then studying for the priesthood. The new Free State authorities suspected him of involvement in the burning of the local Garda barracks while on vacation at home; he may have stood by and watched the fun. They took him to Sligo Prison. Any father might have been distressed, but James McGowan had more reason than most for anger since his son could have been expelled from college and lost his chance of ordination. A furious row resulted in his assaulting a Free State officer, whereupon he, too, was taken to prison in, bizarrely, an armoured car. He made the driver stop the car while he went to buy underclothes, then marched down the street to the shop holding one arm at the customary angle for carrying his missing umbrella. He was quickly released. He was also dismissed from his job, but soon reinstated. No doubt the former INTO president had plenty of influence in the right quarters.

James McGowan's wife, my maternal grandmother Nell Devine, was one of a remarkable clan who lived at Kesh in County Sligo. Whereas Patrick Downey never bragged about his supposedly grand forebears, Nell and her relatives took tremendous pride in their cleric-laden ancestry. They claimed that through the Devines and other ancestors, Fitzmaurice and McDermott by name, they could boast priests in every generation as far back as the eighteenth century. Research ultimately showed that they had understated the facts. Nell's nephew Father Tom Devine traced his ancestors back through eight generations—a considerable feat in Ireland, owing to the lack of reliable records—and found priests in each of them. After his death, relatives who had thought his obsession with ancestry absurd found themselves in possession of a document which proved them wrong.

Some of his discoveries were the product of chance, not diligence. On a pilgrimage to Lourdes, he noticed the name Devine on a shopfront and decided to investigate. He thereby unknowingly obeyed two maxims of journalism, always go everywhere and never fail to follow up a 'lead'. Right enough, the proprietor of the shop informed him that he was descended from a man who towards the end of the eighteenth century had fled Anglo-Saxon rule in Ireland (he may have played some role in the Rising of 1798) by emigrating to Louisiana. He had not lived there long when Napoleon sold Louisiana to the United States. Unwilling to exchange one version of Anglo-Saxon rule for another, Mr Devine emigrated to France, settled there and founded a family.

There are several gaps in Tom Devine's document. It tells us more about the clerical connections than the direct ancestors and gives us little clue to their possessions and living standards. A pity, because in every branch of my family one can see hints, if no more, of how the Irish Catholic middle class developed over centuries: in the church, in the changing patterns of landholding and agriculture, and in efforts to break into the professions. Two of Devine's collateral ancestors in the eighteenth century were British naval surgeons: chosen, no doubt, for their proficiency in sawing off legs during a sea battle and not for more arcane skills.

Of the priests, the farthest back, one of the Fitzmaurices, was ordained in 1697. He must have led a hard life, trying to minister to his flock when the Penal Laws against Catholics were at their harshest, in endless danger of imprisonment or worse; and it is impossible to guess how the family found the money to send him and those who came after him during the eighteenth century to France for their education. Most likely a network existed to fund the expenses and arrange the travel.

Travelling to and from France must have been immensely difficult in the west and north-west of Ireland, compared with the easy access to the continent from the ports of the south and south-east. As to the money, it may well be that people like the Devines, Fitzmaurices and McDermotts always had some in hand, earned by dint of hard work, thrift, and carefully negotiated marriages. In a later age, the turn of the nineteenth–twentieth century, the bride of John P. Devine, one of my grandmother's brothers, brought with her a dowry of £300, a fortune in those days and surely very hard earned. This time the gold coins were real. They were poured out on to a table in Kesh. As the operation proceeded, a shaft of sunlight came through the window and shone on the treasure, a dazzling sight. The table is still there.

Another brother, Michael, was a prize-winning Maynooth student, but not destined for high office in the church. He was an arrogant and quarrelsome character who held the higher clergy in great disdain and spent most of his ministry in the remote and rushy parish of Geevagh in County Sligo (close to the Arigna Mountains and in recent years the scene of damaging mudslides). There is still a splendid photograph of him in the family house in Kesh, taken in 1907, which shows that even as a young man he had a supercilious glare. He exerted himself on behalf of his nieces and nephews in arranging for their education, and I suspect that he got school fees reduced through bullying. It was not unknown then, or in earlier or later ages, for priests to divert church funds for such purposes or keep them for themselves. But avarice was not in Michael Devine's character. He neglected his living conditions and his diet abominably. Stephen Derham, a Sligo solicitor and a friend of my father, once attended a court sitting in Geevagh. In those days the district courts did not sit until midday and the litigants and witnesses had plenty of time to stoke themselves up with Dutch courage in the pub. Devine came in. He refused Derham's offer of a drink, saying that 'I've only come here for my breakfast.' He then ordered and consumed a bottle of brandy and a dozen raw eggs.

As a teenager I attended his funeral, courteously presided over by a bishop who had suffered slights from Michael Devine in his lifetime. There followed the Reading of the Will, the only such event I have experienced: a shame, since readings of wills afforded opportunities for great Agatha Christie-style drama. All the bequests went to parishes and convents, none to relatives.

Michael Devine's uncle, Archdeacon John McDermott, supposedly was the model for 'the old priest Peter Gilligan' in the poem by W.B. Yeats. The legend has it that Gilligan/McDermott arrives home weary after a long day ministering to victims of a disease epidemic, and falls asleep on a chair. A young man arrives to inform him that his father, on his deathbed, needs a priest to administer the last rites. The old man falls asleep again, wakes up suddenly and full of guilt, and rides to the stricken home. He finds the father dead. The people there, astonished, tell him that he has already visited them. The legend takes root that God has sent an angel in his guise. There is a rational explanation. I have witnessed incidents in which people suffering from extreme fatigue could not remember significant actions performed hours or days earlier. McDermott simply could not recall the first visit.

There was a famine, followed by an epidemic, in parts of the west of

Ireland, including Sligo and North Roscommon, in 1879. It hit the affected areas as hard as the Great Famine of the 1840s had afflicted the whole country. However, either the McDermott incident occurred at a later date or the reference to an 'old priest' is wrong. McDermott died in 1931, so he certainly was not an old man half a century earlier.

My grandmother claimed to remember 'the famine', meaning the famine of 1879. She would have been four years old at the time. The Land League, which agitated for tenants' rights, was founded in the same year. She remembered a speech by 'a man with one arm', clearly the founder, Michael Davitt. Her father, Fitzmaurice Devine, became active in the Land League, which campaigned, first for tenants' rights, then for peasant proprietorship. She described him reading *The Nation* aloud in the kitchen to an audience of neighbours who may have been illiterate or, more likely, simply too poor to buy a newspaper. Thus were the opinions of the Dublin nationalist intelligentsia mediated to small farmers in deprived parts of the country.

Nell's daughter Florence McGowan married Patrick Downey, ten years her junior, in 1932. They lived with her in the post office. My birth enlarged the family to four persons, and the arrival of my sister Eva made it five. But not long after Eva's birth, our mother fell ill, stricken with cancer. She died a lingering death before I reached the age of three. The earliest memory of which I am certain is of going to the house of friends a couple of miles away: myself walking, a maid holding my hand while she pushed Eva's pram with her other hand. I suppose we were sent there to get us out of the way during the funeral.

I cannot say what it is like to lose a mother, since I have no recollection either of herself or of how I learned of her death and I was much too young to understand the meaning of death. My experience therefore differs greatly from that of my Leitrim contemporary John McGahern, a man whom I would come to know in adult life. McGahern's mother died when he was eight. He immortalised her in his books, especially his final work *Memoir*, so moving and so beautiful in the writing that it cannot be read without tears. I have no McGahern-type memories either to glory in or to trouble me, no emotional consciousness of deprivation, but I think from time to time of what I must have missed and how much worse it must have been for Eva, a motherless girl.

I sometimes think, too, of Nell's unenviable situation. Before my mother died she had suffered through the deaths of her husband and two of her eleven daughters. Four of the other girls had become nuns in faraway convents, one in South Africa, and she did not expect ever to see them again. Now she faced having to raise two more children. We were brought up by a prematurely aged grandmother and a stern, aloof father who would soon become, for reasons I will explain, often an absent father.

———

The old Dromahair post office was built, early in the twentieth century, on rather eccentric lines. The post office, and the adjoining mail sorting office, fronted on to the village street, opposite the Abbey Hotel. At a right angle were the dining room and sitting room, and a narrow hallway which led to the kitchen and scullery. Upstairs were five bedrooms. The two best overlooked a small garden dominated by two enormous cypress trees. In one of these bedrooms I was born in the early hours of 20 September 1933. My father, who even as a very young man was devoutly religious, went at once to the church to give prayerful thanks for my safe delivery. In those more law-abiding days, churches could stay open all night without risk from thieves or vandals.

Almost all the houses in the district, even those bigger and better than ours, were damp and draughty. In ours, the woodwork was atrocious. There were hardly any modern gadgets, and central heating was unknown: the house was heated by turf and coal fires, and for a time during and after the second world war by briquettes from the Arigna mines. These were quite unlike turf briquettes. They were spherical, made of inferior coal, and burned very badly. My father was preoccupied every autumn with the problem of getting good turf instead of soggy cartloads, and lighting fires was far from easy.

Gran had a different preoccupation. Among her favourite nineteenth-century aphorisms (like 'tell the truth and shame the devil' and 'wilful waste makes woeful want') was the one that puts cleanliness next to godliness. I have no doubt that she regarded it as an indication of social status and good upbringing at least as much as a matter of comfort. She always had a maid, as well as an assistant in the post office, but she did much of the housework herself. She had a particular passion for spring cleaning and watched keenly for a spell of fine weather, by no means a common occurrence in what passes for spring in the West of Ireland. When it happened, the house would be turned topsy-turvy for days on end and living in it became almost unbearable. As to our personal hygiene, few children in the period can have been more often or more thoroughly scrubbed.

Our upbringing was strict in the extreme. Corporal punishment was then all but universal: casual or calculated, depending on class more than location. Small farmers and their wives might inflict a blow of a fist on their children, or beat them with whatever instrument came to hand. In a later generation, I encountered an old woman on Achill Island while on holiday there with my wife and daughters, then aged about nine and seven. She commented on the girls' good manners, which she attributed to their having had 'many a skelp of a buachallán' (lash of a ragwort stalk) and would not believe me when I told her that I had never laid a finger on them.

Middle-class and upper-middle-class parents, in Ireland as in Britain, kept canes or leather straps in their houses, brought out for the pettiest offences. They believed in regulation and deprivation. In the pre-Dr Spock era, mollycoddling children was regarded almost as criminal. For example, breast-feeding of babies was very rare, and it was thought proper to allow them to cry rather than break the routine of their bottle feeds. Snacks outside meal times were equally rare. In that respect at least, children of all classes were better off than those of the present day.

Such were the practices and principles—'spare the rod and spoil the child'—of normal decent people. They were as much part of the accepted fabric as Gran's Victorian maxims. In my childhood I was of course unaware of the abominations which have since become the subject of so much controversy and shame, from the violent attacks of John McGahern's deranged father on his children to the sadism in state institutions run by religious orders and the excesses in schools, even elite schools. The system in our respectable home was quite enough to instil fear into us.

Along with fear went guilt, and for that we can blame, above all, the Catholic church. I do not mean to add much to the abundant literature on the subject. Enough to say that I believed, like millions of others, that every one of my peccadilloes contributed to the suffering of Jesus and that I lived in imminent danger of eternal damnation. We were urged to frequent performance of the Stations of the Cross, reflecting on each stage of Christ's journey to his agonising death. Holy Week, when these reflections reached their greatest intensity and the church ceremonies their greatest length, was an orgy of guilt and fear, for which joyful Easter hardly compensated.

Perhaps—although of this I am uncertain—my feelings of guilt and fear were alleviated by an unorthodox view held by my pious grandmother. She believed that Hell existed but that God was too merciful to send anybody there.

'Not even Hitler?'

'Not even Hitler.'

A greater consolation, no doubt, was the assurance that we could find salvation in the one true holy Catholic and apostolic church. Confusion reigned as to whether this guarantee was exclusive to Catholics. We had numerous Protestant friends and neighbours and my father entered the Protestant (Church of Ireland) church for funerals when the Catholic church still forbade its members to attend. Could these friends and neighbours achieve salvation too? Well … yes, but it was harder for them because they ate meat on Fridays and had misguided ideas about justification by faith and some were Presbyterians who believed in predestination. But as good people they had as much chance as ourselves of reaching Heaven—not that anyone would bet on our own chances.

These good people were more numerous than is usual in rural Ireland. Still more unusually, they belonged to all grades in society. Humphrey Kelleher from Cork, who married my sister Eva, said he had never met a poor Protestant until he visited Dromahair. The man he met was a farmer, not in fact particularly poor. Another was the village postman. But most of our Protestant neighbours were shopkeepers or relatively prosperous farmers, or members of the upper middle class. Doreen Robinson, the daughter of a small shopkeeper, taught the piano in a dark little room dominated by pictures of King George VI and his queen and stuffed with the kind of furniture that filled my paternal grandmother's dining room and sitting room in Drogheda. Doreen was a patient teacher, but I was not an attentive or skilful pupil.

For Catholics, direct clerical influence was not confined to the shadow of all those priestly heroes in my more or less distant ancestry. We were surrounded by footsoldiers of the remote and revered Pope. Everyone accorded them a degree of deference and esteem which would be unbelievable in the present age.

We were visited by my uncles Father Michael Downey and Father Charles McGowan. They were untypical footsoldiers; rather, to me they appeared persons of awesome sophistication. Both had very Anglicised accents. Walking one day with Uncle Charles, we strolled along an avenue of trees. I called them elms, pronouncing the word 'ellums' in my Leitrim accent. He tried to get me to pronounce it something like 'woms'. In fact they were lime trees.

Well or poorly educated, sophisticated or crude, rational or eccentric, all the priests I knew in my youth had this in common, that they totally believed in the doctrines they preached and in the validity of their work. In adult life I was shocked to learn that some Protestants thought them cynical because they wrongly assumed that priests did not believe in the doctrine of the Real Presence. Eventually I was more shocked to discover that this was true of a good many of them, including bishops and cardinals.

Teachers lived under a dual tyranny, of the church and of the government inspectorate. Much school time was devoted to Christian doctrine classes, and a priest, specially appointed by the Catholic diocese for the purpose, conducted rigorous annual examinations. More widely, it is only a slight exaggeration to say that much of the population lived under a clerical reign of terror. One or two orders of priests specialised in 'missions', usually annual and lasting several days, at which they delivered sermons on hellfire similar to that famously described by James Joyce in *A Portrait of the Artist as a Young Man.* Their theme was always the same, the sins of the flesh. One who preached in my time to the boys at Newbridge College claimed to have witnessed a young couple hit by a bolt of lightning, 'struck down in the midst of their sin'. No doubt that was standard fare. In Carlow, I would find, pubs were obliged to close while the missions were in progress. Hundreds of thousands of men belonged to confraternities, of which the most notorious was the 'archconfraternity' in Limerick. Often their social status and even their livelihoods depended on regular church attendance and other symbols of piety, such as making pilgrimages to the Marian Shrine at Knock in County Mayo. Neighbours spied on one another and commented on whether those they watched came up to the mark.

However, in my early life the most common talk about priests, even among the devout like my father, concerned neither their sanctity nor their tyranny but their foibles. One of our parish priests drank great quantities of cider and often turned up late for Mass. Another denounced members of his own flock as 'Stone Age savages' and had a particular aversion to the 'sharpshooters' who knelt on one knee at the back of the church. He managed to force them into seats. He encouraged Catholics to assault Jehovah's Witnesses and devoted sermons to mocking Protestant doctrine on the Eucharist. This happened as late as the 1960s, by which time fewer people were willing to tolerate the insults or the bigotry. When

I visited the village on holidays, I thought the sermons very amusing, but my father did not find them at all funny, and he was right.

Dad's chief clerical friend Father John Keaney, parish priest of a neighbouring parish, preferred to talk about food and wine. He had been educated at the Irish College in Paris and spoke fluent French with an accent identical to that of Edith Piaf. Early in his ministry he had found himself obliged to help out some former students of the same college. It seems they had been evacuated to escape the revolution of 1871 and ordained on the promise that they would somehow complete their education. The promises were seldom kept, and half-educated clergy were baffled by church documents circulated to them from time to time. The documents were neither in English nor in French but in Latin, which Keaney had to translate for them.

He drank whiskey copiously, a practice which may have strained his inadequate income and stoked up his intense dislike of bank officials—by which he meant humble tellers, not the fat cats who have brought us so much trouble in our times. Yet in their numerous tête-à-têtes, he and my father talked about theology, not the iniquities of banking. And Dad accorded the clergy of all ranks and all characters the same excessive respect which they enjoyed from the uneducated.

———

Gloom was not confined to one's prospects in life and eternity; it was tangible as well. The local climate might have been specially designed with misery in mind. Because Dromahair lies among low hills, rain and mist, quickly blown away on the coast, linger for weeks on end. Shades of grey are the prevailing colour. For all the beauty of the surrounding countryside, the colours of the landscape are subfusc during most of the year. The scenery north of the village may resemble the Dolomites and the Italian lakes on a tiny scale when the sun shines, when Lough Gill is blue and calm and the gorse blooms, but it takes a rare brilliant day to make the drumlins look other than grey and brown. And in even the best of Irish villages—and ours was one of the best—the paint pot was used very sparingly when money was scarce.

Daily life was as dull as the drumlins. I have often been struck by the delineations of urban working-class life in the many memoirs and works of fiction on the subject. The authors may set out to describe unrelieved deprivation and misery, but most of them give us, in addition, some notion of the colour and movement of urban life—and, yes, the excitement. There was very little excitement in my childhood.

Yet there were compensations, and naturally it is the high and colourful points that I remember best: the shops dressed for Christmas, children's noses pressed against the windows in the classic manner; the bustle of the turkey market; Easter picnics, regardless of the showers; scones in a house where they served tea beside the Glencar Waterfall; day trips, sometimes a full week's holiday, in Strandhill or Rosses Point; trips to Bundoran with rides on the dodgems, the bumpers as we called them; picking fraughans on Bilberry Hill and blackberries and hazelnuts near the Loughnahoo marsh.

The highest point of all was our annual holiday in Drogheda, with side trips to the seaside and to our Meath relatives, my father's bachelor uncle at Grangegeeth and my grand-aunt Kate McGuinness's family in Nobber. Sometimes we were joined by our Dublin cousins, Uncle Gerard's children. The girls were exceedingly pretty: Eva and I thought them as glamorous as film stars. In those days the place was idyllic. By the roadside a stream ran along a fringe of mature trees; beside it a field of barley, higher up a rugged pasture. Uncle Tom Goodwin bred gigantic but docile Clydesdale horses, more I suppose as a hobby than for profit, and there is a photograph somewhere of three or four small children, our Downey cousins from Dublin, on one horse's back.

But if Uncle Tom and Aunt Kate treated us kindly, nothing could exceed the love lavished on us by our grandparents, Mamma and Pappa (as we called them, following the example of our father and aunt), by Aunt Mary, and by her husband Jimmy O'Reilly, one of the nicest men I have ever known. They and their six children were a model of a loving family, equalled in my experience only by the Hughes family, of whom I will write in due course. All of them were, like my father, devoted Catholics.

As a child I took time to learn that the treats we enjoyed were the preserve of the middle classes and farming families with decent incomes. Those naturally included people, like teachers, public officials, tradespeople and gardaí—of whom there were a great many, who must have been seriously under-employed—who lived at a level of comfort comparable to our own, as well as the truly affluent. From my earliest youth I was conscious of sharp social and economic differences, partly because Gran had a keen sense of her own social status, but not until I reached adulthood did I understand them clearly. And not until my teens or later did I understand fully that our little village must be one of the great inhabited sites of Ireland.

———

Just outside Dromahair—or rather, nowadays, inside it, since the Celtic Tiger housing boom—stands a 'fairy fort', a prehistoric passage grave. Nearby, where the River Bonet takes a sharp right turn and flows through a little gorge, are the remnants of a castle built in the fourteenth or fifteenth century, popularly known as 'O'Rourke's banqueting hall'. On the rising ground above it are a fortified manor house from the early seventeenth century, much better preserved, and the Lodge, in my childhood the residence of yet another land agent, Captain George Hewson. The building work on the site did not stop there. The late twentieth and early twenty-first centuries brought holiday homes and a French restaurant.

As the river flows alongside the village it descends through a series of rapids. It resumes a calm flow for its last couple of miles before it debouches into Lough Gill, close to the Lake Isle of Innisfree. On its right bank stands the crumbling wall of what supposedly was another O'Rourke castle. Legend has it that in the twelfth century Dervorgilla, wife of Tiernan O'Rourke, prince of Breffny, eloped from there with Diarmuid MacMurrough, king of Leinster. The elopement is the subject of a poem by Thomas Moore, whose friend Lord Byron thought the incident, which led to the Norman invasion and, in the popular imagination, all the subsequent woes of Ireland, the most romantic story he ever heard.

In a later age Margaret O'Brien, the wife of another O'Rourke prince, built Creevelea Abbey, on an eminence on the left bank of the Bonet opposite Dromahair. It is not an abbey but a Franciscan friary, the last founded in Ireland (1508) before the Protestant Reformation. Among its features are a carving, on a pillar in the cloister, of St Francis preaching to the birds; the grave, from the early nineteenth century, of a priest whose clay is said to produce cures; and the eighteenth-century grave, with a tombstone, now almost illegible, of an O'Rourke bishop. I once saw in Clonalis House in Roscommon, the ancestral home of the O'Connors, a remarkable document, a letter from the German emperor to Queen Anne, seeking a safe conduct for O'Rourke from the continent. He was permitted to return to Ireland and carry on his ministry.

Towards the end of the sixteenth century Breffny was ruled by Brian O'Rourke, known as Brian na Murtha ('of the battlements'). After the failed Spanish Armada expedition of 1588, the English decreed that survivors of Armada shipwrecks should be slaughtered. O'Rourke and allied or subordinate Irish chiefs, notably MacClancy of Kinlough, gave them succour. Captain de Cuellar, survivor of a wreck off Donegal, wrote a famous account of his travels through wild country to MacClancy's castle. Notwithstanding his gratitude for the shelter, he did not forbear to describe his discomfort in a building which he found primitive.

O'Rourke was in Scotland hiring mercenary troops—probably with Spanish gold, but just possibly with English, since some Irish lords thought nothing of taking money from both sides—when he was arrested. King James VI, afterwards James I of England, sent him to London, where he was executed. His son, another Brian, was one of the three princes who defeated the English at the Battle of the Curlews in 1599, the others being Hugh O'Donnell and Conor McDermott.

A remnant of O'Rourke power survived the final Irish defeat at Kinsale in 1601, and the family fought to some effect in the Great Rebellion of the 1640s.

Modern Dromahair, however, is the creation of a much later period, the turn of the nineteenth–twentieth century. It was laid out, largely by Wilton Vaugh, to resemble an English village, rather like those of the Lake District.

The local people, of all classes, were proud of this island of beauty and (for some) affluence in a sea of indigence and decline. They took pride, too, in the area's romantic history and folklore, and particularly in the exploits of the O'Rourkes, but there was at least equal romance in prehistory and legend. Nearby is Ben Bulben, the mountain to which the legendary Fionn Mac Cumhall pursued the fugitive lovers Diarmuid and Gráinne. There are two huge megalithic cemeteries, dominated by Knocknarea with a cairn, 'Maeve's cairn', on the summit. It is unlikely that an Iron Age queen is buried there; most probably the cairn forms part of the megalithic complex. But in those days we did not know the awesome age of these monuments.

As a child I did not recognise the decline, but from an early age I could see the poverty, in the village as well as the countryside.

Under-employed labourers lived in wretched, insanitary dwellings. Their children wore threadbare, ill-fitting clothes. Their diet consisted mainly of potatoes, bread with margarine or lard, a very few vegetables, a chicken at Easter, a turkey or a goose at Christmas, occasionally bacon. They hardly ever ate fresh beef or mutton, 'butcher's meat'. Young men, and some not so young, congregated under a lamp post: thanks to the Jeiters, Dromahair had its own electricity supply, powered by water. They were called corner boys—unfairly, since they were neither work-shy nor criminally inclined, but merely lacked opportunity in life. Neither were they drinkers, for they had no money for drink. They stood for hours, frequently in a drizzle, chatting and sharing cigarette ends.

Very early in life, too, I learned that there were people very much better off than ourselves. The villagers, like all villagers, were great snobs and said that the Hewsons and Vaughs were 'not real gentry'. The former land agents, however, had the last laugh. Hewsons married into very grand families, like the Whites of Newtownmanor, descendants of the Beresfords, in former times pillars of the Anglo-Irish ascendancy. George Hewson's son followed him into the British army and became a brigadier. While he was away at the war his two daughters came to live at the Lodge, where Eva and I sometimes played with them. I remember most vividly their kitchen garden, with sweet golden gooseberries the size of plums, altogether different from the hard, sour, unripe gooseberries on sale nowadays.

Wilton Vaugh made money and accumulated property in various parts of Leitrim. He was a notorious miser, who was said to dine on a bun while his wife ran a normal household on the income from her marriage settlement. His deathbed will (accessible on the Internet) is an intriguing document. At one point, while dictating numerous bequests, he interjects that his wife, to whom he left nothing, was well provided for under her marriage settlement. The two witnesses present at his bedside must have expostulated.

His daughter Charlotte, known as Lottie, was as generous as he was miserly. She married Frank Whyte, who came from a Catholic land-owning background in Wexford and was related to Count Francis Xavier Whyte, one of the prisoners released by the French revolutionaries from the Bastille in 1789. Their three daughters were brought up as Protestants under the old system whereby in mixed marriages the boys followed their father's religion and the girls their mother's. The youngest, Marguerite, married a Church of Ireland rector but after his death adhered to the Orthodox church. She taught me to ride. My mount was a pony called Tipsy, old and fat but good enough to get around the course at a gymkhana.

The Whytes built themselves a house on the lake and devoted themselves to maintaining and improving the woodlands on their property. Both were friends of my father. During the war Dad, as an officer in the Local Defence Force (LDF), worked closely with Lottie, a stalwart of the auxiliary nursing corps.

Just outside the village lived Miss Mary La Touche, whose considerable income derived from investment. She suffered in the Great Depression which followed the Wall Street crash of 1929. She told Dad: 'Mr Downey, I am now a pauper.' Her income had been reduced to £1,500 a year. As a teacher, he might have earned one-sixth of that sum.

A house in the hills above the lake was occupied by Harry Palmer, a bachelor squireen. A century earlier, the place was visited by Sir Robert Peel, then Chief Secretary, who may have been a distant relative of the Palmers. A spot on Lough Gill below, where he bathed, is still known as Sir Robert's Point.

———

I took in my own family's politics with the air and water. It was based on the 'traditional nationalist' view of Irish history which has since gone out of fashion. We had fought for our freedom for centuries; then the English had abolished our parliament, betrayed Parnell and cheated his successor John Redmond. Unable to achieve Home Rule peacefully, we had been forced to resort to armed revolution. Those dissatisfied with the 1921 Treaty had then rebelled against the new, legitimate government. My mother might have been a minor revolutionary heroine, but she and Uncle Joe had undoubtedly taken the wrong side in the civil war. Yet the legitimacy of Mr de Valera's government was never questioned, and our rulers of whatever party were considered, rightly for the most part, benign. When the second world war broke out, there was almost universal support for de Valera's policy of neutrality, of which more in a moment, but no doubt as to 'whose side we were neutral on'. Hitler, as must be obvious from the anecdote about Gran, was regarded as the epitome of evil long before we learned about the Holocaust, indeed before the Holocaust began. Some, recalling the Black and Tans less than twenty years earlier, might have wanted the British to get a bloody nose, like the man in another part of the country who said 'I'd like to see England nearly bet', but only a handful of diehards, and none to my knowledge in our locality, wanted Germany to win.

The war affected us in many ways, some far from obvious. We suffered hardly at all from food rationing, though I remember the 'black bread', in point of fact an unpleasant shade of grey. We did have to endure shortages of other commodities, especially clothes, and there was much patching and mending. But my chief memories are military in character.

Before the 'Emergency', de Valera had augmented the army by setting up a Volunteer force. Then came the part-time LDF (Local Defence Force, later the FCA) and the Local Security Force. Dad immediately joined the LDF: he eventually became a commandant in the FCA. I watched the drilling and marching and longed for an invasion which our brave lads would repel. Little did I know of the frightfulness of war; almost as little about the reality of de Valera's well-judged version of neutrality.

Twenty miles or so from us was the 'Ballyshannon corridor'. British pilots stationed in Northern Ireland had permission to fly a short distance over Free State territory to reach Donegal Bay and the Atlantic and thus save themselves a long detour. Often they strayed outside the corridor. People would run out of their houses to see the rare sight of an aircraft. If the airmen were looking for installations of military interest, they found none. They may have wandered off course, or merely wanted to see the scenery. The tiny border post at Manorhamilton, eight miles from Dromahair, was commanded by Lieutenant Jack McQuillan, who later embraced radical politics and made a name for himself as an honourable and quixotic man. McQuillan claimed to have shot down one of the British warplanes. It is perfectly possible to down a small plane at close range with machine-gun fire. I hope the crew survived.

Had I known about the incident as a small boy, I would have thought his action proper. My father most certainly would have disagreed. He thoroughly approved of de Valera's policy, which consisted of giving Britain all the help and support he possibly could short of allowing British troops on our soil. The authorities confiscated a two-way radio from the German diplomatic mission in Dublin. They passed on weather forecasts, unavailable to the Irish public, to the British. They interned stranded German prisoners—in easy conditions—while allowing captured British servicemen to go free. They bought arms from the British, who had little enough to spare. De Valera's confidant Frank Aiken sought American arms as well. He went to Washington and met President Franklin Roosevelt. The incident is recounted in Robert Fisk's book *In Time of War*. Roosevelt said he felt it reasonable to help the Irish to resist a German invasion. 'Or a British invasion,' Aiken put in. Roosevelt was so infuriated that he gave the tablecloth a ferocious tug which pulled it completely off the table.

Some have blamed Aiken for prompting a dreadful mistake on de Valera's part, visiting the German diplomatic mission in Dublin to sign a book of condolence when Hitler died in the ruins of Berlin. De Valera's weak justification was that the head of mission, Eduard Hempel, had always behaved well, unlike his American counterpart David Gray. We still do not know the full truth behind the incident.

We do, however, know the truth about the Irish military plans, which were highly realistic. In the event of a German invasion, de Valera would have called at once on the British for aid and they would have responded immediately. The Germans for their part made unrealistic plans, which would have involved occupying a chunk of the south-east, consolidating, and resting for a while before pressing on. The British would have crossed the border from Northern Ireland and, along with whatever elite forces we had available, met them as soon as they broke out. A German defeat, probably sooner rather than later, would have been certain.

Not for some decades afterwards did I learn that Dad had played a role in these matters: a minor role to be sure, but one well beyond his normal duties in the LDF. I have called him a largely absent father. During the war we saw little of him except at school. He frequently spent weekends close to the border or across it, in Fermanagh. There he both spied on the RAF and liaised with them on preparing for the crisis that never came. His work paid off when one of his contacts smuggled the plans for a new air base across the border in her underclothes.

Even as a small boy I knew where his sympathies lay. Like most of the population, he saw no contradiction between being a patriotic Irishman and wanting Britain to win. From his Intelligence contacts he would have known, as the general public did not, about the attempts by IRA extremists to support a Nazi invasion. He also knew something of Nazi methods which the wartime censorship kept out of the newspapers. When I was about ten years old I discovered two pamphlets in his desk, which he had left unlocked, presumably in the belief that I would not pry into it. These were British documents aimed at Irish 'opinion formers'. They gave horrifying accounts, based mostly on the evidence of Polish officers who had escaped from prison camps, of German atrocities. A year or two later came the liberation of the Belsen death camp and the devastating pictures of the survivors. On both occasions I thought that only Germans could do such things. I would grow up to learn much more—too much—about human depravity.

Strangely, however, I also remember the period as one of social activity. My father had many friends in Sligo and across North Leitrim, naturally including the Regular officers posted to Sligo and Manorhamilton. There were exotic visitors to the Abbey Hotel, like the left-republican Mulcahy sisters from Sligo and the Clissmann family who had connections with the Abwehr (German military intelligence, often said to be at odds with the Nazi regime). There was also a certain Mr Vorster, who lamented the bombing of Hannover—'my beautiful Hannover'—and told me that Hitler had done some good things, like building flats for workers. As for their hosts the Jeiter family, I suppose their sympathies took quite another direction. Old Josef Jeiter had named his sons Francis and Joseph. Frank had an album full of Austrian stamps from the imperial period. If these people of Rhineland origin felt nostalgia for a dynasty, it may have been the Habsburgs and not the Hohenzollerns.

Dromahair had its own station on the railway line which ran from Enniskillen to Sligo. The go-ahead railway company ran diesel-powered railcars, much like trams, as well as steam trains. In 1944 Northern Ireland was crowded with American servicemen posted there in preparation for the D-Day landings. They frequently came across the border on the railcars for 'rest and recreation'. They wore handsome uniforms which put the wretched uniforms of Irish soldiers to shame. And they carried arms. They showed us their guns and made exaggerated claims for the speed of their aircraft. So much for neutrality.

| 1937: SCHOOL

School was awful, though I never saw any rats. The worst part was the lavatories. I will not attempt to describe them.

After a few years, my father moved from Kilcoosey to Ballintogher, four miles from Dromahair on the Sligo side, and took Eva and me with him daily. The Ballintogher school was older, dilapidated and impossible to heat properly. It was also filthy.

In both places the classrooms were bleak, with ancient desks, uncomfortable seats and rotting floorboards. Décor consisted of a map of Ireland and posters enjoining farmers to pare their donkeys' hooves (widely and callously ignored) and clear their land of 'thistle, ragwort and dock' (ignored then and now, with the poisonous ragwort flourishing).

I was just under four years old when I started at Kilcoosey. I had already learned to read, at least to the extent of making out newspaper headlines. The work was far too easy, and this would be the case also at Ballintogher and at secondary school. So I developed bad habits. And bad habits are hard to shake off.

Much of my education came from books, most of which I found in our own house, along with bound volumes of the *Boys' Own Paper*. Others I borrowed from the Whytes, who had several books by the wonderful Jack London, and from a Garda, Tom Craig. He and his wife Nora had a full set of Dickens, my lifetime favourite, and Wilkie Collins. By the time I went to secondary school I had begun to read Dostoevsky, Thackeray, George Eliot (I fell in love with Maggie Tulliver, as I later fell in love with Elizabeth Bennet), the Brontë sisters, Liam O'Flaherty and other Irish novelists. Then, inevitably, there was *Tom Brown's Schooldays*, which made Irish schools look like easy going—though I would come across quite a few Flashmans in later life. In addition to novels and short stories, I gobbled up the collected works of Patrick Pearse—the set had belonged to my mother; I still have it—and more daunting works like *The World Crisis* by

Winston Churchill and a history of Europe by H.A.L. Fisher.

My reading of both kinds fortified the notions of honour and courage instilled in me by my upright father, who associated the highest standards of behaviour with Christianity. I had no trouble absorbing the history, though I found it puzzling that the British were always portrayed as the Good Guys, but with the novels I developed another bad habit, gobbling them up too fast. My powers of recall were not sufficient. In middle age I re-read Dickens—more slowly—and came across characters and incidents that I had barely remembered. I have always envied people, like Brian Lenihan senior and the journalist Con Houlihan, whose facility for recall was equal to the speed of their reading.

I am happy that I came so young to the world of books and the imagination, but I knew even then that it did not substitute for two other things I needed and lacked, education appropriate to my talents and the companionship of boys of my own age. Eva had the friendship of three neighbouring girls, with whom she played elaborate housekeeping games in the sorting office—deserted for most of the day—but I had no male friends before I entered my teens. This was mainly because we went to our father's schools at Kilcoosey and Ballintogher and had little contact with the boys who attended our own village school, of which after our time he became principal. When I grew old enough—ten or eleven—I had to content myself in my breaks from the books with Wordsworthian wanderings over the hills. They were not then covered with coniferous forests; there were well-worn paths everywhere, used for moving cattle and drawing water from wells, through heathlands and rough pastures.

At this time or a little later, Dad was turning his mind to two important questions, his remarriage and our secondary education. He settled the first question when he married my stepmother Gertie: Gertrude McAllister, Gran's assistant in the post office. Her family had the distinction of being the only one in the village, apart from ours, to split in the civil war; all the others supported the Anglo-Irish Treaty and the Free State government. Two of her brothers served in the Free State army, two on the rebel side. They fought against each other when the republicans besieged Markree Castle in County Sligo, then occupied by Free State forces—or rather did not fight, for all four later assured their mother, truthfully or otherwise, that they fired to miss. Gertie was a tiny girl then. Her sister Minnie, twenty years older, was engaged to one of General Michael Collins's colonels, Joe Ring. Collins had nominated him for high office in the new police force, but he was killed in action before he could take up the appointment. While the McAllister household mourned him, soldiers who did not know about the family's connection with both sides in the civil war raided and ransacked it. Gertie when she grew up became a lifelong supporter of Fianna Fáil.

The marriage was long and fruitful. It gave me two new sisters, Frances and Maria, and a brother, Tony, with all of whom I enjoyed delightful relationships in adult life. Unfortunately, however, we have always been separated by geographical distance and the same is true of Eva. After her marriage to Humphrey Kelleher they lived first in Cork and then, after her husband's appointment as the district judge for South Kerry, in Kenmare, a beautiful place but hard to reach. Tony became a headmaster in England, Maria the deputy principal of the Loreto Convent school in Cavan. Frances, having lived in various parts of Ireland, eventually returned to Dromahair with her husband and two sons. We have had splendid family reunions, with four generations represented.

My father, like Napoleon, never apologised or explained, and he did not explain his decision to send me to the Dominican-run Newbridge College, on the other side of the country. Late in life he remarked that he liked the Dominicans for their religious orthodoxy, but that is not an explanation. Neither is the theory that he wanted Uncle Joe, who lived in Newbridge, to keep an eye on me: I was in the care of the Dominicans. It has been suggested that he had heard stories of paedophilia in one or other of the more accessible Catholic church diocesan colleges, but that is most improbable. The obvious thing was to send me to Summerhill College in Sligo, alma mater of several uncles and grand-uncles, and Eva to the Ursuline Convent, also in Sligo. He may simply have wanted to get us out of the way while he began a new life. In any event I went to Newbridge and Eva to the Cross and Passion Convent in Kilcullen, a few miles away.

Schools, like all institutions, have their ups and downs, and postwar Newbridge was having a down. Old boys educated there both earlier and later have spoken to me of it with affection, but I arrived there to experience the terrible winter of 1946–47. That was the winter of the fuel crisis in Britain, when the Attlee government gambled on coal supplies and lost. The shortage drastically affected Ireland. Steam trains, for example, had to be fuelled by turf instead of coal. That entailed frequent stops to clean out the furnaces, because peat produces so much ash. When I went home for my first Christmas break, the train to Sligo, eleven miles from Dromahair, made such frequent and prolonged stops that it did not reach its destination until 2 o'clock in the morning. At Newbridge, coal for central heating ran out. For weeks on end the water froze in the taps. We sat in the classrooms with our overcoats on and jogged around the tennis courts during the breaks to warm ourselves a little.

There were other shortages. For some years we had no blazers or flannels—though we always seemed to have rugby equipment. This game was mandatory in all weathers, so that useless players like myself endured the miserable experience of togging out daily to be pulverised by our betters.

The school authorities exerted themselves for our wellbeing and tried to give us good food. They failed. They were not alone. I once went to Terenure College, a very similar school, with one of our rugby teams—as a touch judge, not a player—and found the food even worse than that at Newbridge. It may have been better at very grand places like Clongowes Wood, but not much.

Members of the senior team were of course the school's elite, but even they were little pampered. One whom I met in later life, a man who had gone on to make a national name for himself as a player, still complained of the terrible food. Another—of a different bent, the kind who might have been voted 'the boy most likely to succeed', and he had indeed succeeded in his profession—complained that he had once been unjustly punished thirty years earlier. Once in five years! For me, punishments, usually well deserved, were a weekly occurrence.

There was another elite, those who shone academically. Whether or not I belonged to it was doubtful. I was both lazy and rebellious. Either learning came too easily to me or I neglected it. Yet I won prizes, the main one at the end of my school career: the first award of the Prior's Cup for essay writing. I have never set eyes on the cup itself. The last I heard, it was still being awarded annually. I have to praise the Dominicans for taking pains to be fair to this thorn in their flesh.

I have to praise them, too, for trying to give us an education broader than that demanded by the official curriculum. Of my introduction to the arts, I will write in a moment. The older boys got a sketch, not much more, of philosophy, which meant essentially Plato, Aristotle and Thomas Aquinas. It 'stuck' only to the extent that in adult life I read a little of Aristotle and Jacques Maritain. Modern philosophy, which I encountered much later, was quite beyond me. I much preferred history and, with age, biography, a common enough path for those with a sceptical cast of mind.

Church history figured high on the list of subjects. Little was concealed, not even the Dominicans' evident embarrassment over how to approach the career of Girolamo Savonarola. We learned about the political and personal antics of Renaissance popes. Martin Luther was treated with delicacy and a degree of sympathy, notwithstanding that some of his loudest and best justified complaints were against the Dominicans. But we had it instilled into us that the behaviour of unworthy popes did not diminish the holiness of the church; rather, it showed a staying power in the face of such adversity which proved divine guidance. As to necessary reform, that had all been settled by the Council of Trent. A comfortable way of looking at things.

They taught us about the Enlightenment, but assured us that it did not really contradict Christian, specifically Catholic, teaching. I accepted what one may call their close reasoning at the time. In matters of conduct, I was more rebellious.

I often got away with disobeying the rules. Leaving the grounds was forbidden except on specific occasions, and boys constantly broke this rule to augment the goods available in the school tuck shop. That did not suffice for my more adventurous spirit. At the age of fifteen I 'bunked out' to the Curragh to see my first race meeting and ventured my only shilling on the outcome of the Thousand Guineas. This, however, was small potatoes compared with the activities of a few senior boys, who climbed down drainpipes at night and went into the town to meet girls; what kind of girls, I don't know. Newbridge had once been a British garrison town, and it is just possible that one of the establishments catering for soldiers' physical needs had survived under the puritanical new regime.

This had long been bloodstock country as well as military country. The Aga Khan, celebrated patron of Irish bloodstock and racing, had (and the present Aga Khan still has) a stud farm near Newbridge; the great Shergar was stolen from there by the IRA. His son Aly Khan had a house near Kilcullen. Locals claimed to have seen one of his glamorous wives or girlfriends walking naked on the terrace. A leading trainer, Paddy Prendergast, lived in a fine house, now a hotel, in the town. His sons Kevin and Paddy attended our school. Both followed their father, successfully, into the racing game.

On Sunday mornings, rich stud-farm owners used to attend Mass in the beautiful college chapel. We admired their huge, luxurious American cars, a rare sight indeed when few Irish people had cars of any kind.

My own laziness, and the faults of the curriculum, were more to blame than the masters, clerical or lay, for my failure to do better at French and Latin. A writer in any European language must profit from a knowledge of

Latin, and it is a great pity that classical languages are so little learned in Ireland now. As to the curriculum, Cicero and Horace are not suitable authors for boys in their early teens, and our teachers did not impart their wisdom and sophistication to us, or at any rate to me.

In my time, however, there were two outstanding teachers. One was a layman, James Murray. I have always regretted that I did not come under his tutelage for mathematics until the Leaving Certificate course. He had to throw me out of the honours class when I failed to master the differential calculus.

Henry Flanagan was a Dominican, young but bald. It must be a terrible thing for a prematurely bald young man, indifferent to rugby or racing, to have to confront a class of teenage savages. But those who shared his interests could not have had a better man to enlighten them. He conducted the choir and mounted productions of Gilbert and Sullivan. He ran the 'gramophone society': in music his passions were Haydn and Italian opera. He encouraged me to write, not that I needed much encouragement. At the beginning of the Leaving Certificate course in English, he announced to us that the curriculum was too narrow and that he intended to devote the first term to art and architecture. To Henry Flanagan I owe much of my imperfect knowledge of these sublime things.

He had other admirers. The great singer Christy Moore was one of his pupils some years after me. Moore corresponded with him until the end of Flanagan's life, writing him letters from any part of the world in which he happened to be performing.

At the other end of the scale was Michael Casey, who had been a scientist in the public employment. He liked to carry out foolhardly chemical and optical experiments. It was alleged that he almost blinded himself in one of these and vowed that if he recovered he would give up his job and study for the priesthood. Whatever the grounds for that story, he joined the Dominicans, who sent him to Newbridge. He was a truly dreadful teacher who combined sarcasm, an occupational hazard, with adherence to what I would come to suspect were out-of-date versions of science, especially atomic theory. He showed off to the class by screwing two or even three thick lenses on to his spectacles to determine their effect. He kicked up a tremendous row if anyone performed a chemistry experiment clumsily. And his notions of punishment bordered on the loony.

Newbridge maintained, by the prevailing standards, an unusually civilised regime of corporal punishment. It was administered only by the prior (head of the Dominican community), the headmaster, the dean of studies or the dean of discipline, and normally consisted of six blows on the hands, twelve for more serious offences, with a leather strap. The force of the blows depended on the personality of the priest inflicting them. At worst, they were bearable for a not particularly tough boy like myself, but they did cause considerable physical and psychological pain to more sensitive types.

That did not suit Casey's ideas, doubtless derived from the regime in English public schools. In place of reporting a boy to the appropriate authority for punishment, he offered the choice of accepting from himself a couple of light blows on the bottom with a T-square, which must have hurt less but humiliated more. I was one of those who refused to bend over and who were therefore 'sent up' more often.

This was very silly and fairly harmless, but just once I witnessed something much worse. His superiors seldom allowed him to preside over study sessions, attended by the whole school—or at meals, when disorder broke out in the hope, often realised, of provoking him. One evening in the study hall he caught a boy engaged in some trivial misbehaviour. He struck him on the side of the head, so violently as to make him sway. As the boy regained his balance, Casey struck him again on the other side of the head. In the end he was transferred to Maynooth, where the students were older, not subject to corporal punishment, and, presumably, better behaved.

Of the numerous punishments inflicted on myself, I have only one vivid memory—oddly, more pleasurable than otherwise.

At the age of (I think) fourteen, on the way back to school after Christmas holidays, I saw my first professional theatrical production. In one way the stage was not new to me, for we had had amateur 'concerts' in Dromahair and Ballintogher. These did not remotely resemble classical or rock concerts. They began with a long series of songs and sketches, sometimes extremely well done: a dramatisation of *The Croppy Boy* in Ballintogher was most impressive and there was a general gasp of horror when the 'priest' hearing the young rebel's confession flung off his clerical garb and revealed himself in the uniform of a Yeoman captain. Following the minor entertainment came a three-act play, usually a comedy by Lennox Robinson. Suspension of disbelief hardly existed. At a rare romantic moment when a young couple kissed in front of an audience composed of their neighbours the players would turn their backs, visibly embarrassed, amid a storm of shouts and whistles. An Edwards-

MacLiammoir production of a comedy entitled *Home for Christmas* took me into a different, enchanted world which would never lose its magic for me. On getting back to Newbridge, very late, I tried to pretend that I had missed a bus. I was punished for the tardiness and the lie.

Legitimate excursions to Dublin were mostly associated with rugby, for international matches and when our teams played Dublin schools. Naturally it was a matter of honour to attend the school matches. Attendance at the internationals was not mandatory, but I did have the good fortune to see at least one Triple Crown victory for the Irish team, probably the best of all time, at Lansdowne Road. Notwithstanding my own ineptitude at the game, I had enough knowledge of it to recognise the glory of Jack Kyle. His artistry on the pitch rivalled that of Hilton Edwards and Micheál MacLiammoir on the stage.

When I grew a little older, these trips afforded opportunities to meet girls, several of whom went to school in the Dominican Convent in Eccles Street. In later age, at a party, I met a very pretty woman who reminded me that she had once been my girlfriend. But that did not mean then what it means now. Older boys told astonishing stories of the liberties permitted to them, but I was timid and in any case these yarns, and the boasts of adult men, were less than credible. Most of us were experts on the subject of sexual repression. A kiss might be dismissed as a venial sin, but the hand under the blouse or up the skirt set you on the path to perdition. And by all accounts it was worse for the girls, who were told by the nuns that their guilt was greater if they led the boys on.

Crude and unfunny adolescent jokes circulated, as did tattered copies of books like *Lady Chatterley's Lover*, but as well as I can remember, I never discussed sex with any of my school friends. These tended to be sensitive and serious-minded, members of the Gramophone Society and readers of classics like myself. Some had a religious bent. I was most unhappy when one of the closest, John Hayes, disappeared from the scene. I heard nothing of him for several years, when he sent from California a card celebrating his ordination as a Dominican priest.

When I was about sixteen, and on holidays at home, I got one memorable glimpse of another and starker form of sexual deprivation, and of how some tried to alleviate it, in another milieu, a dance hall a few miles from Dromahair. This place closely resembled the original Ballroom of Romance at Glenfarne, not far away, and was equally unromantic. The most salient feature of such venues was the dreadful shortage of girls, which must have been due to the tendency of girls to emigrate at an earlier age than boys. My companions and I arrived late, to find what looked like a pitched battle in progress among dozens of youths, somewhat older than ourselves, on the dance floor. We asked the man selling the tickets to explain. He said that a fight had broken out over a girl, whereupon the others had joined in. He pointed out a girl sitting in a high window seat. She may have been no more than twenty, but to me she looked much older (because of her heavy make-up) and quite unattractive. She was clearly enjoying the show. Why her? I asked. The man gave me a contemptuous look. I have never forgotten that look of pity for my ignorance.

At that time or a little earlier, I was in love, albeit chastely, with Edie White, whom I had come to know, along with her numerous brothers and sisters, through my unusual holiday job, delivering telegrams. Her father was the principal teacher of a school in a very poor district, Killavoggy, in the drumlin country five miles south of our village. The Whites were very lively people. With them I played parlour games and danced 'half-sets', a variety of Irish dancing much despised by purists who favour elaborate figures which I have never mastered. Soon, however, Edie disappeared from my ken. She was unofficially adopted by an American uncle—a common enough procedure in those days—and settled permanently in the United States.

The Whites were of course better off than most of their neighbours. It is time I wrote about these small farmers and their way of life.

———

Poverty came, in the first instance, from the soil itself. There are patches of fertile land almost everywhere in Ireland, but the drumlins are exceptionally unfavourable territory for agriculture. The topsoil can be as little as an inch thick, with impermeable daub or marl, known in Leitrim as 'yellow clauber', underneath. One can grow oats and potatoes and a few hardy vegetables, but for the most part the land is suitable only for grazing and making hay. For this last, and for turf if you have turbary rights, the never-ending rain makes life much more difficult. In my youth the hay was dried twice, first in small mounds called 'laps', then in cocks; yet many a crop had to be abandoned. After 1985, 'the year of the floating haycocks', almost all small farmers abandoned haymaking in favour of silage. In Leitrim the problem had already been largely solved by the abandonment of the land.

In 1841 the population of the county was 155,000. To think of how the majority lived—often in mere holes in the ground, and close to starvation in circumstances not even of famine but merely of an inadequate potato crop—is enough to make one flinch. By the end of the twentieth century the population had fallen to 25,000. It then recovered to 30,000, but the recovery was far from uniform. Carrick-on-Shannon became a boom town and my own Dromahair a suburb of Sligo ('Sligo Four') but the depopulation of North Leitrim continued. By the year 2007 forty townlands had been completely abandoned. The young had, quite simply, fled.

They had fled living conditions which resembled those of the time of the Great Famine more closely than what was considered acceptable in the mid-twentieth century. I do not exaggerate. Those who managed to make some kind of decent living might plant fruit trees and have roses round their doors and keep their houses clean. Examples were Dad's friend Willie McMorrow and his spinster sister Bedelia, and the McBride family, close neighbours of the Whites of Killavoggy; and there were intriguing characters at another level of knowledge and aspiration. Tom Carty, a bachelor who lived two miles from the village and whom I often visited, kept bees, tended an apple orchard, looked like Cicero and read Gibbon: he liked to quote the passage which described the early Christians as enemies of human kind. But far more houses, if they deserved the name, were at best ill-tended and at worst nearly uninhabitable. They usually consisted of three rooms, a kitchen and two bedrooms; in the better houses one of these was not a bedroom but a parlour, a place of musty furniture and deathly cold, used only on a rare occasion like a funeral. The roofs were of slate or thatch; a tin roof was regarded as a sign of penury. Quite frequently the roof of one of the rooms fell down and was not replaced but left as a ruin. Light came from oil lamps; the poorest used candles. The kitchen was wretchedly equipped and furnished. Food, mostly potatoes, home-baked bread and little else, was cooked in pots hanging from a crane over an open fire. The predominant smell was of smoke and soot, which caked the rafters and permeated the drinking water, drawn with great labour from wells, some a considerable distance away. The crude kitchen furniture usually included a settle bed, which by day turned into an excruciatingly uncomfortable seat for two or three people. Settle beds notoriously attracted fleas. Worse pests were rare. I recall an outbreak of head lice at the school in Ballintogher, but such outbreaks occasionally occur in suburban schools to this day.

Down to at least the 1960s, small farmers had almost no cash income. The lucky ones got part-time employment as road workers or received remittances from emigrants. They had oaten cakes, 'free' cattle fodder in the form of hay, and turf for fuel. The usual way to get cash was to sell a bullock or a heifer, and the death of a beast gave occasion for mourning. Young cattle—'stores', which dealers would sell on to graziers in rich eastern counties—were driven many miles to fairs (markets) and too often driven back home again when no bidders could be found.

Worse than any of this was the familial, social and cultural breakdown. In the 1950s the phenomenon of late marriages or no marriages contributed to the drastic population decline which prompted authors to write about 'the vanishing Irish'. Along with it, of course, went a decline in trade and a depression which lay over even the fortunate ones in public employment. No area suffered more than ours. In the village, Gardaí and other public-service employees might have large families, but the countryside was populated by bachelors and spinsters and the few young people who would soon escape. My father had to explain to me that marriage and child-rearing were supposed to be the norm, not the exception.

Traditional music survived only in patches. The powerful Gaelic Athletic Association, far the most important cultural and social organisation in rural Ireland, could not muster a football team in Dromahair for years on end. In one year, Leitrim had a promising county team. By the beginning of the next football season, fourteen of its fifteen members had emigrated.

In terms of individual satisfaction, those at the very bottom were not the under-employed in the villages but the 'relatives assisting'—a much-derided euphemism—on farms owned by their siblings, uncles or cousins. Theirs were lives of unending misery and deprivation. Drudgery alternated with idleness, depending on the weather and the seasons. They had no money apart from whatever pittance the owners chose to give them. They had virtually no recreations: Michael D. Higgins has written a poem about the highlight of a spinster's week, going to Sunday Mass on a 'High Nellie' bicycle. They had no prospect of marriage and family. They could never know joy.

Farm life, at any rate for owners and their wives, was relieved somewhat by pride of proprietorship—and citizenship. For they were citizens in a sense that the urban underclass was not then and is not now. Almost all of them voted in elections. They listened to the news on the radio. Women cycled into the village with battery-powered radios for recharging. They were well informed about the progress of the war—so far as the censorship would allow—and the rise of Soviet power. They treated teachers as well as priests with great respect; Dad must have been one of the last schoolmasters to be addressed as 'Master'; but in some ways society was much more egalitarian than it later became.

Still, they led terribly restricted lives, dominated by the lack of money and opportunity and by the inexorable demands of the land. They were hard pressed, as indeed the middle classes frequently were also, to buy clothes and shoes for growing children—or themselves. During the war my father, accompanied by a Regular officer, attended a meeting in a hilly district to recruit volunteers for the LDF. They lectured the young men in the audience on the glories of defending their country against invasion. At the end they asked for questions. Silence. The request was repeated. At last one of the more articulate, pressed by those around him, rose and asked a simple question: 'When do we get the yellow boots?' A pair of boots was a treasure.

John Healy told a more poignant story. An emigrant opened his cardboard suitcase for examination by the British Customs at Holyhead. It contained nothing but a pair of Wellington boots. Not so much as a change of clothes.

They broke out of the tedium of their hard lives in various ways, some less conventional than others. Fair days brought excitement, and frequently they brought violence. Men unaccustomed to alcohol would get drunk after consuming a couple of pints. Inevitably fights broke out with roughly cut sticks, 'ash plants', as weapons. Many a head was broken, and a good deal of blood was shed. This, however, was much less fearful than it appeared. As anyone can see on a football pitch, a slight head wound produces a lot of blood. I never saw the police breaking up any of these fights, as they surely would have done if things had started to look serious.

Sometimes in the hills in winter, the curious custom of 'joins' was observed. People clubbed together to buy a keg of Guinness and a quantity of poteen, and hold house parties which could go on for days, complete with music and dancing. Usually they did not drink the poteen neat, but made punch with it. Even so, it could cause a temporary, and occasionally a permanent, loss of wits. The priests thundered against illegal distillation, and in several dioceses it was a 'reserved sin', one for which absolution could be granted only by a bishop. They had sense on their side. Bad poteen could cause dreadful conditions like loss of sight and serious mental incapacity. No doubt the priests also had in mind what in those days was the ultimate sin, extra-marital intercourse.

Another condition, presumably caused by isolation, kept the psychiatric hospitals busy. Middle-aged men would be afflicted by whirling 'fits', somewhat like epileptic fits, and fall down unconscious. When found by their neighbours, they would be taken off to hospital until they recovered temporarily.

Thousands suffered from more serious, in fact deadly, conditions. Tuberculosis, the 'white plague', was still dreaded. It carried off whole families. Our grandfather's sister-in-law, whom we knew as Aunt Mary Anne and whom as children we often visited in her house near Collooney, lost her husband and all of her ten children. Other families lost children to diphtheria. When I was in my teens, an epidemic of polio struck victims of all classes, usually teenage boys, everywhere in Ireland. One sufferer was Patrick Cockburn, youngest son of Claud and Patricia Cockburn, with whom I would become friendly in adult life. Patrick Cockburn overcame his condition by sheer fortitude and, like his father and his two elder brothers, made a sparkling name for himself in journalism. But many others died or lived out their lives with serious physical disability.

As compensation for their grim lifestyle, did the country people have the 'opiate of religion'? I am very sceptical about the Catholic middle-class notion, then common, that the antidote to doubts about religion was 'peasant faith'. I think peasant faith was mostly skin-deep. Conor Cruise O'Brien has told a revealing anecdote about a conversation with Monsignor Pádraig de Brún, uncle of O'Brien's wife Máire Mhac an tSaoí. Asked what people in a remote part of Kerry really believed about the afterlife, de Brún said that they believed three things simultaneously: one, the orthodox Catholic teaching; two, that death was the end; three, that the ghosts of the dead continued to hover about us, perhaps with malevolent intent.

Numerous writers have asserted that in those days every rural house had a red lamp permanently lit under a picture of the Sacred Heart of Jesus. I can tell them from personal experience that they are wrong. In my teenage years the many rural houses I visited were as likely to hang a Victorian print as a Sacred Heart lamp; and in recent years, as I followed political candidates on their election canvasses, I have seen only one in a rural area and none in a town. A few years ago I was intrigued to read an article in the *Sunday Independent* by a young Protestant woman who wrote that she had encountered this startling (to her) sight in the house of one of her Catholic friends. This is a rare sight indeed in upper-middle-class South Dublin.

Whatever about South Dublin, did traces of an older religion and older customs survive in districts like ours? Perhaps. Many undoubtedly believed in fairies. In some places certain families were thought to have the power of cursing their enemies. In my childhood a 'wise woman', a healer, was said to live on the slopes of Killerry Mountain (which features in innumerable pictures of Lough Gill). But the face of the Catholic church was set sternly against heresy, and what the church could not eradicate, it took over. 'Holy wells' proliferate throughout the country, on what are unmistakably pre-Christian, in fact pre-Celtic, sites. The church tried to ban gatherings at these places, and when prohibition failed, cleverly turned them into locations for Catholic ceremonies. It also took over the Feast of Lughnasa, renaming the ancient Celtic harvest festival Garland Sunday. As to healing by amateurs, the church thought it would be wiped out by modern medicine. No such thing has happened. Across the world there are hordes of healers without formal medical qualifications, armies of charlatans but also people with genuine skills. It surprises me that some people continue to look down on bone-setters and water-diviners whose ability is beyond doubt.

But in my time, for the Catholic middle class and the more prosperous farmers religion was as rigid as contempt for antique medical practices was complete. When the flood of emigration swelled in the postwar period, one could hear fears expressed, not about the discrimination or the atrocious living conditions a young boy or girl might endure in England but that he or she might 'lose the faith'. A more real and present danger, for the girls, was that they might be enticed or forced into prostitution. Pimps hung around Euston and other English railway terminals, keeping a keen eye out for the vulnerable. Catholic agencies did strenuous, and successful, work to counter them.

Of course emigration was not merely a postwar phenomenon. It took on a special and highly unpleasant flavour during the war when able-bodied Irishmen were greatly in demand for an English labour market denuded by the conscription of huge numbers of British into the armed forces. These young Irish constituted a form of bonded labour and underwent what John Healy called 'rites of passage' which included the shaving of their pubic hair. But the postwar emigration was on an incomparably larger scale. In five years during the 1950s, a quarter of a million left the country. And the pattern was far from uniform. Richer areas were little affected, whereas for the poor parts—and Leitrim was the poorest—the flight was a calamity: a disaster for the region, and God knows how many thousands of personal tragedies.

There was a place in the Curlew Mountains called Kilfree Junction, where the train from Sligo to Dublin stopped to take on passengers. On my way back to school after holidays, I witnessed harrowing scenes there. Owing to the custom of late marriages, the fathers of the young emigrants were often elderly. The sight of an old man weeping as he parts with his children is a dreadful thing.

Once, when I was sixteen or seventeen, two girls, not much different in age from myself, shared a compartment with me on the Sligo–Dublin train. Clearly the elder girl had spent a year or two in England and was now bringing her sister to join her. Throughout a journey of three or four hours both of them wept and sobbed ceaselessly. They scarcely spoke, even to each other: occasionally one would try, but both were so overcome, and so breathless, that they could not utter a coherent phrase.

I could give them no comfort beyond an offer of lemonade which they were unable to drink. They may have found some consolation when they boarded the Holyhead mailboat at Dun Laoghaire. Those boats contained overflowing lavatories and decks awash with beer and vomit, but they also contained kind and strong older men who had fiddles and accordions and other means of cheering them up.

Official and voluntary agencies (the former, however, exceedingly parsimonious) worked hard to warn against the dangers, and ease the conditions of life, which they would encounter in Britain. At home, a Save The West campaign demanded measures to bring trade and industry to the West to stem the flow. Bishops in the region, alarmed at the devastation of their flocks, played a large part. Yet other bishops continued to preach the virtues of 'the small family farm' and to laud the virtue of a supposedly 'natural' way of life. Healy would become the most admired and most eloquent of the campaigners. He railed against depopulation in newspaper articles and in his most famous book *No One Shouted Stop*, alternatively entitled *The Death of an Irish Town*.

Healy's work attracted much favourable notice for his forceful writing style and his sincerity and humanity. But he put forward no practical solutions. He deplored the 'Mansholt Plan', named after a European commissioner, which foresaw a reduction in the number of viable ('commercial') Irish farms to a few thousand, but something very like the Mansholt Plan scenario was certain to happen—and has happened. The best guess at present (2008) is that the number will fall quite soon to 15,000 or 20,000 at most. If the population of the West has stabilised, that is owing to improvements in trade and industry and the numbers employed in the public service.

Not until 1969 would a coherent proposal appear for regional policy. The Buchanan Report advocated the nomination of 'growth centres'. Enterprise and population would be centred in the obvious provincial cities and larger towns, and the spin-off effects would bring equally obvious benefits to smaller places. The report was immediately shelved for reasons of Irish localism and of political cowardice and inanition. Eventually, at the beginning of the twenty-first century, the Fianna Fáil–Progressive Democrat coalition put forward a very similar plan in its 'spatial strategy'. This in turn was killed off by the crazy decentralisation programme on which hundreds of millions of euros were fruitlessly expended. It was eventually abandoned, but it will have calamitous and long-lasting effects on the efficiency of the administration. No such thing as joined-up government exists in Ireland.

Chapter 3 ∿

1951: INK AND LEAD

N ewbridge, the Spartan conditions notwithstanding, was a world removed from the deprivation of the west of Ireland. Most of the boys came from very comfortable urban backgrounds. When they left school, a considerable number would go on to university, and a greater number could look forward to spending much of their lives on the golf course or the rugby field, where they would make contacts and advance their careers. Their ambitions, though limited, were much less narrow than those of most of their contemporaries. But horizons were still greatly restricted. You could aim for the civil service, 'The Bank', or some similar occupation which would bring you a pension after forty years of tedium. Or you could go to university and, after three or four years idling, face a career decision which, more often than not, meant teaching, regardless of fitness for the job. Many of my contemporaries would enter a family business, others would become solicitors or accountants or engineers. Rebels did not thrive: one man spent his life on the fringes of the theatre and came to a sad end. There would be a few doctors; no barristers to my recollection. The word entrepreneurship was scarcely known, and only one of my classmates had a talent for it. He took a degree in engineering and set up a successful engineering works. As to myself, my ambition was firmly fixed from at least my mid-teens. I always wanted to be a journalist.

Looking back, I believe that I made this decision partly for an entirely logical and quite unromantic reason: the desire to employ my one undoubted talent, writing, to the best effect. But in addition, the romance of the trade entered my bloodstream at a very early age. Although to my recollection I did not read books like *The Street of Adventure* before adulthood, from childhood I was a 'news junkie', devouring the reports in the newspapers—almost always the *Irish Independent*, the staple of every Irish middle-class Catholic household. I fancied, wrongly, that I could follow the progress of the war, and marvelled at the privileged position of a war correspondent, chronicling the progress of the armies that fought for civilisation. And although I was almost equally ignorant of the realities of politics, I was on the way to becoming a political junkie too. I recall a delegation from the short-lived Clann na Poblachta visiting our house in 1948, trying in vain to persuade my father to stand for the Dáil (he rejected similar invitations from Fianna Fáil and Fine Gael). And I overheard conversations between him and a frequent visitor to our house, Dr Don Deasy from Drumshanbo, who declared: 'We have to face it. The Irish language is dead and partition is permanent.' It seemed to me that whether he was right or wrong about the language or partition, writing about politics must be an exciting job.

Indeed it is; and it would give me half a century and more of hard work and sheer pleasure. I would grow to love the smell of ink and lead, the thrill of the scoop and the satisfaction of directing the production of a newspaper on great occasions. But of course in my teens I knew nothing of these things. I hardly knew how to start. At school, my ambition mystified both my contemporaries and the masters. The Dominicans did their best in the way of career guidance, but they had no training or expertise and, like the boys they tried to help, they could seldom see beyond the narrow horizons I have mentioned. My very limited contacts told me that I must begin at the bottom, somehow finding a place as a trainee on a weekly newspaper, and work my way up.

This ambition, conceived so early, got in the way of the academic ambitions which should have taken precedence. I did not think it worth my while to aim for a university scholarship, so I neglected my school work. My father had made a mistake by sending me to Newbridge a year late; then, when I performed poorly in the Intermediate Certificate, he decided that I should spend an extra year catching up. It has always baffled me that a man dedicated to education failed to see that I had started on the wrong foot and that the extra year was an encouragement to idleness. In the event, I achieved good results in the Leaving Certificate in 1951, but in those days good results in any subject other than English did not impress provincial editors.

My precocious interest in politics was not matched by grasp of social or economic matters, and I had only a worm's-eye view of the disastrous social and economic trends which, happily, would be reversed after 1959 by the efforts of Seán Lemass and T.K. Whitaker. My only concern was to find a job on a provincial paper.

But jobs were scarce, even wretchedly paid jobs for trainees. I made contact, each time without avail, with a number of papers. At last my father found me a place of sorts with the *Sligo Champion*, simply because he happened to know one of the directors of the company that owned the paper. The deal was that I would be paid so much per line for contributing the 'Dromahair notes' and nothing at all for whatever work was assigned to me in the office in Sligo by the editor, Tom Palmer.

Palmer was a colourful professional and one of the 'characters' of Irish provincial journalism, but he did not exert himself in the matter of training. Much of my work consisted of reading the proofs of the Donegal electoral register, which the company printed. Very likely it made me one of the best proof-readers in the world, but it did not much advance my knowledge of journalism.

I was rescued by my stepmother. A frequent visitor to Dromahair was Kees van Hoek, a Dutchman who wrote a column in the *Irish Independent* and who evidently had good contacts in the emergent continental Christian Democrat parties. He also had what would prove for me far more important, a friendship with Liam Bergin, the editor of the *Carlow Nationalist*. For some reason van Hoek had occasion to send frequent parcels to Dublin, and in the course of these transactions he struck up a friendship with Gertie, who explained my situation to him. By chance, Bergin had a vacancy on his paper. It arose in an extraordinary way. The incumbent was Costa Hempel, son of Eduard Hempel, who had been the German envoy to Ireland during the war. Costa Hempel had been struck down with tuberculosis and gone to Switzerland to recover. On van Hoek's recommendation, Bergin made me his replacement without ever having met me. So Hempel's misfortune was my good luck.

I arrived in Carlow on a bleak night in January 1952 and made my way to the respectable boarding house chosen for me by Bergin or someone on his behalf. Its respectability was a symbol of the kind of organisation I would now work for, and when I moved, for the sake of a few shillings a week, to a more downmarket location—where for a while I slept in a room with four beds, all occupied—on what was then 'the wrong side of the river', the right bank of the Barrow, my change of address did not meet with Bergin's approval. But I was content in both places.

Bergin and all who worked for the *Nationalist* prided themselves on the newspaper's standing in the town, the region and the country. It had a long and honourable history. For example, it had sent its own reporter to cover the Home Rule debates at Westminster in 1886. When the Irish parliamentary party split on the issue of the Parnell divorce, it took the anti-Parnellite side. (As the descendant of fervent Parnellites, I was quite upset when I discovered that, and it took me a long time to accept that the Uncrowned King's opponents had a case.) It was rightly considered one of the best regional papers, perhaps bettered only by the *Kerryman* of Tralee. Accuracy and objectivity were prized. The design and typography were exceptionally good, reaching standards of handsomeness and legibility very rare then in provincial papers, not to say national papers. I was extraordinarily lucky to receive my training on a newspaper that upheld standards like these and that commanded so much respect from the local establishment.

Bergin took a keen interest in training. He regarded himself as the mentor of future stars, and boasted of the successes of former pupils. Of these, the outstanding man was Desmond Fisher, who went on to become editor of the *Catholic Herald*, one of the top executives in RTÉ, and ultimately Bergin's successor as editor and managing director of the *Nationalist*. The pattern continued long after my time. Among the Bergin trainees who made national names for themselves was the brilliant current affairs broadcaster Olivia O'Leary.

Homer nods from time to time, and the *Nationalist* nodded sometimes. Half a century on, I came across documents relating to the wartime censorship in the National Archives. The owner of an engineering works in the town had died. His obituary mentioned that his factory had worked for the Department of Defence and the British Admiralty, the latter clearly a gross breach of neutrality. Presumably the Germans never read it: no bombs fell on Carlow. But the censors were alarmed and demanded an explanation. The company pleaded that Bergin was seriously ill at the time and the office manager was in charge. The censors imposed no sanctions.

But by the time I came to the *Nationalist* Bergin had recovered and was at the height of his powers. From him and from the news editor, Paddy Ginnane, I learned a lot about journalism, including sub-editing—grammatical, spelling and punctuation errors were not tolerated—and the rudiments of design, an art in which I would never excel. In the course of my work I also picked up, bit by bit, a knowledge of two things of which at the age of eighteen I was largely ignorant, commercial agriculture and the class system.

As a paradigm of agricultural practice, Leitrim was at the bottom of the heap, no more than one layer up from subsistence farming. As I have mentioned earlier, store cattle raised in the west were sold cheap for 'finishing' in the rich eastern counties. I had seen the end result in Meath;

and I had seen the stud farmers' gorgeous cars in Kildare. Carlow was an example of an equally rich but more advanced kind of agriculture. Rotation of crops was practised on the basis of the 'Three BS', beef, sugar beet and barley. The barley went for processing to make a fourth B, beer. The beet went for refining to the sugar factory in Carlow. There were then four such refineries in the country. It was a highly artificial arrangement. The sugar company was a state-owned monopoly, and we could have bought better sugar from the West Indies for half or one-third of the price. Adam Smith would have deplored the system. But it brought the beet growers great prosperity, and it brought employment to the towns in which the factories were located.

It seemed to me that the more a region industrialised, the more stratified the class system became. The divisions between the old ascendancy, the prosperous farmers, the business and professional classes, the small traders, the artisans and the labourers were reinforced by the divisions in the sugar factory and other industries between skilled, semi-skilled and unskilled men. In time, I would learn much more about trade unions and the hollowness of working-class solidarity. In my youth, the effect on me was the development of egalitarian views, very different from those familiar to me in my childhood and at Newbridge.

I covered town and county council meetings, courts, inquests and, on Sunday afternoons, Gaelic football matches. I had no interest in joining the tennis club or the rugby club. My chief recreation, apart from the cinema, was the FCA, which I had joined while at school. Unlike my father, I never rose to any higher rank than corporal. The highlights were the rare trips to the firing range—I was a tolerably good marksman—and the annual camp at Gormanstown. We trained with Lee Enfield rifles of World War One vintage and equally antiquated machine-guns. The authorities, no doubt sensibly, were very sparing in their allocation of ammunition. Just once, at Gormanstown, I had the dizzying honour of being appointed guard commander on the main gate for one night. Our chances in the unlikely event of an IRA attack would have been poor. The ammunition for our rifles was kept in a locked cell in the guardhouse. In an emergency I would have had to run to the officers' mess and apply to the officer who kept the key. Better than allowing men, or rather boys, to blaze away at a bush or a sheep or, infinitely worse, some wandering drunken innocent.

As soon as I gained some proficiency in my work, I began to think of promotion. This meant an appointment as one of the district correspondents. But I was too young. When a vacancy arose in Portlaoise,

Bergin gave the job to Michael Finlan, a beautiful writer but quickly bored in a job far below his capacities. Their relationship did not last long, and in Finlan's place Bergin appointed a young man of a different stamp, Pat Nolan, who would rise to be an eminent labour correspondent for the *Irish Times*. There he became famous for his tendency to use as compliments the words 'diligent' and 'industrious'. They certainly applied to himself. However, unknown to Bergin he had a little weakness. Drink went to his head, sometimes with spectacular results. It was said that he once rode a motor-bike across the roofs of several cars parked in a row.

When Nolan arrived in Portlaoise, Finlan was still 'working out his notice', and he showed his replacement around the district. He introduced him to contacts in Mountrath, ten miles from Portlaoise. The trip ended in a pub, where Nolan drank too much and started to smash bottles and glasses. The owner, a widow, appealed to Finlan and asked him what she should do. He replied in his strangely Americanised accent: 'Call the cops.' Many years later, in a conversation with me, he denied this version of the story, saying that he was in another room when the incident occurred and someone else called the police. One way or another, the Gardaí arrived, arrested Pat Nolan and threw him in a cell for the night. Soon afterwards he attended his first session of the Mountrath district court in the dual capacity of reporter and defendant. He sent an item to the *Nationalist* to the effect that 'Patrick Nolan, a reporter, of the County Hotel, Portlaoise' had been fined forty shillings (say, one-fifth of a week's wages) for being drunk and disorderly. It was greatly to his credit that he wrote the item, and equally to Bergin's credit that he published it.

Soon another desirable job fell vacant, that of district correspondent in Portarlington, and Bergin appointed me although I was not yet twenty years old. Thus began one of the happiest years of my life, and I have always retained a great affection for the county of Laois and Portarlington in particular.

The town lies in good farming country between the midland bogs and the pretty Slieve Bloom Mountains. In my time, long before the building boom, it was surely unique among Irish towns in physical size and shape, two miles long and no more than two hundred yards wide. When I read a novel by Emma Cooke, *A Single Sensation*, I realised at once that the fictional town described in it could only be Portarlington. 'Emma Cooke' turned out to be the nom-de-plume of Enid Blanc, an acquaintance of the olden days. Her Huguenot name is not uncommon in the area. Huguenots settled there three hundred years ago, and some of their fine houses, with their backs to the street and their fronts to the River Barrow, are still occupied.

My work was in one way ridiculously easy, in another quite hard. Young journalists in an age of daily violent crime and political sensation must find it impossible to imagine a tranquil time when the national murder rate, not counting undetected domestic killings, averaged six per year—in one year only three murders were recorded—and the only lively feature of the political scene in the Laois–Offaly constituency was the antics of Oliver J. Flanagan, then an independent Dáil deputy who would shortly join Fine Gael and rise, first to the rank of parliamentary secretary and ultimately defence minister.

Flanagan was a useful rentaquote long before the term was invented. When some minor controversy blew up, he had no objection to my writing the predictable terms of his reaction myself. This, however, changed when he joined the ranks of the parliamentary secretaries (since pompously renamed ministers of state) and assumed an air of gravitas quite out of keeping with his notorious earlier utterances. In 1943 he had made a vehemently anti-semitic Dáil speech. Although the full horrors of the Holocaust had not then been disclosed, the fact of Nazi persecution of the Jews was notorious. In his constituency he adopted a radical posture. It surprised me to find that the process of land division, which had started at the beginning of the century, was not yet complete. Flanagan demanded the division of estates as small as three or four hundred acres. Since then, the process has been well and truly reversed.

I covered the local courts and went to Portlaoise for sittings of the circuit court and county council meetings. The meetings were well-conducted; not so the court hearings. The circuit judge, Michael Binchy, had a reputation as a fine lawyer, but as a judge he suffered from a serious handicap, deafness. Partly for this reason, the cases dragged on unconscionably. One, a dispute between two farmers concerning a right of way, took two full days, in the course of which the lawyers argued interminably over maps and photographs. Disputes of this kind were and are common, and not only in Ireland. Half a century later, at a journalists' congress, I met a Bavarian colleague whose husband was a lawyer. One of his clients won a trifling court award against a neighbour, something like five Deutschemarks a year. The lawyer warned him of the consequences of insisting on payment: 'He won't deliver your mail to your house if you are away. He won't bring his tractor to drag your cow out of a ditch.' The farmer replied: 'I know, but it will be worth it to see his face when he has to hand over the money.' Cases like these could and should be settled quickly and cheaply, but rural litigants like their day in court.

In Carlow a member of the *Nationalist* staff was regarded as a person of great status and probity. Not so in Laois or in another part of my district, Monasterevin in County Kildare. I could count on my fingers the bribes I have been offered in all my career, and most of them came in one year, in Portlaoise, Mountrath and Monasterevin. Uniformly the purpose was to keep a defendant's name out of the paper, and usually those who offered the bribes were surprised when they were rejected. On one occasion in Portlaoise a good contact of mine offered me an unspecified sum not to report an action against a friend of his. I listened to the evidence and concluded, as did the judge and everyone else in the court, that the plaintiff had no case whatever. Nevertheless, publication would have unfairly damaged the defendant's reputation. I met my contact in the bar of the County Hotel and assured him that the *Nationalist* would not publish my report. This did not satisfy him. He pulled out banknotes of large denominations. I told him to put them back in his wallet.

Incidents like these, however, were rare compared with the day-to-day work of scrabbling for mundane news items. And conscientious though I was, it left much—too much—of my time for social activity. I played a lot of poker. I joined a gun club which engaged in target shooting, nothing more lethal. I was invited to an illegal cockfight on condition that I wrote nothing about it. There was an uproar when a report appeared in the *Daily Express* and I was blamed. The anonymous author must have been Tony Gallagher, my predecessor as the *Nationalist* correspondent in Portarlington, who had maintained his contacts there.

———

I left Portarlington, and the *Nationalist*, after only a year. Much as I loved the place and the paper, I was glad to go. My relationship with a sweet and lovely girl was in bad shape—something for which I was entirely to blame—and my career was about to take a remarkable step forward.

Éamon de Valera founded the *Irish Press* in 1931 as an organ of Fianna Fáil propaganda and a counter to the pro-Treaty opinions of most national and regional newspapers. Under two outstanding editors, Frank Gallagher and William Sweetman, the new publication made a name for itself for thorough and innovative news coverage, sport and features.

Among its stars were Jack Grealish, Liam Mac Gabhann, Terry Ward and the novelist and man-about-town Benedict Kiely. It modelled itself to an extent on Beaverbrook's *Daily Express*, then, notwithstanding all its eccentricities, one of the greatest newspapers in the world. Vivion de Valera, who eventually succeeded his father as 'controlling director', admired Beaverbrook and had the tumbledown offices on Burgh Quay, a former music hall, rebuilt somewhat in the style of the 'Black Lubyanka', Beaverbrook's spectacular London headquarters.

When 'tatie hokers' from Donegal, working on the potato harvest in Scotland and living in frightful conditions, died in a disastrous fire, Grealish as news editor hired a small aircraft to take Mac Gabhann to Scotland, avoiding the tedious rail and sea journeys he would otherwise have had to take. This dashing and innovative move must have caused distress in the *Irish Press* management, which was notorious for its parsimony as well as its dictatorial style.

The *Sunday Press* was launched in 1949. Like its elder sister, it became an instant success. For many years it was the leading Irish Sunday paper by circulation. Among its remarkable features were an up-to-date layout and massive sports coverage. But it is best remembered for several series which are lumped together under the title of the first in the line, 'Four Glorious Years'.

It was edited by Colonel Mattie Feehan, one of the most bizarre characters ever to reach prominence in Irish journalism. Feehan's military title referred to his wartime service. Heaven knows how he attained such an exalted rank. A man who served under him when he was a young lieutenant commanding a machine-gun post on Carnsore Point told me a story about aircraft identification. The instructions were that any British warplanes flying over the south-easternmost point of Ireland should be ignored but that German planes should be shot down and their crews rescued and interned. Feehan, according to this man, reversed the instructions.

'Four Glorious Years' and its successors glorified the fight for independence. The various series mostly ignored the political aspects of the struggle and concentrated on the fighting, portraying every petty ambush as a major battle. Brendan Behan, who wrote beautifully crafted pieces for the morning paper, said he was afraid to enter the Sunday Press office 'for all the bullets flying about'.

Sometimes the articles strayed away from the derring-do and rehearsed tales of British injustice. One described the trial of the Manchester

Martyrs, three men sentenced to death for the murder of a policeman. Close to deadline time, it was found that there was no caption to go with a drawing of the three men in the dock. The chief sub-editor, Tom Hennigan, was asleep at his desk (this frequent phenomenon was not owing to drink but to some medical condition from which he suffered). They woke him up, whereupon he wrote a caption: 'the Manchester Martyrs pleading for mercy in the dock'. The whole point of the story was that the men did not plead for clemency but adopted a defiant posture, crying out: 'God save Ireland!' Feehan was not pleased.

Nor was he pleased with the review by the film critic, Vinny Doyle, of George Morrison's historical movie *Mise Éire*. The film is best remembered for the musical score by Seán Ó Riada. To make up for the paucity of pictorial material from the period, Morrison used montages of newspaper headlines. Doyle scathingly described it as 'the best film I ever read'. His colleagues expected him to be sacked, but his editor instead engaged him in an earnest conversation, puzzled that he did not find the work inspirational.

In the end, it was the unfortunate Feehan who got the sack, discovering in the process the deplorable methods employed by the *Irish Press* management which he had served faithfully for many years. He was sent to meet the company secretary, and found him in floods of tears. The executive informed him of his dismissal and the trifling compensation he would receive.

The *Evening Press*, which first hit the streets in September 1954, was organised on very different principles. The management wisely decided that an evening paper aimed mainly at an urban readership should eschew political propaganda. But how could it take an editorial line which was unfavourable to Fianna Fáil or at least neutral? The problem was solved by a decision not to carry any editorials whatever.

The key policy point was not political or even editorial, but ruthlessly commercial. Dublin could not support three evening papers. The *Evening Press* therefore would have to kill off one of the existing publications, the *Evening Herald* (owned by the Irish Independent group) or the *Evening Mail*. It went after the *Mail's* circulation by 'lifting' vast numbers of classified advertisements from the *Mail* and reprinting them free of charge. The tactic worked.

As editor, Vivion de Valera appointed one of the rising stars of the Irish Press group, Douglas Gageby. Gageby, then in his mid-thirties, had already had a most remarkable career.

He was born in Dublin but received much of his education in Belfast where his Northern-born father, a civil servant, moved at the time of independence. Under the terms of the Anglo-Irish Treaty, officials of the British administration in Dublin had a choice of staying in place under the new regime, taking a position in London, or going to Belfast to serve the Stormont administration. Douglas Gageby attended a Belfast school with a unionist ethos and went from there to Trinity College Dublin, then a heavily unionist and Protestant institution, but at an early age he embraced Irish nationalism and throughout his life he remained a fervent advocate of a united Ireland. In this he was influenced by the opinions of his wife Dorothy, daughter of Seán Lester, the last secretary general of the League of Nations.

During the war he served as aide-de-camp to the Chief of Intelligence, Colonel Dan Bryan. He was only a lieutenant, but formal rank does not matter greatly in intelligence services and he had a close relationship with Bryan which survived his military service. The importance of his position is illustrated by a photograph reproduced in the book *Bright, Brilliant Days*, edited by Andrew Whittaker. It shows him in uniform, sitting at his desk. On the desk are three telephones; at the time, a single telephone was almost unobtainable in Ireland. Bryan's job of course was intense co-operation with his British counterparts, and Gageby must have known many secrets. He was thus close to the top of the network which my father at the same time served in a humbler role on the Leitrim–Fermanagh border. Yet he was one of the most Anglophobic people I have ever met. He thought he saw British spies under every bed, and he had an obsession with the principle of neutrality which would cause me some grief in later times. I have sometimes wondered whether he picked up his Anglophobia on Burgh Quay, where the phenomenon seemed more intense to me than in the Fianna Fáil Party generally.

Not that Fianna Fáil supporters, or the generality of *Irish Press* readers, were free of Anglophobia—or bigotry. Numerous readers complained, often openly, of the appointment of a Protestant to one of the most influential jobs in the group. They found it impossible to accept that he was 'one of us'. Back on Burgh Quay, he was regarded (as I have written in my essay in the Whittaker book) not so much as a token Protestant as a trophy Protestant: a man who followed the teachings of Wolfe Tone and Thomas Davis and also believed in Fianna Fáil, not just for the usual reasons but as a party that supposedly aimed at the establishment of a liberal, non-sectarian, united Ireland.

That belief system was not then, and is not now, entirely in accord with reality, but it was insignificant by comparison with his powerful personality. Gageby got things done. He made people do things. They trusted his judgment against their own instincts. He was a great editor. He could also be a bully, and unscrupulous.

On the *Evening Press*, he prevailed in the face of a serious lack of resources. A notoriously penny-pinching company employed too few people, and the few outstanding sub-editors were outnumbered by those brought in to fill gaps during their sober moments. The chief sub-editor, John O'Donovan, complained that he was surrounded by alcoholics and drug addicts. This was a wild exaggeration, but certainly his staff included at least one drug addict and another man who worked brilliantly until the pubs opened, after which time his capacity, even his attendance, fell to vanishing point. O'Donovan himself had his little eccentricities. He wrote music criticism, and plays in (he hoped) the manner of Bernard Shaw. He maintained that Italians could not write great music; only Germans could attain the heights of the art. 'Germans' included Austrians, so lovers of Mozart could presumably feel comfortable.

The news editor, Jack Smith, had worked for Reuters as a war correspondent and published two books about his experiences. He was a man of wit and kindness and a true professional. He had a full-time reporting staff of only two, myself and Jim Flanagan; John Healy contributed a good deal of work to the evening paper, but failed to get himself assigned there full-time. There were exotic creatures in the form of an elderly nature columnist and a sports columnist who specialised in rows with sports governing bodies, foolish people who employed such silly and counterproductive tactics as banning him from press boxes at matches. There was a sweet man, Jim Edwards, who had a lovely light touch as a columnist. There was Reg Cullen, a man of wit and gentle humour quite unlike the more normal gallows humour of his native Belfast. And there was the inimitable Terry O'Sullivan, who wrote the Dubliner's Diary. Everything you want to know about him can be found in the magnificent memoir *Are You Somebody?* by his daughter Nuala O'Faolain.

For the rest, Smith had to rely on co-operation with the main *Irish Press* newsdesk, dominated by Bill Redmond. Redmond was a competent news editor, but tyrannical and almost sadistic. Two of the many books about the *Irish Press* come close to describing him but pull their punches. One is by the darling but tragic Michael O'Toole. The other, by Healy, is not a book properly speaking but a collection of pieces put together by his daughter after his death. Both are too soft.

Flanagan, a man of good sense and judgment, got his job by virtue of his long experience in the provinces. Nobody ever told me exactly how I got mine. Healy in effect head-hunted me, but I don't know how he or Gageby, or anyone else, had heard of me. I cannot say that my fame preceded me, since I had not earned any fame. I suppose Healy had come to learn, perhaps from Tony Gallagher, of a promising young man on the *Nationalist*. Gallagher, like Healy, came from Mayo. Both would have been favourably disposed to anyone from the province of Connacht.

———

James Joyce said that if Dublin were obliterated it could be rebuilt brick by brick from his description of the city in *Ulysses*. If anyone attempted such an exercise I could lend a hand, for the city I lived in in the mid-fifties resembled the one described by Joyce more closely than the Dublin of the twenty-first century.

There are better descriptions than any I could offer; for example, *The Ginger Man* by J.P. Donleavy and *Dead as Doornails* by Anthony Cronin, as well as the classic *At Swim-Two-Birds* by Flann O'Brien (Brian O'Nolan, Myles na gCopaleen) in which he prefigured Mel Brooks with a climactic scene in which the riders in a cowboy movie come to chaotic life in a suburban cinema.

The chief characteristics of the city were poverty and decay. Donleavy, an American, portrays his hero wandering among the Georgian houses, amazed by the poverty. In those crumbling buildings, once the homes of the Anglo-Irish ascendancy, the underclass lived in squalor and insecurity equal to anything described by Seán O'Casey. In the course of my work I visited many of the slums and stood amazed, like Donleavy, at the conditions of the poor. Picture a woman with eleven children living in one room with no electricity, no running water, no sanitation, and rotten floorboards through which a careless person could easily put a foot. Picture a system on the docks—which one wrongly thought had been abolished by Big Jim Larkin—in which workers were divided into 'button men' (permanent employees) and casuals with virtually no rights. Various forms of corruption, petty and not so petty, flourished then and later on the docks and on the cross-channel boats. The most notorious concerned the 'ghost' workers, who were theoretically employed to accompany cattle on the boats but who in fact stayed at home, like Fleet Street printers. I doubt if they would have done much good on the boats. Every Wednesday morning herds of beasts were driven from the cattle market on the North Circular Road to the pens on the docks. The sparse traffic was disrupted and the streets filled with filth. The drovers were extraordinarily incompetent. They lacked so much as the skill to prevent the cattle from wandering on to the footpaths and knocking over old women carrying shopping bags and handbags.

I lived in boarding houses and in bachelor flats of indescribable squalor: I never learned the art of housekeeping. But my life was enjoyable and even privileged. A young unmarried man with a little money in his pocket could have a very good time.

With friends from Burgh Quay like Jim Edwards and Reg Cullen, I frequented the fringes of the Bohemian society of the day. I made the acquaintance of the near-legendary 'characters' who figure in so many memoirs and novels, like Cecil Salkeld (who appears in *At Swim-Two-Birds* and whose daughter married Brendan Behan), Patrick Kavanagh and, a little later, Myles na gCopaleen. Kavanagh's reputation as grumpy and quarrelsome is well deserved. Numerous anecdotes about him have lived on in print and legend, but my favourite Kavanagh story is less well known. It comes from the actor and director Jim Fitzgerald. One morning the two found themselves sitting together in McDaid's pub in Harry Street, neither with enough money to buy a drink. A friend arrived with a copy of the *Irish Times*. It reported that Kavanagh had won an international literary prize worth a handsome amount in cash. They rushed round the corner into Grafton Street, to a bank known as the 'Royal Show Bank' because the manager, one Mr Colthurst, lent money to theatre people on flimsy collateral or none. He told them, regretfully, that the *Irish Times* story did not constitute grounds for any more loans. They returned to McDaid's, where the bar filled up with people eager to congratulate Kavanagh and buy him drinks. But he still sat gloomy and silent. At last he turned to Fitzgerald and said: 'That fellow Colthurst. Do you know he's a cousin of Bowen Colthurst, who murdered Frank Sheehy Skeffington in 1916?'

'Good Lord! Can that be true?'

'No, it's not true, but I'm going to put it about!'

Behan was the one I knew best. I admired him for his talent as a writer, and most of all for his wonderful ear for dialogue, in which he rivalled

O'Casey. But it was impossible to admire him as a person. He was a gurrier, unwashed, violent, delighting in every kind of misbehaviour, lazy, an abuser of his marvellous talents, and, worst, mean-spirited. In his final years he would swagger from pub to pub, ignoring his old friends and accompanied by hangers-on, flashing the large cheques he received from American publications for work into which he had put little or no effort. A far cry from the pieces he had earlier contributed to the *Irish Press*, for which he was poorly paid.

But to my way of thinking his worst characteristic was begrudgery. I did not see the original production of *The Hostage* in Dublin under the Irish title *An Giall* and cannot say whether the work in that manifestation was all his own, but certainly the London production was written chiefly by Joan Littlewood. *The Quare Fella* was rewritten from beginning to end by Carolyn Swift, from what amounted to no more than raw material supplied by Behan. She staged it in the little Pike Theatre, which she ran with her husband Alan Simpson. When eventually it reached the Abbey stage, I sat and listened to a drunken curtain speech in which Behan called the Abbey version the definitive production. I thought that unforgivable.

Elsewhere, the coterie surrounding the editor of the *Irish Times*, Bertie Smyllie, continued after his death to meet in the Pearl Bar in Fleet Street. One of their mainstays was Donagh McDonagh, playwright and district judge—and son of Thomas McDonagh, executed by the British in 1916. Behan called him 'the national orphan'. McDonagh, who reciprocated his hatred in full measure, said that his own work would still be performed when Behan's was forgotten. He could not have been more wrong.

The *Irish Press* journalists had their own pubs, the White Horse, the Scotch House and Mulligan's. The White Horse was frequented by strange fellows, with stranger accoutrements like shooting sticks, who claimed knowledge if not actual membership of the IRA or splinter organisations. Even if one believed their yarns and had some way to establish their veracity, writing anything was made almost impossible by the restrictive legislation in force. The IRA could be described only as 'an illegal organisation'. This made it difficult to report on the campaign which broke out on the border in 1956, in which more extreme groups, notably Saor Éire, figured in addition to the IRA.

To meet real IRA men, one did not have to go as far as the White Horse. The 'chief of operations', Seán Cronin, afterwards Washington correspondent of the *Irish Times*, worked as a sub-editor on Burgh Quay. He was arrested and sentenced to six months' imprisonment. Relations between the 'freedom fighters' and the security forces were casual, even friendly. While Cronin was in prison, the Special Branch continued to tap his telephone. Each time his American wife went shopping, she would first lift the phone and tell the tappers that they could relax for an hour or two.

Benedict Kiely liked the Scotch House and its customers. He told me that he first set eyes on me sitting there between Terry Ward and Liam Mac Gabhann and that my proximity to two great old-timers gave him the clue to my personality.

Kiely, a prolific novelist, was one of those who suffered most under the shameful censorship. Classics, and the works of most contemporary Irish writers of any standing, were banned on grounds of indecency by censors with twisted minds. The most notorious case was the banning of *The Land of Spices* by Kate O'Brien, a writer of the utmost delicacy, on the strength of four words. In a climactic scene, the central character sees her father and a young man in 'the embrace of love'.

The film censorship, at a time when the cinema was the main recreation of the masses, was grotesque. More infuriating than the outright banning of movies was the mutilation of many which passed the censor, to the point where it became impossible to follow the plots. There was no pre-production theatre censorship, but in one infamous incident the legal costs incurred in proceedings against the staging of *The Rose Tattoo* by Tennessee Williams forced the closure of the Pike Theatre in 1957. The playgoers' choice was very limited. After the destruction by fire of the Abbey, the national theatre set up shop in the Queen's in Pearse Street, a former music hall. There it staged mostly third-rate kitchen comedies, some of which portrayed the sad social conditions of the period as something to celebrate. For years on end argument raged about the rebuilding of the Abbey on the original site, resolved at last by the adoption of an appalling design by Michael Scott which produced an unshapely auditorium and backstage arrangements of extreme discomfort for the players.

I went to the cinema with girlfriends or with one or other of my Downey cousins, the same who as little girls had been photographed together on one of Uncle Tom Goodwin's draught horses. A bigger and rarer treat was a trip to the opera, sometimes with Aidan Hennigan (afterwards London editor of the *Irish Press*) and two cousins from the other side of my family, Petria and Mary Hughes. The standards of the chorus and the orchestra did not remotely approach the heights both have since reached; and the jokes, frequently cracked across the world and not just in Ireland, about twelve-stone sopranos singing roles like that of the frail Mimi in *La Bohème*, were not far from the truth.

I worked much harder than I had done on the *Nationalist*, and the work was more interesting. By comparison with the provinces, the capital naturally offered a far more lively and exciting news scene. But these things are relative. Crime, the staple of an evening paper, was almost entirely at the pettiest level except for the numerous incidents of street violence. I covered the robbery of £10,000, a fortune in 1955, from the Ballast Office, the headquarters of the Dublin Port and Docks Board. The story, for what it was worth, stayed on the front pages for several days. When I was sent with a photographer (Sheamus Smith, who in more liberal times became the film censor) to cover my first murder story, I felt that I had hit the big time. In fact, this was not much of a story. A deranged poor devil in an out-of-the-way rural district was suspected of killing his wife. The police for some reason were slow to arrest him. I interviewed him on his farm, where he was making hay. While we spoke, he kept jabbing his pitchfork at me. I was torn between concern for my safety and fear of losing face if I stepped too quickly or obviously out of the way.

I don't suppose that my life, whatever about my dignity, was greatly at risk on that occasion. Indeed, for all the length and variety of my career, and leaving aside the minor unpleasantness of having petrol bombs exploding at one's feet, I think I was seriously in danger only once. This happened in 1956, during the IRA 'border campaign' organised by Seán Cronin. On a dark winter evening I was in a car driven by a photographer, on an 'unapproved road', i.e. one on which it was forbidden to cross the border. We heard a sound and felt a shudder which made it appear that a missile had struck the car. I got out to investigate, found nothing, and clambered back in. Before we could restart, we saw two Royal Ulster Constabulary (RUC) men inches away from us at the two front windows, each with a pistol trained on us. They had fired on us from a distance of half a mile or so across fields, then rounded a bend and caught up with us when our car stopped. We persuaded them of our innocence and they directed us to the right road. Only afterwards did I reflect that at least one of them had been in the local RUC barracks when it was attacked the previous night and that the smallest suspicious move could have made them pull their triggers.

In Monaghan, on the southern side of the border, the hotel was crowded with journalists who had been trying to track down a sensational story. The RUC had fatally wounded two IRA men in a gun battle. Their bodies were taken across the border, and a secret inquest was held. John Healy, already pontifical in his twenties, stood in the middle of the hotel lobby and proclaimed: 'There are no bodies. There was no inquest.'

By then, Jim Flanagan and I had become quite famous for a strange reason, far removed from gun battles and inquests. We found missing babies, three of them, who had been stolen at different times by desperate childless women. One had been taken to Belfast many years earlier by a woman who had brought her up until the age of twelve or thereabouts, lovingly and in greater comfort than her family in Dublin could have provided, and who had persuaded her husband that the child was theirs.

The *Irish Press* newsdesk, piqued at the success of upstarts like ourselves, reacted in a way that showed Bill Redmond in his true colours. He sent Healy, a married man with small children, to Belfast to interview the husband, thereby destroying his holidays that Christmas. He could as easily have found an unmarried man to do the job.

The 'missing babies' stories lingered on in the public recollection for decades, and journalists and others often asked me to relate the details long after I had forgotten most of them. I used to reply that such was the paucity of real news, we found not only missing babies but stolen cats. That was true to the extent that Flanagan rescued one cat, the property of a rich elderly woman in Sandymount. A ransom may have been paid. The overjoyed owner celebrated by feeding chicken to her pet. The sight outraged Flanagan. Chicken then was a treat, altogether different from the 'rubber' variety which would soon become common. Few of the poverty-stricken families we encountered in our work could afford it.

Gageby and Smith recognised my ability to write good and clear English, and write it fast and accurately. I was rewarded more than once with an enviable assignment, to contribute the Dubliner's Diary when Terry O'Sullivan was absent. This meant a nightly tour of what passed for the Dublin social round, finishing by writing the column as late as 3 a.m. Many of the events I covered were little more than public relations exercises, but the work had its glamorous moments. Among the celebrities I met, then and again some years later in a similar role on the *Evening Mail*, were Ava Gardner, Margot Fonteyn, Liberace, and Bill Haley. In my young and impressionable days, Ava Gardner appeared to me like a creature different from ordinary human kind. Not only was she beautiful, she had about her an almost tangible aura of something on a higher plane than ordinary sexual attraction. Margot Fonteyn was charming, Liberace sad. Bill Haley, regarded as the pioneer of rock and roll, was a most frustrating interviewee. When I asked him to describe the origins of his style of music, he merely replied that at a concert performance he and his band (the Comets—what else would he call them?) had decided to play with 'a heavy beat'. My efforts to get a bit more analysis resulted only in the repetition of the phrase.

I visited the greenrooms of the theatres and made the acquaintance of actors and directors, including the glorious Edwards and MacLiammoir. I loved actors, their faults as well as their virtues. In their unrequited ambitions, their self-regard, their insecurity and their fondness for the minor vices, they were very like journalists. But, again as with journalists, I found them, or thought I found them, free of the major vices. In both cases that would change when it became at last possible for Irish theatre people and newspaper people to make serious money, but when they accumulate cash in bank accounts or try to cheat the taxman they act out of their ineradicable insecurity much more than greed.

———

My pleasant social life, however, could not blind me to the depression and inertia that surrounded us and worsened with every year that passed. It was clear from the most casual observation that nobody in authority had any answer to the desperate condition of the country. Unemployed men marched in their thousands to Leinster House; one of them got himself elected to the Dáil and briefly sat as a powerless independent deputy. Conservatives affected to fear revolution—as if there were anyone to lead a revolution. The Catholic church maintained its iron grip on the people's manners and morals. Its agents, as much as the Special Branch, spied on the tiny left-wing groups. So greatly was the very word 'communist' feared that the main group rejected it and called itself the Irish Workers' League. In public life the choice lay between the Fianna Fáil gerontocracy and the even more conservative Fine Gael, who could achieve office only with the help of minor parties. Labour and the trade union movement were split (a touch of church influence here as well) and Labour's role in the two coalition governments of 1948–51 and 1954–57 was well summed up by the Fine Gael leader James Dillon, who said that their cabinet members had been 'as quiet as mice'.

I witnessed the despairing reaction of the second coalition government of 1954–57 when Jack Smith sent me to cover the panic measures twice brought in by the Fine Gael finance minister, Gerard Sweetman. Neither he nor his colleagues, nor—as yet—the Fianna Fáil opposition, had any better answers to negative economic growth and the poor state of the public finances than special tariffs on imports. Yet it was the same Sweetman who identified a young rising star of the civil service, T.K. Whitaker, and made him secretary of the department.

My own reaction was to embrace left-wing politics with fervour. I had begun to move in that direction as early as the age of nineteen, and by the mid-fifties my views had become firm. Let me try to explain them.

First, they derived more from intellectual conviction than emotional commitment. I was never a Marxist, much less a Marxist–Leninist, but I believed, as countless intellectuals did, that central control of industry and finance was right practically as well as morally and could be brought about by democratic means. I admired, again like countless others, the staggering achievements of the Soviet Union, first in wartime production, secondly in scientific advance. Such views may appear eccentric, almost ridiculous, in the twenty-first century, but they were common in the 1950s and 1960s. They went along with a naïve hope for democracy and human rights in the communist world: what one of the Czechoslovak reformist communist leaders deposed by the Russians in 1968 called 'socialism with a human face'.

The Soviet achievements were real, and it was reasonable, though mistaken, to think that the USSR could overtake the United States as the greatest power in the world. That, by the way, was what the Soviet leader Nikita Khrushchev intended when he said that 'we will bury you': he meant by beating the US in the economic and scientific fields, not in war— though he nearly started a world war with his Cuban adventure in 1962. But the arms race, the space race and the hopeless inefficiencies of the communist system would soon destroy the Russian economy, and it is hard to suppose that the establishment of democracy and human rights in communist countries was ever more than an illusion.

People like myself were ignorant of the sheer power and size, never mind the complexity, of the capitalist system. Few in Ireland had any notion how banks and markets worked. Our model for reform was essentially British. We thought that a government could simply decree the nationalisation of major industries and set up first-class public services on the precedent of the British national health service, funded by insurance or taxation or a mixture of both. We were equally ignorant of the immense difficulty faced by any Irish government in expanding its small revenue base; and we could not foresee a time when the question would be solved, temporarily at least, by the introduction of 'let her rip' capitalism, stoked up by state aids and tax reliefs but founded essentially on rapacity.

Our trouble, as we saw it, lay in finding or creating an organisation through which we could attempt to achieve our aims. We could hope for little or nothing from the existing political parties or the trade union movement.

I sat for a while as the National Union of Journalists' representative on the Dublin Council of Trade Unions and found it divided into three parts: those under church influence, communists and their allies, and non-communist, idealistic socialists epitomised by the unjustly forgotten Mattie Merrigan. I would have considered myself a member of this third tendency, but I found little appeal in the notion of 'working-class solidarity'. My left-wing views notwithstanding, I was a middle-class individualist at heart; and nobody could work in the printing trade without seeing the divisions within the working class.

Fianna Fáil, once radical, had grown old and tired in their sixteen uninterrupted years of office between 1932 and 1948, and appeared to us as conservative as the dyed-in-the-wool Fine Gael leadership. Labour, even after the reunification of the party, were hopeless.

We did not know that salvation would soon come from what appeared to us most unlikely quarters at the centre of the establishment: the Fianna Fáil Party and the bureaucracy. The aged Éamon de Valera would retire as Taoiseach in 1959 and hand over to Seán Lemass, still vigorous and determined at the age of sixty. Lemass would form an axis with T.K. Whitaker, the foundation of the country's economic progress. The likes of us were irrelevant to this dynamic.

Some of us had placed our faith, in greater or lesser degrees, in a promising new party. Seán MacBride—a former IRA chief of staff and son of Major John McBride, executed in 1916—founded Clann na Poblachta in 1946. It was an instant success, winning two by-elections and gaining ten Dáil seats in the 1948 general election. But its support derived overwhelmingly from disaffected Fianna Fáilers, and these deserted it when, to their dismay, MacBride and Dr Noel Browne entered a coalition government led by the old enemy, Fine Gael.

Moreover, the conduct of MacBride as foreign minister and Browne as health minister was extraordinary, as were the negotiations for the formation of the coalition. Both Clann na Poblachta and Labour refused to accept the Fine Gael leader, General Richard Mulcahy, as Taoiseach. The job went to John A. Costello, an eminent lawyer and onetime Cumann na nGaedheal attorney general. MacBride had the government secretary, Maurice Moynihan, an impeccable civil servant, excluded from cabinet meetings because of his former closeness to de Valera. And then MacBride kept Ireland out of the North Atlantic Treaty Organisation on the flimsy grounds that Nato membership would mean recognising the partition of the country. Partly, as has always been presumed, at his urging, Costello declared Ireland a republic and took us out of the British commonwealth. De Valera privately opposed this move, thinking that it would hamper our feeble efforts to end partition. I greatly doubt if remaining in the commonwealth would have helped us on partition or in any other way, but the whole business was downright silly since we could have become a republic and still retained our commonwealth membership as India did.

MacBride's 'solution' to the unity question was an anti-partition campaign aimed at rousing sympathy in Britain and farther afield for Irish aspirations. The campaign failed spectacularly, and no wonder, since his only weapon was hot air.

He enlisted the support of de Valera, who knew very well that the operation consisted of nothing more than pointless rhetoric. Conor Cruise O'Brien was then a junior official in the Department of External Affairs. He was also an excellent mimic, though not alone in his ability to emulate de Valera's strange speaking style. In later life he liked to tell a story which casts light on all three men.

In 1973 he became a minister in Liam Cosgrave's Fine Gael–Labour government. De Valera, then President, entertained the new ministers to dinner at Áras an Úachtaráin and gave them a first-class piece of advice: Stick together.

Chatting with O'Brien after dinner, he said: 'Dr O'Brien, we have met before. You came to see me with Mr MacBride to discuss the anti-partition campaign. They think I am blind, but I have a little of what is called tunnel vision. I could see you when Mr MacBride was speaking, and I noticed that you were not watching him. You were watching me. And I said to myself, that young man is interested in politics!'

But the fatal flaw in the coalition and the party made itself manifest through domestic issues and personalities. MacBride was a difficult enough person in all conscience, but Browne was impossible: petulant, self-regarding, arrogant and, weirdly, a social snob.

He had been brought up in straitened circumstances, and traded on his claim to have shared the experiences of the poor. But as a boy he was informally adopted by a rich Dublin family and educated at an elite English Catholic school and at Trinity College. Thereafter he was constantly on the lookout for social solecisms on the part of those whom he openly considered his inferiors. He recorded one of the queerest in his memoirs *Against the Tide*: one of his episcopal adversaries, Bishop Michael Browne (no relation), lit a cigarette while drinking a glass of champagne. This happened long before smokers became outcasts. As to champagne, presumably bishops as well as ordinary mortals may drink what they please.

Noel Browne quarrelled with old friends, on flimsy grounds or none. One was Michael McInerney, long-time political correspondent of the *Irish Times* and kingpin of the National Union of Journalists, a man as decent as he was naïve. He was devastated when Browne snubbed him because he wrongly supposed that McInerney had somehow let him down. Browne's memoirs contain grotesquely unfair pen-pictures of former friends and political colleagues. He was totally intolerant of alternative viewpoints (though he often changed his own) and of common human failings, and he portrays himself as both superior and infallible.

He is remembered for a triumph and a catastrophe. Having himself survived tuberculosis, he set out, as health minister, to eradicate the disease and largely succeeded. There is no doubt about the triumph or the credit due to him—or the means by which the campaign was funded, the use of Irish Hospitals' Sweepstakes money. However, it was characteristic of him that in his memoirs he showed himself reluctant to share the glory with his chief medical officer, Dr James Deeny, or other officials in the Department of Health. His success also owed a great deal to the recent development of new 'wonder drugs', unknown to earlier generations.

He went on to devise the Mother and Child Scheme, a plan to revolutionise medical treatment for mothers and children up to the age of sixteen. It was a daring and imaginative departure, but he did little to share his vision or his tactics with his party or his colleagues in government. He seldom attended cabinet meetings. Instead, he engaged in long and complex—and doomed—negotiations with the Catholic bishops, who eventually denounced the scheme as contrary to faith and morals. Costello and MacBride repudiated him, and he resigned. The government fell soon after, on an unrelated issue, but the collapse has always been attributed, correctly, to the Mother and Child Scheme controversy.

It remains a matter of contention to this day, not because of the issue itself (settled more or less satisfactorily, after Fianna Fáil's return to office in 1951, by de Valera and Dr James Ryan, who knew better how to negotiate with bishops) but because of the church–state confrontation and Browne's role in it. Innumerable people believe, first, that he single-handedly conquered TB and, secondly, that he bravely and nobly stood up to the bishops when others bowed the knee, literally and figuratively. In point of fact, he equivocated on the question whether they had the right to dictate to the politicians on issues which they chose to nominate as matters of faith and morals. Unquestionably he towered over the politicians who rushed to declare themselves Catholics first and Irishmen second, and it is no wonder that he achieved and retained the passionate loyalty of many fine people. But he is severely to blame for his mishandling of the controversy, which served to copperfasten our deplorable 'image' as a society dominated by the church.

——

One fine man who stuck by Browne through thick and thin was Jack McQuillan, whom we have met in his wartime role. Along with Browne and others, he founded a new party in 1958, the National Progressive Democrats (not to be confused with the right-wing Progressive Democrats) and, like Browne, he eventually joined the Labour Party. This, however, was a step too far for the electorate in his constituency, Roscommon. John Healy had a favourite story about another Roscommon deputy, Johnny Beirne, who rejected a pay increase for deputies. The voters decided that if he could do nothing for himself, he could do nothing for them. In McQuillan's case, however, his loss of his Dáil seat owed more to the reluctance of the voters in that constituency to elect anyone with a Labour label. In elections to come, other Labour candidates would find out the same thing, to their cost.

But the Browne supporter who attracted the most public attention in several manifestations—and the one with the most outstanding intellect and charisma, to employ a much-abused word—was David Thornley. I first met him, not in a political context but as the fiancé, afterwards the husband, of my cousin Petria Hughes.

Her father John was the husband of Dympna, my mother's sister. He was a remarkable man, 'politically correct' before the term came into use, a feminist, and a loving and indulgent father who quietly made sacrifices for the education of his five children. He was also a practising Catholic, but he did not look on the clergy with the same reverence as my father.

He came from Armagh, where he joined the IRA when in his teens. He fought in the civil war on the republican side—more or less by chance, in a period of confused conflict and contradictory loyalties. He therefore partly shared a background with my Uncle Joe, who married John's sister Eithne. In the 1930s, however, their political paths diverged sharply. Whereas Joe maintained his loyalty to Fianna Fáil and sat for a time as a local Fianna Fáil councillor in Newbridge, John Hughes conceived a vehement hatred of the party and of de Valera personally. He said that he had voted for the party only once, to 'get my friends out of jail' in 1932, but de Valera soon began to lock up IRA members again, and executed several of them. Nevertheless John Hughes considered himself a staunch republican. He saw no contradiction between this allegiance and his fondness for Jacobite songs and coalitions led by Fine Gael.

I first visited their house in Clontarf while still a schoolboy. I soon made friendships which would last a lifetime with all the family, but especially with the two girls closest in age to me, Petria and Mary. Sunday evenings in Clontarf were one of my joys, with singing, parlour games and fierce arguments. The arguments took away nothing from the love and warmth, but I usually found myself bested in them by David Thornley and Aidan Clarke, who married Mary. I remember one long argument with Thornley in which my pitiful dialectical powers were wholly unequal to his defence of the Catholic version of the 'natural law'.

Thornley was born in London, the son of an English father who died young and an Irish mother who had inherited wealth and who moved back to Dublin after her husband's death. David became a star student in the Trinity history department. He earned his doctorate with speed and ease, with a thesis published under the title *Isaac Butt and Home Rule*. He was appointed to the staff and was a notable figure in the college by his mid-twenties. Aside from his academic achievements, he fancied himself as a tenor and as a boxer. He played cricket, as did his brother-in-law Aidan Clarke, whose academic career at the time paralleled Thornley's; and, like Petria and most unlike myself, he was a keen rugby fan. It would be a grave understatement to say that he spread his enormous talents too thin, but the sport and music were insignificant by comparison with his involvement in politics and, later, television. However, his musical tastes gave a clue to his personality. He loved the emotional, the sentimental, the rich and ornate—and the popular. He adored Mario Lanza when purists preferred Jussi Bjorling. At Christmas time he indulged himself by re-

reading all of Dickens's Christmas books. And he admired larger-than-life characters like himself. He aimed for the top in whatever career he adopted for the moment. Sadly, he never reached it in any of them, and when he died aged forty-two he had achieved nothing commensurate with his abilities.

With the sharpness of his intelligence and the fluency of his writing style, he might have been the leading Irish historian of the twentieth century. He might have been provost of Trinity. He might have been (had such an option been open, as in countries like France, to persons of varied backgrounds) editor of a national newspaper or magazine. He might have attained much greater eminence in television. But he did not follow up the projects he had begun. For example, he wrote a pamphlet on the confluence of the national, religious and land questions in the late nineteenth century, a staple theme of modern Irish historians, but did not produce the major work the subject cried out for. He planned a biography of Patrick Pearse, but never wrote it.

This gap was filled eventually with an excellent biography of Pearse by Ruth Dudley Edwards. However, the views of these two authors on the events of the early twentieth century in Ireland differed radically. For Thornley in his youth embraced simultaneously and paradoxically Catholicism of an old-fashioned kind, extreme nationalism, and left-wing politics.

Not very left-wing, though. At the beginning of our acquaintance, he asked me for support for some cause or line of action, appealing to me as a 'fellow Fabian'. I was nothing of the kind: as I have explained, my opinions then were a long way to the left and had not begun to moderate into social democracy inspired by egalitarianism, an unfashionable philosophy but one which I have never abandoned. In his sad final years he would consort with Trotskyists, who claimed that he had become a Marxist. I doubt that.

In politics he was the leading light of the 1913 Club, a left-wing discussion group. Much more significantly, he devoted himself, while still an undergraduate, to Noel Browne, who after falling out with Clann na Poblachta joined Fianna Fáil, which he saw as the nearest thing to a radical party the country possessed. His accession was greeted with fervour by huge numbers of the rank and file, but resented by one of the party's most powerful figures, Seán MacEntee, with whom he shared the Dublin South East constituency. So intense was Thornley's commitment to Browne that he followed him into Fianna Fáil, much to Petria's dismay, and conceived

an enthusiasm for the modernisers in the party. But in 1957 MacEntee saw
to it that Browne did not get a nomination to contest a sudden general
election. Browne's coterie, led by Thornley, decided that he should stand
as an independent candidate 'by popular demand'. They arranged a
meeting of supporters in a trade union hall in Fleet Street, over the road
from the Palace Bar, where they waited for the predictable result. I was
chosen to propose or second (I forget which) a motion calling on Browne
to stand. I remember the meeting well, not so much for my own role as for
three other reasons. The smoke (there really were smoke-filled rooms in
those days) was thick enough to make breathing difficult. Máirtín Ó
Cadhain, the great Irish-language writer and Trinity College colleague of
Thornley, made a speech which I found hard to follow but was apparently
based on the proposition that we were engaging in too much socialism and
not enough republicanism. And a sly little man was eager to know who I
was and what or whom I represented. Fianna Fáil always have their spies
everywhere.

I did not resent being used as a cat's paw in this way, and I worked
ardently in the election campaign, which Thornley ran brilliantly and
ruthlessly. Browne spent most of it in Ringsend, the working-class part of
the constituency, with a faithful servitor who seemed to have no political
views but admired the great man for eradicating tuberculosis. The rest of
us canvassed the majority middle-class and upper-middle-class areas. We
had strict instructions not to mention political theory or even the
appalling condition of the economy, but to concentrate on the supposed
heroism with which Browne had confronted the bishops. The word
socialism was banned. One bitter February night in Rathmines, door after
door was opened by people with a warm aura of affluence about them,
who uniformly told us, usually without being asked, that of course they
would vote for the man who had defied the bishops.

This was not the only campaign run by Thornley for Browne, or the
only occasion on which he neglected his own best interests. He got poor
thanks for his arduous work. Browne in his memoirs dwelt cruelly,
ungratefully and gratuitously on Thornley's physical deterioration in the
years before his early death. He was petty enough to write that he feared
his right-hand man might have political ambitions of his own. Why not?

Browne believed, rightly, that a deputy needs to work through a
political party if he hopes to achieve anything of substance. He had
forsaken two parties, and neither Fine Gael nor Labour (in its then
condition) had any appeal. He decided to found the NPDS.

The launch of the new party was carefully organised. A preliminary meeting, much like that of 1957, was held. Then a second meeting took place, at which membership forms were handed round. I attended the first in the company of Niall Andrews, son of the Fianna Fáil stalwart Todd Andrews and afterwards a Fianna Fáil deputy and member of the European Parliament. He always insisted that both of us filled in membership forms and said that when he went home his mother 'beat me round the kitchen' for daring to think of leaving the grand old party. There would be a curious echo of this a generation later, when his brother David agonised over an invitation to join yet another new party, the Progressive Democrats, but decided that he could not bring himself to abandon Fianna Fáil. David Andrews eventually became Foreign Minister in the short-lived Fianna Fáil–PD government under Albert Reynolds.

Niall Andrews was mistaken. I did not attend the second meeting. By the time it was held, I was out of the country.

| 1957: HOME AND ABROAD

S hortly after the launch of the *Evening Press*, Gageby had a confidential conversation with Jim Flanagan and myself. He said that he expected us to attend meetings of the chapel (house branch) of the National Union of Journalists and report back to him on the proceedings.

Neither of us obeyed the injunction. I took office in the chapel and became active in the overall Dublin branch of the NUJ, but I never reported back to Gageby. Michael McInerney believed that I was afterwards victimised for my union activities, but I cannot confirm that. I can only report what happened in 1957, less than three years after I joined the paper.

The American ambassador, Robert Taft, was leaving Dublin. In that less security-ridden era it was common to report items like that and for the friends of the grandee to go to the airport to see him off. I wrote a paragraph in which, by some stupid slip, I gave the wrong day for Taft's imminent departure.

Gageby went into one of his rages. He decreed that I should be suspended without pay for three days. This was a kind of punishment frequently inflicted, and it did not much upset me. However, he also decreed that I should lose a 'perk' I happened to enjoy, writing film criticism in the absence of the regular critic, Kevin O'Kelly. That struck me as vindictive and unacceptable. I did not see it as an issue for the union, so I simply sent in my resignation.

The long-term consequences may have been disastrous, but I have never regretted my action. I had made my protest and was willing to bear any consequences. I was young and single, unlike people who have to put food on the table for their children. 'He that hath wife and children,' wrote Francis Bacon, 'hath given hostages to fortune.' To revert to the vernacular, it's proverbially a mistake to cut off your nose to spite your face, but there's great satisfaction in it.

Since I refused to seek the aid of the union, an unofficial delegation of senior journalists came together and met Vivion de Valera. They got nowhere. He told them that an organisation like the Irish Press group could be ruled only 'by the whip'.

Then I had a tremendous stroke of luck, all the more remarkable at a time when jobs were exceptionally scarce. Jim Edwards had left the *Evening Press* for the *Times Pictorial*, a weekly paper owned by the *Irish Times*, and he persuaded the editor, Tony Gray, to take me on as a writer and sub-editor on a casual basis. I moved round the corner from Burgh Quay to Westmoreland Street, and I did not look back.

——

Gray and his deputy—his level-headed brother Ken, imperturbable and sound as a bell—were both excellent journalists. Tony Gray had lately been one of the bright young Protestants thought from time to time to be in contention for the editorship of the *Irish Times* when Bertie Smyllie departed. But the *Pictorial* was not a classic-winning horse in the *Irish Times* stable. Its appeal, as the title suggested, lay farther down the market. It had little in the way of staff and money. The standard of printing was at best fair, and there were no colour photographs.

Still, it provided an entrée to the *Irish Times*, and a front-row seat from which to view some of the cataclysmic events about to unfold in Westmoreland Street.

The *Irish Times* was founded in 1859 by Major Lawrence Knox. The paper was edited for many years by a Church of Ireland clergyman, the Rev Dr George Wheeler. He was in effect the first editor, though he was preceded for a matter of weeks by his brother-in-law. Wheeler varied his journalistic duties with a cure of souls at the vast British military camp on the Curragh. He customarily travelled by train at weekends to nearby Newbridge, and from the station to the camp in a horse-drawn carriage. One day the carriage overturned. He died of his injuries.

The paper supported the mild Home Rule movement led by Isaac Butt. It regarded the Anglo-Irish Protestant ascendancy as the natural leaders of a semi-independent country firmly fixed within the British empire. After Knox's death it was sold to the Arnotts, a rich business family. From then on it adopted a vehement brand of unionism, and during the first world war it would enthuse at the sight of young Irishmen joining the British army and shedding their blood in France for the empire.

Under Smyllie's reign (1934–54) the *Irish Times*, having come to terms with the new regime after independence, came to terms also with de Valera's accession to power, which had occurred in 1932. But Smyllie did not repudiate the newspaper's, or his own, unionist roots, much less the liberalism that supposedly went with its Protestant heritage. The liberalism for the most part was only skin-deep, but it was enough to make the paper compulsory reading for Catholics, as well as Protestants, with any sort of independent bent. The *Irish Times* took an even-handed line in the Spanish civil war (1936–39) when Catholic Ireland loved Franco, and it thundered against the Catholic bishops when they devoured Noel Browne in 1951. It published columns by Smyllie himself and better ones by Sheila Greene, estranged wife of Professor David Greene of Trinity and lover of a trade union leader, Christy Ferguson, with whom she often drank in the Pearl Bar. The paper's commentaries were, if not particularly well-researched or well-written, at least more informative and independent than most of the reading material available elsewhere.

Besides, Smyllie employed two of the most famous columnists in any age of Dublin journalism. One was Brian O'Nolan, who wrote for the paper under the nom-de-plume Myles na gCopaleen and as 'Flann O'Brien' published the immortal *At Swim-Two-Birds*. He drank heavily and morosely, but he rose early each morning to produce his Cruiskeen Lawn pieces for the *Irish Times*, biting satire and impeccably typed (in an age when many writers, journalists included, still wrote by hand). The other was Patrick Campbell, who inherited the title Lord Glenavy and who wrote *An Irishman's Diary*, full of literary gems. Later he made a name for himself in England as a television personality.

The office manager was Cully Tynan O'Mahony, a Catholic unionist whose career had been, if the stories can be believed, exceptionally colourful but comical rather than dramatic. According to these yarns, he had served during the war of independence in the Auxiliaries, known as 'Auxies', a special force recruited by the British to put down the Irish insurrection by fair means or foul, mostly foul. They were much like the notorious Black and Tans, with this difference, that they were recruited from officers who had served in the first world war. After independence he joined the Palestine Police (Britain then ruled Palestine). One day he was walking on a beach with a brother officer. An Arab from a nearby village approached them and offered to sell them a parcel of land. They told him to clear off. As they walked away, one said to the other: 'Do you know the name of that village?'

'Tel Aviv.'

O'Mahony had an artificial foot. It was said that he had not lost a foot by reason of enemy fire but had cut it off himself with a penknife when it stuck in the doors of a lift. The story is more credible than it may seem because of the construction of old-time lifts and because men of his kind customarily carried large penknives. According to one of the many Westmoreland Street legends, his artificial foot fell off one day as he was climbing the Pearl stairs. Myles na gCopaleen, following behind, said: 'Ah! O'Mahony! Footless again.'

One day a stray, motherless kitten wandered into the Irish Times front office, faintly mewing for milk. O'Mahony fetched a saucer of milk, but the kitten did not know how to lap, so he knelt on the floor to lap it himself and give the little animal a practical lesson. Thereafter he was always known as Pussy O'Mahony. The word would have a different implication nowadays.

His son Peter worked with me long after as an assistant chief sub-editor. He was a fine man and a dedicated journalist, but a perfectionist in a trade in which sticklers (myself included) need to learn compromise and the tyranny of the clock. On one occasion his perfectionism lost us an entire first edition. Thankfully I was not present.

Another of O'Mahony's sons was David, who as Dave Allen became a British television star, one of my all-time favourite comics. But he was more than a stand-up comic: his humour had depth and point and underlying sadness. I think Peter helped to write his scripts.

Smyllie himself was quirky in the extreme. It was widely believed that he used to 'hide' in the pub to avoid board members when he wanted to publish something more radical than usual, but I don't believe that. He bore a grudge against Trinity College, which he thought should have awarded him an honorary MA. He had grounds for resentment. As a Trinity undergraduate he had taken a holiday job in Germany in 1914, and the outbreak of war caught him in Germany, where he was interned, like poor Josef Jeiter in reverse, and thereby unable to finish his degree. He had queer ideas about style, possibly related to the fact that the Great War had shaped his mindset, more likely owing chiefly to pomposity. He sprinkled his editorials with Latin tags, a practice derided by Douglas Gageby, who said that Smyllie knew hardly any Latin and the phrases were only such as, to quote the old phrase, 'every schoolboy knew'. In my own time we still clung to 'to-day' and 'to-morrow', and the weird spelling 'Yugo-Slavia'. In later times I would try strenuously, with limited success, to modernise the style and to wage war on the proliferation of hyphens. My colleagues were so conservative that I could not persuade them to change the style of dates to, for example, '13 July 1985' in place of 'July 13th, 1985'.

Daft style rules were nothing new to me. The *Irish Press* group had had many. They had insisted that the forename Éamon should be spelt with one N only in reference to de Valera and all other Eamonns must have two Ns, regardless of their own preferences; and that we must use the Irish version of town names which had been changed officially to Irish. According to the office folklore, a sub-editor found himself confronted with a reference to 'the bishop of Nara'. He thought this must be a mistake, and changed it to Navan. It was then revised to the Irish version, and appeared, mysteriously, as 'the bishop of An Uaimh'.

In the *Irish Times*, stylistic absurdies were small beer compared with the long struggle to come to terms with independence, and with the change of government in 1932. At first, the process had strict limits. Long after the foundation of the Irish state, a reference to 'the government' still meant Whitehall, not the new regime in Dublin. The Protestant business and professional classes retained much of their wealth, power and influence long after the land-owning ascendancy dwindled into irrelevance; it would take them another generation at least to become fully assimilated. The *Irish Times* still had few Catholic readers. The journalistic staff were mainly Protestants—some unionists and Freemasons, some not—and that was true also of many who worked on the business side or as printers: the Protestant working class had not yet been wiped out by the deplorable *Ne Temere* decree which insisted that the children of mixed marriages must be brought up Catholics, or by a more benign phenomenon, embourgeoisement.

During the second world war, Smyllie had engaged in many quarrels with the censors. He scored a famous but boyish victory over them when the war in Europe ended. The front page featured photographs of the Allied leaders, scattered about in no particular order. For the late editions, he had them rearranged in the shape of a v—v for Victory. He employed George Leitch, a charming man but utterly incompetent, as chief photographer merely because Leitch had served in the British forces in the first world war. He was unhappy when Patrick Campbell joined the Irish naval service (part-time) instead of the British navy. (In this he was the opposite of Gageby, who called a man who had served in the British armed forces 'you fucking traitor'.) When an Irish naval officer in the British service survived the sinking of his ship, a paragraph appeared which celebrated his safe emergence from 'a boating accident'. The censors did not spot the true meaning.

A decade and more later, the yarns might be equally good but the state of affairs was not promising. The declared circulation was a little above 30,000, not only a wretched figure but an inflated one; the true circulation may have been as low as 20,000. The newspaper might not survive, certainly would not flourish, as the house organ of the Church of Ireland and Trinity College. It would have to change, or fade. By the time I arrived in Westmoreland Street in 1957, the board was putting its mind to spectacular change.

Something else would have to change besides the ethos. The editor's office floated on a sea of whiskey. Not only did Smyllie drink excessively, in the office as well as in the Pearl Bar, so did his assistant editor Alec Newman and the next man in line, Bruce Williamson. Both of these were highly educated and cultivated men who were not well suited to the rough newspaper trade. Much of their work consisted of reading proofs and spotting mistakes and solecisms. These abounded, for the paper's reputation for upholding literary standards was undeserved. When sub-editors were unsure of a date or the spelling of a name, they often checked the *Irish Independent* version. A deputy chief sub-editor, a Scot called Morrison Milne, inflicted horrors like 'General Issimo' and 'in Communicado' on the readers. Then and later, subs waited nervously for eruptions from the editor's office. This continued into my time. Late one night a far from sober Bruce Williamson plonked down a proof in front of a young (and very literate) sub, Noel McFarlane. It referred to 'a hand-written manuscript'. 'Another milestone,' he huffed, 'in our never-ending search for obscurity.' I remembered the incident when I came across a reference to 'the well-known German composer, Ludwig van Beethoven'. But by then we had entered the present age of illiteracy.

Whether or not larks like these fortified literary standards, they were a world removed from the needs of a modern newspaper. The board decided on daring departures, some of which proved appallingly unwise. The chief moves, not necessarily in chronological sequence, were as follows.

Major Thomas Bleakley McDowell joined the board and bought, first a tiny proportion and later a large chunk of the voting shares. He came from Belfast and had served in the British army as a legal officer, organising courts-martial. Gageby was enticed from the Irish Press group to become joint managing director. He too bought a slice of the voting shares. There was irony in his appointment, for Smyllie had once asked him why a bright young Protestant was not working for his paper and Gageby had replied: 'I don't want to work for your bloody paper.'

The company launched the *Sunday Review*, a brave experiment in publishing a middle-market tabloid which deserved better success. It bought the *Radio Review*, a listings magazine, whose owner, J.J. McCann, joined the Irish Times board. This was a crazy decision. All Dublin knew that an Irish television service would soon be launched and that Radio Telefís Éireann, as the expanded broadcasting service was entitled, would produce its own listings magazine and wipe out the *Radio Review*.

A more catastrophic move was the purchase of the moribund *Evening Mail*, when the Irish Times board had no clue whatever as to the *Mail's* calamitous finances. There is no doubt that the motivation was purely sectarian, a desire to prop up a Protestant newspaper. Gageby objected, and no wonder: only a few years earlier his own work as editor of the *Evening Press* had made the *Mail's* survival impossible. Long afterwards he told me that he was persuaded to vote for the purchase with the time-honoured plea, 'let's make it unanimous, Douglas.'

The *Times Pictorial* was renamed the *Irish Pictorial*. Tony Gray went off to London as features editor of the *Daily Mirror*, and a very odd fellow, Peadar Ward, succeeded him. Ward had previously edited the *Catholic Standard*. Under his editorship and that of his predecessor Peadar O'Curry, the *Standard* had spied on communists and denounced people who dared to make trips to the Soviet Union. By a curious chance (or perhaps not by chance) Gageby went on to bring O'Curry into the *Irish Times* as a sub-editor.

It soon became obvious that the poor old *Pictorial*, starved of resources, would not last long. It would be the first of three publications to fall victim to the board's misguided policies, and it would be time for me to change course again.

———

At twenty-four, I had seen very little of the world. Previously I had ventured no farther than London, where I had been dazzled by the lights of Piccadilly Circus and bewildered by the throngs in the streets at night. Now the chance had come to improve on that. I set off for France, Italy and Spain, and after a couple of false starts spent six months teaching English in Gijon, in the province of Asturias in north-west Spain.

In Paris, I lodged for a little while in a garret straight out of *La Bohème*, and did not mind the climb up the innumerable stairs. I discovered that the stories of Parisian waiters' rudeness were true, and that Parisians, unlike the provincial French, sneered at crude efforts by foreigners to speak their language. (Nowadays the immigrants who work in the cafés are much more polite.) I visited the *Folies Bergères* in the company of an English medical student whom I had met on the train from Dieppe. He was horrified at the near-nudity of the gorgeous girls in the show. That struck me as eccentric in a medical student. I went to the Louvre and gawked at the *Mona Lisa*. I discovered cabarets in which the audiences roared with laughter at anti-German jokes. I went to the races at Auteuil and backed a couple of winners.

In Madrid, I met a fascinating family, to whom I introduced myself as a friend of Deasún Breatnach, who wrote for Dublin newspapers under the pen-name Rex Mac Gall. Breatnach, his affluent origins in Rathmines notwithstanding, was a fervent socialist and republican. In later life he would support the Provisional IRA. His son Osgur was one of the men wrongly convicted of carrying out the Sallins train robbery, a cause célèbre in the 1970s. His daughter was Lucilita, at one time secretary of Sinn Féin.

Deasún Breatnach had lived in Spain as a very young man and married a Basque whose brother had served in the volunteer division sent by Franco to fight for the Germans on the Russian front. This brother-in-law had become a prosperous businessman. He lived in some style in an apartment in the centre of Madrid and owned a villa in the mountains nearby. A younger member of the family took me to the wonderful Prado gallery, to my first bullfight, and on tours of tapas bars, evenings which featured excessive consumption of snacks and wine followed by a late dinner. Whatever the Spanish may have said then or say now, this is not good for the digestion. But I began to learn about food at a time when haute cuisine was largely a mystery in Ireland.

Deasún Breatnach's aunt was a nun in a convent not far from the Atocha Metro station, in recent times the scene of one of the worst al-Q'aida bombings. The Countess of Barcelona, wife of the Pretender Don Juan, had been educated there. The aunt informed me that the countess often visited the convent and that on her last visit she had expressed confidence that Franco would honour his pledge to restore the monarchy. In this hope she would be disappointed. Her husband would never be king. The throne would pass to their son Juan Carlos, who would play a notable part in the restoration of democracy in Spain.

Miriam Swanton, a former member of the 1913 Club, taught English in a language school in Aviles, near Gijon. Her brother married a girl from the Asturias provincial capital, Oviedo. Miriam found me work similar to her own in Gijon. I had little aptitude for teaching and I learned more Spanish than my pupils learned English, but such was the eagerness of the Spanish to learn English that I had no difficulty in finding private students in addition to those who attended the school.

Two of the private students were rich shipbrokers. Both had served as pilots in Franco's air force during the civil war. I also struck up an acquaintance with the local Falangist chief, a man my own age who in several long conversations fiercely contested my notions of democracy. These people, however, were untypical in socialist and republican Asturias, the scene of heavy fighting and many atrocities in two civil wars. The friends I made there hoped not only for democracy but provincial autonomy. They hated Franco and particularly detested his use of Moorish troops. They told me a story which I could have heard only in Asturias.

The region produces cider, not wine. Gijon is full of *chigres*, pubs where the barmen pour the bitter and refreshing brew, much like English scrumpy, at seemingly impossible angles. The drink is strong stuff, and public drunkenness, then unknown in most of Spain, was common. During one of the civil wars, a toper staggered towards the statue of the legendary Gothic King Pelayo which stands near the waterside and cried out: 'Pelayo, you drove the Moors out of here once. Now drive them out again!'

He was referring to the fascist use of Moorish troops, and to the Asturian claim that they were never fully conquered by the Moors and that in the Middle Ages Pelayo began the 'reconquest' of Spain at Covadonga, in the foothills of the Cantabrian Mountains, which they rather grandly call Los Picos de Europa. The enterprise had the advantage of supernatural aid. The Blessed Virgin Mary appeared at Covadonga to encourage the king in his endeavours. I went to her shrine on an excursion to a fiesta, and from there up the mountains, where we witnessed shepherds in a 'hill-leaping' contest. They jumped, perilously, extraordinary distances. Near the summit the sky clouded over and there followed a spectacular thunderstorm.

I also made, with another busload, an expedition to the forests on the border of Galicia, Spain's most north-westerly, and supposedly most Celtic, province. Wolves and bears were said to live in those forests. I saw neither. The nearest I came to contact with ferocious wildlife was the sight of a shepherd near Covadonga who carried on his shoulders a wineskin made of a wolf's hide.

More interesting for me than the sightseeing was observation of the local mores and the local economy. I had expected to see desperate widespread poverty, and I would indeed have seen it in the south of Spain then. Not so in Gijon, an important port, or Oviedo, an industrial city. There were beggars, usually in or around the church porches, but few poorly dressed or underfed people in the streets. The middle classes liked to say that 'we are poor but we live well.' The men often survived by holding down two jobs. Opportunities for women were dreadfully limited, but they were limited in Ireland too, as witness the 'marriage bar' which prevented married women from working in the Irish civil service. Young Spanish women of the middle and upper-middle classes may have suffered more from the restrictions on their private lives—though the girls I knew in Gijon were jolly and at least half-liberated.

After the advent of democracy, all that would change, and greatly for the better; and republican Asturians would give due but unenthusiastic credit to the constitutional monarchy. In 2006 I attended a journalists' congress in Oviedo, where I met a man who told me that he had not become a monarchist but merely a 'Juancarlista', a supporter of Juan Carlos who would also support the heir to the throne, Prince Felipe, if in due course he reigned on the same principles as his father. Perhaps that would have pleased the Countess of Barcelona. Or perhaps not.

———

Much as I enjoyed Gijon, I had no wish to stay there more than a few months. A career as an English teacher was bound to pall soon, and I did not see myself as a reporter on a Spanish newspaper. In the first place, my command of the language was insufficient. In addition, although I did not find the Franco regime particularly oppressive in terms of daily life newspapers were subject to a censorship which I would surely find unbearable. In the autumn of 1958, after a brief visit to Rome, I headed back to London, the one place where I was certain to find work.

My little mainland interlude had left deep impressions on me. In Ireland we pictured continental Europe, thirteen years after the worst war in history, as a scene of desolation. We had no idea that the miraculous postwar recovery had begun. Business leaders at home had told us that we could never aspire to British living standards, only continental standards. Now I had found that mainland countries had begun the process of overtaking Britain.

London was a shabbier place than Paris or Rome, or even Madrid. Postwar reconstruction in Britain was proceeding at a dismally slow pace. Paris and Rome showed no sign of war damage, and neither did Madrid, notwithstanding the bombardments it had endured in the civil war. Piccadilly Circus and Leicester Square might compare with those cities for bright lights and throngs of people, but they had nothing to match the glories of the Champs Elysee or the Via Veneto. Parisian elegance and the beauty and sophistication of the French and Italian, and perhaps most of all the Spanish, women had left me breathless. The main lesson I learned from my travels was that if you want to find something out, it is well to go and have a look for yourself. Seeing is believing.

I would soon grow to love London, but my first six weeks were discouraging, and not only because the signs of the city's slow recovery were visible. I spent those weeks in a job much inferior, in terms of satisfaction, to my employment in Gijon. It was the time of year when the giant ICI manufacturing company determined the dividends to be paid to its shareholders. To check the figures, it employed casual staff, usually students, and I joined them in this tedious but quite lucrative work.

The students surprised me by their political conservatism: student revolts lay a decade in the future. The regular staff with whom we mingled regarded me as an oddity—not because of my political views, in which they had no interest, but because of my reading habits—and thereby gave me my first real glimpse of the oddities of the English class system. They read the *Daily Express* and *Daily Mail*. One of them assured me that you could believe everything you saw in the *Express*. Nobody would say that nowadays. They assumed that the workers in the company's factories read the *Daily Mirror*, another great newspaper which would soon enter a period of sad decline in quality. They found it hard to believe that I came to work every day carrying the *Guardian*, whose circulation they assumed to be confined to intellectuals.

No doubt the people at the top preferred the *Financial Times*. The chief clerk occupied an intermediate position, in reading habits as much as in status. He read the *Daily Telegraph*. This elderly and kindly man had been born on a Scottish island and spoke fluent Gaelic. I discovered that we could carry on a conversation if I spoke to him in Irish and he spoke to me in Gaelic. But we did not have much to say to each other. All I wanted was to get out of ICI and into a newspaper office.

My wish was granted when I went for interview to the offices of the most extraordinary newspaper group for which I have ever worked, the Express and Independent, based in Leytonstone in East London. I recognised the good old smell, ink and lead, as soon as I entered the headquarters.

This building—a ramshackle shed—and the other peculiarities of the company have been described by Leslie Thomas in his autobiography *In My Wildest Dreams*. Shortly before my arrival he had been called up for national service (conscription, imposed by governments that had not yet abandoned their imperialist legacy, was still in force) and it has been suggested that I took his place, but the dates don't fit exactly. He wrote a best-selling novel, *The Virgin Soldiers*, inspired by his experiences in Malaya, and made a fortune from this and his other works.

The Express and Independent published several newspapers in various parts of London. I was assigned to a concrete hut in Woodford in Essex, a pleasant and prosperous, but dull, suburb best known for the fact that Winston Churchill represented it in the House of Commons. I rubbed shoulders with the great man on one of his rare visits to his constituency, when he made a nonsensical speech about 'merchant venturers'; and I heard his wife Clementine speaking at a Conservative garden fête. Her theme was the awfulness of the Labour Party's left wing. I don't know how much of it she believed. Clementine Churchill was not a Tory but a life-long Liberal.

My work was much like my previous activities in Carlow and Laois, with this exception, that so little ever happened in Woodford worthy of publication in a newspaper. There was plenty of cultural activity, and I was impressed by the standard of the local dramatic and musical productions, but more newsworthy events were lacking. My time was better occupied in covering the magistrates' court in nearby Epping (minor sexual offences featured strongly) and at a weekly event in Leytonstone at which staff from all over London gathered to read the final proofs of the various Express and Independent papers.

These operations took place in a caravan parked outside what I have described, and Leslie Thomas has described in more detail, as the ramshackle shed which constituted the group's headquarters. We were not responsible to any editors, because the newspapers we worked for did not have editors: the only person of real authority was a sort of editor-in-chief known only as 'Mr Harold'. Unlike the colourless Mr 'Arold, the assembled

journalists were lively fellows from every part of England, Ireland and
Scotland. They drank coffee, sometimes stronger brews, and told jokes.
Whatever their origins, almost none of them saw the Express and
Independent as a job for life. The usual ambition, which of course I
shared, was to move to Fleet Street, still the Street of Adventure with all its
traditions, its glamour and its opportunities for fame.

I saw a little of the Street of Adventure, or at least its fringes, when I met
Tony Gray in a pub frequented by the *Mirror* staff and popularly known as
the Stab in the Back. It afforded a glimpse, not so much of glamour as of
intrigue and boot-licking. I renewed my acquaintance with Paddy
Ginnane and Tony Gallagher, who were both working in London for
United Press International. Through them I made the acquaintance of
Australian journalists who, whenever they could, spent their afternoons in
drinking dens off the Strand. English pubs then were closed by law in the
afternoons, but there were plenty of 'drinking clubs' with lax membership
rules. And I met that wonderful man, Donal Foley, with whom I would go
on to work closely, in the *Irish Press* London office.

My first visit there coincided with the advent of my old drinking
companion Brendan Behan. He had been living in the Canary Islands, not
yet the scene of mass tourism but an underdeveloped backwater, and I
have often thought that he should have stayed there and taught himself to
write in a disciplined manner. He probably would have ruined himself
with drink and neglect anyway, but the lionisation in which he would revel
in London, New York and Toronto certainly contributed.

Joan Littlewood was about to stage her version of *The Hostage* in
Stratford, East London. One of my girlfriends worked on it in the humble
capacity of assistant stage manager. Among her many duties was to keep
Behan as quiet as possible and in particular to prevent him from making
drunken and incomprehensible curtain speeches. She had to put up with
frequent sexual harassment, but she knew how to handle it.

In the meantime I made as much as I could of the limited opportunities
offered by the *Woodford Times*; and I made many friends. One, Bob Bird,
became a friend for life. He was a true Cockney, born within the sound of
Bow Bells, the son of a docker. He lived with his parents in a council
maisonette close to the Mile End Road, very well-designed and
comfortable. I became a lodger there, and took an enormous liking to the
vivid life of the East End.

This was a different place from what it would become in the next half-
century. The huge Bangladeshi immigration had not yet begun. The

people were mostly native English, descendants presumably of migrants from the Essex countryside who had moved in to work on the docks and in the factories at the time of the Industrial Revolution. There were a handful of Irish, some of whom had prospered by running the boarding houses in which their compatriots lived in wretched conditions. Others worked in the gigantic Ford car plant in Dagenham. There were hardly any blacks and, to my surprise, hardly any Jews. Their ancestors had arrived in the late nineteenth century, illiterate and verminous, fleeing pogroms in Czarist Russia. The existing Jewish community—affluent, cultivated and assimilated—viewed the phenomenon with mixed feelings, but quickly decided that it was their moral duty to help the immigrants. Whether because of this or because of their celebrated flair for trade and finance, the East End Jews soon prospered and moved to desirable residences in the suburbs. There was a further but smaller immigration in the 1930s, of people fleeing the evil and crazy Nazi rule in Germany, but that did not affect the East End. So many of the refugees, some of them among the world's leading intellectuals, settled in North London that taxi drivers called the Finchley Road 'Finchleystrasse'. By my time, the remaining East End Jews had become the aristocracy of the area, much respected for their business acumen and their moral values.

Gangsters abounded, including the notorious Kray twins. We often drank in the Blind Beggar pub, scene of one of the Kray gang murders. But although gangsters sometimes frequented the same pubs as ourselves I never to my recollection spoke to any of them: I obeyed a firm injunction to have nothing to do with them and not so much as to look at their women.

Once again, I was leading an enjoyable life and I expected it to continue for at least a year or so. My course would soon take another turn.

Chapter 5

1960: WESTMORELAND STREET

I n August 1959 I went back to Ireland to attend my sister Eva's wedding to Humphrey Kelleher. I stopped off in Dublin and made for the Pearl Bar. There I met Tony Gray, whom I had last seen in London. He told me that he was helping to launch a new local weekly based in Dun Laoghaire, the *Post*, and offered me the job of editor. I accepted on the spot.

I lasted only ten weeks before getting the sack. I could call myself the victim of teething troubles. New publications commonly spend more money, and make less, than their budgets allow for, and frequently a proprietor's reaction is to sack someone. And the *Post*, although it survived for a year or more, was never going to succeed because it was ahead of its time: in a later period Dublin local papers, run on better marketing principles, have flourished. But in any case I was too raw and inexperienced to edit a newspaper.

Then I had another stroke of luck: the birth of the *Sunday Review*. The news editor, the same Liam Mac Gabhann with whom I had sat in the Scotch House, offered me frequent casual work. I joined just in time to help write the lead story in the first edition.

Or not quite the first edition. The editor—John Healy, brought over by Gageby from Burgh Quay—and the managing editor, Ted Nealon, had got hold of a story which they thought would launch the paper with a bang: the birth of a baby to the young wife of an aged man. But on the night, things changed. An American cruise ship ran aground on the Daunt Rock, off Cork. There was talk of casualties. In the end all the crew and passengers survived, but it was a big story none the less. Throughout the evening, we made frenzied efforts to establish the details while the editor and managing editor agonised over whether they should give their scoop lesser prominence and lead with the story of the shipwreck. Finally they decided, correctly, that for the later editions they must make the shipwreck the lead story. I contributed as much information as I could gather. Mac Gabhann was impressed by my work, but it was not much out of the ordinary.

Healy is remembered, in addition to his Mayo polemics, for the creation of the Backbencher column, a new departure in Irish journalism. Nealon, who collaborated with him on the column, deserves equal credit. It is not too much to say that between them they transformed political coverage. Hitherto this had consisted largely of long and dull reports of speeches in the Dáil and elsewhere, along with editorials and analytical articles which, with rare exceptions like the thunderings of the *Irish Times* at the time of the Mother and Child crisis, were not particularly good. Backbencher featured pithy comments, shenanigans in constituencies and leaks of stories from the 'Three Musketeers' in the Fianna Fáil government: Donogh O'Malley, Charles J. Haughey and Brian Lenihan senior. These leaks were said, almost always wrongly, to have the approval of the Taoiseach, Seán Lemass. In time, all the other Irish newspapers would copy the Backbencher style, with varied success.

After the death of the *Sunday Review* in 1963, Healy would go on to take the column into the *Irish Times*, where along with Douglas Gageby he would make it, not a conveyor of information and excitement but a parade of prejudices. His admiration of Haughey, 'our last hero', exceeded all rational bounds. In so far as he engaged in any criticism of his idol, he mainly confined it to the proposition that Haughey was unfortunate in his choice of friends. In reality Haughey's true character was obvious from the beginning to those with a less rosy viewpoint, and it would ultimately be revealed in a lurid light.

As an editor, Healy was as inexperienced as myself—more so, indeed, for he had virtually no knowledge of sub-editing or production. He had ambitions beyond his means, since the board, in its usual way, starved him of staff and money. He wanted to make the paper sophisticated and modern, or what he considered modern. He told me: 'It's the affluent society!' The affluent society lay some distance in the future, and left-wingers such as myself—paradoxically, like the business leaders who had talked about continental living standards—doubted its achievement. But he was right and we were wrong in an important way. The Labour Party and the unions were irrelevant to the new Ireland emerging in the 1960s. The road map had been sketched by Lemass and Whitaker. The Fianna Fáil modernisers would travel the road—until the past came back to bite us.

Soon Healy would suffer from the *Irish Times* convulsions, whereas I would profit from them. The *Irish Times* news editor, Alan Montgomery, had been appointed editor of the *Evening Mail*. Monty toured the *Mail* building in the company of a 'native guide', a staff member. He was astounded by what he saw of the working methods. There was virtually no layout and no planning for the position of the material on the pages. Sub-editors would write superficial instructions on the slips of copy paper (flimsy sheets, offcuts from the reels of newsprint) and send them to the composing room for setting into metal type. When the overseers there judged that they had sufficient type to fill the paper, they would inform the sub-editors that they need not bother to send them any more copy.

On his tour, Monty came to a closed door. When he made to open it, the native guide said: 'Oh no, Mr Montgomery, you mustn't go in there!'

'Why ever not?'

'It's Mr Gormley's office, and he always takes his afternoon nap at this time.'

This was George Gormley, sports editor of the *Mail*, greyhound owner, widower, father of three athletic daughters, and uncle of Myles na gCopaleen. He often related that as a small boy he was put out of his bed so that Myles could be born in it. He was better known for a yarn so rude that I will refrain from telling it. It ended with the punchline 'Good Man Me Da!' Michael (Mickser) Hand, who would become one of the 'characters' of Dublin journalism, called him 'Good Man Me Da' in honour, or dishonour, of the line. It stuck.

When the *Mail* moved, as it shortly did, from Parliament Street to Westmoreland Street, Gormley was demoted to the rank of news sub-editor. He sat with his back to the clock and, since he did not wear a watch, he constantly asked the person opposite him to tell him the time. At precisely 10.30 a.m., the time the Pearl Bar opened, he would descend in the lift, cross the street and lash down the 'lovely grub', a whiskey and a pint of stout, which the barman would have prepared for him. He always returned within five minutes, although he suffered severely from gout.

At least George Gormley was alive. Other elderly sub-editors who had transferred to Westmoreland Street seemed to belong to the ranks of the undead. They would stare helplessly at a piece of copy, perhaps only a paragraph, for half an hour on end. And they had nobody to guide them. Understandably, the *Irish Times* did not rush to move their best and brightest on to the *Mail*. Apart from Monty himself, only one person of status went there. This was Jim Murphy, a pedantic nitwit, who became chief sub-editor. His deputy was Norman Clarke, who had been the *Mail*'s managing director and now underwent a precipitous demotion. Murphy had the bad habit of supplying the composing room with far too much copy, giving unnecessary work to the overstressed Linotype operators and compositors. Clarke sent far too little, leaving gaps which we were at our wits' end to fill. Murphy called him 'a great man to cast off a paper' (calculate the quantity of copy required to fill the pages). Neither would ever learn a happy mean.

Monty offered me a staff job, and I accepted eagerly. It was a much better prospect than casual work on the *Sunday Review*. But it was far from satisfying. Ken Gray did most of the page designs in his quiet and efficient manner. For the rest, I alternated on layout and 'stone work', in the composing room supervising the making up of the pages by the compositors, with Frank Cairns, one of the very few competent people who had come from Parliament Street. Hand, with some help from the two of us, did almost all the sub-editing. He sat with enormous piles of copy on his desk, scribbling instructions, writing headlines, correcting grammatical and spelling errors. The quality of the work can be imagined. He barely had time to read the copy, much less improve it. Murphy in the meantime struggled to keep his desk clear and usually achieved his weird ambition simply by flooding Hand with work.

From this chaos Monty extricated me by making me the gossip columnist, a function identical to the one I had performed on the *Evening Press* during Terry O'Sullivan's absences. Terry-O was still in the same slot for the *Evening Press*, complete with photographer, limousine, chauffeur, bottles of good stuff showered on him by grateful contacts, and worldly advice of which the best and most frequent was 'stay alive'. The *Evening Herald* man was the same Tom Hennigan who had fallen asleep in the *Sunday Press* office. Whatever the condition that had caused his somnolence, it had not improved. His colleagues told us that when he returned to Abbey Street in the early hours he would still fall asleep over his typewriter, for all the black coffee he drank in his efforts to stay awake.

Luckily, though, I would shortly get a serious and worthwhile job.

The *Irish Times* convulsions were nearing their climax. The board had decided to get rid of Alec Newman. They summoned him to a meeting and offered him a 'kick upstairs', a title and a sinecure. He returned to the office which he shared with his deputy, Bruce Williamson, and said: 'The bastards have got me!' Both of them resigned, as did Newman's secretary,

Marion FitzGerald. Alan Montgomery was appointed editor, and brought me with him to the *Irish Times* as a sub-editor. My career had started in earnest. I had settled down at last.

Others had not settled. The shifts and manoeuvrings in the hierarchy continued. Many of the journalists saw the hand of Gageby in the changes, assumed that he intended to take the editorship for himself, and were surprised at Monty's appointment. They then supposed that Gageby would edit the paper at one remove. In later life Gageby told me that that had not been his intention and that he saw Monty as an authoritative and long-term editor, but it is impossible, for me at any rate, not to entertain suspicions.

In any event, his mind was soon made up by an incident which remains one of the great stories of Irish newspaper lore. Guinness planned to appoint their first public relations officer. They asked Monty to advise them. He recommended himself. It was considered a terrible come-down in the world for the editor of the *Irish Times*, but it probably paid double the salary. Gageby became editor, probably the greatest and certainly the most dazzling in Irish newspaper history. Meanwhile, as a parting gift to mark Monty's eminence and long service, the *Irish Times* gave him two weeks' pay.

When the *Mail* went, predictably, out of business, John Healy returned to editing the *Sunday Review* and Ted Nealon, who had edited the paper in his absence, was demoted from editor to 'managing editor'. Long afterwards, Gageby told me he had been surprised to find that Nealon was most upset by the demotion. How could he have expected him to feel otherwise?

Healy and Nealon did not hold those jobs for very long, for the *Review* soon followed the *Mail* into oblivion—all the more sadly since it had almost reached the point of turning the financial corner. The board felt, very naturally, that they could not tolerate any more threats to the survival of the *Irish Times* itself. Healy was widely blamed for 'burying' two newspapers, but that was entirely unjust. These disasters were not of his making.

––––

Moira Stevenson was born in India, but her English-born father and her mother, the daughter of an impecunious Irish adventurer, took the family to London a few years after Indian independence, when Moira was in her teens. We met on holiday in Croatia, then part of Tito's Yugoslavia. We were married in London in April 1963. She had never visited Ireland before our engagement, during which we spent Christmas with Eva and her husband, who then lived in Cork. She found Ireland so backward that much of our society and way of life reminded her of India. This amazed myself, for whom the signs of modernisation were everywhere, but I had to agree with her criticisms of the chaotic political system and administration and the dominance of the clergy. We would both have stronger grounds for criticism of Irish society when corruption took hold.

We would go through some hard times and endure many misfortunes together, most of which hit her harder than they hit me. They included two miscarriages and the death of a baby the day after her birth. To compensate, we have two beautiful and high-minded daughters and four lovely grandchildren.

We lived at first in a dismal flat in Blackhorse Avenue. Its only redeeming feature was a view over the Phoenix Park from the bedroom. After a year or so we bought a house in Tallaght, now a vast complex but then little more than a rural village although only six miles from the centre of Dublin.

If she found Dublin shabby and behind the times, she saw what struck her as the lifestyle and customs of a much earlier age on our visits to Leitrim. One of the practices that shocked her was the donation of 'offerings' in church at funerals. These varied with the supposed incomes of the donors and the extent of their acquaintance with the families of the deceased. A layman stood at the altar rails with the priest and called out the names and the sums offered. I had been familiar with the custom since childhood. When Dad was away on FCA duty, I had had to march up the aisle and hand over his contribution at funerals of people he scarcely knew. Each time the man would call out: 'Master Downey, half a crown.' ('Master' meant my father, not me.)

In some places, the money was placed on the coffin. Thankfully I never encountered this grim custom, but the words 'Master Downey, half a crown' still ring in my ears.

Moira at first assumed that the donations were for the families. She got an unpleasant surprise when she found that they went to the priests. They were part of their stipends, along with the Christmas and Easter 'dues'. These too were announced for all to hear, and some priests complained publicly if any parishioners contributed, to their way of thinking, too little.

One victim, in County Cavan, was a Garda sergeant, the father of the writer Shane Connaughton. It beggars belief that a priest could shame people in this way in front of their neighbours.

She was taken aback by how badly most countrymen dressed. They might wear black broadcloth on Sundays, but through the rest of the week they contented themselves with ancient, holed and patched garments, often 'best suits' demoted to working clothes. Little could be seen of proper working clothes. Photographs survive of county council workers in ill-fitting suits instead of protective clothing.

But Moira's most frequent, and best justified, complaint concerned hygiene. Then and for long afterwards lavatories in pubs and other places of public resort were in an unspeakable condition. If wash-hand basins existed, they usually came without soap or towels. At fairs and carnivals, lavatories hardly existed. Resort might be had to a filthy bucket. And in the countryside, large numbers of people who farmed properly and who kept themselves, their clothes and their houses clean had no indoor sanitary facilities, and often not so much as an outside lavatory.

Conditions, however, were improving rapidly, and the poorest were among the most notable beneficiaries. The process began in the 1950s, with rural electrification, a revolution. The light literally came into their homes. The dark was banished, and with it much of the old superstition. In a famous phrase, rural electrification killed off the fairies.

An education programme was set in train to persuade people of the blessing of 'the electric'. Almost everybody signed up. Emigrants in England sent money home to cover the cost. Those who hoped to inherit land would in time enjoy the benefits themselves.

Then the authorities came up with an excellent though limited housing scheme. They persuaded bachelors and spinsters, less frequently whole families, to move from their tumbledown homes a long way up hilly boreens into roadside houses with piped water. The new dwellings were built with the help of generous grants which in effect paid 100 per cent of the cost. Predictably, the standard of construction was not high. The houses had concrete floors, and they came nowhere near the level of comfort that anyone would expect in the twenty-first century. But they were a tremendous improvement on the homes their owners had abandoned.

The politicians and administrators who took these humane and imaginative initiatives and who at a higher level had begun the process of industrialising and urbanising the country deserve thanks, not oblivion, from the present generation. Their quality, however, was hardly reflected then, and is not much reflected now, in the quality of the Dáil backbenchers, to say nothing of the dimmer sort of ministers. In Dublin and elsewhere, Moira met a few of them and was not impressed. She could hardly believe that they had been elected, much less promoted. When we went to a MacLiammoir one-man show in the Gate Theatre, we both laughed helplessly at his portrayal of the 'stage Irishman'. This greatly amused an audience who knew MacLiammoir (born, by the way, in England) as the ultimate stage Irishman. But we enjoyed it more for another reason. The character he played was in every respect, from accent to mannerisms to physical appearance, identical to a rustic politician of our acquaintance.

She was equally unimpressed by the idea that the church could lay down the rules for the population at large on such issues as divorce and contraception. Although herself a good Catholic, she rightly considered these private matters, not to be subjected to dictation by church or state. It would be a very long time until the majority agreed with her views.

She was astounded at the cruelty, which she had never known in England, inflicted by the Catholic church in Ireland on couples in mixed marriages. In Dublin, Archbishop John Charles McQuaid enforced the rules with special rigour. Catholics who wished to marry someone of different beliefs in a Catholic church had to get a dispensation, and the 'non-Catholic' partner had to undertake to bring up the children as Catholics. In addition, McQuaid decreed that the ceremony must take place early in the morning, with attendance confined to the immediate families. Under this rule, Aidan Clarke and my cousin Mary Hughes were married in a side chapel in St Andrew's church in Westland Row. Others suffered more. Noel Fee, deputy chief sub-editor of the *Irish Times*, waited twenty years for a dispensation to marry a Catholic.

Our home life, meanwhile, was constrained by my working hours, which worsened with my various promotions. Typically I worked late shifts, finishing at 4 a.m. and even later, and slept until lunchtime. This had a few compensations, like having time to take afternoon tea in the Gresham Hotel, where we occasionally ran into lively acquaintances. One was the much-loved Eoin O'Mahony, genealogist, failed politician, spender of money on good but lost causes, and cousin of Pussy Tynan O'Mahony. He was nicknamed The Pope because his genealogical pronouncements were said to be infallible. I suppose his clients thought them so, since he could somehow find that they descended from kings—

like Ronald Reagan, but I will come to him later.

Still, the occasional agreeable encounter did not make up for the inconvenience of my hours of work. This would soon become worse and more troublesome during Moira's pregnancies and later when our children were growing up. I spent far too little time with them. Luckily they had a devoted mother, and both of them would develop an intense family feeling which extended to their armies of uncles, aunts and cousins.

—

The chief sub-editor of the *Irish Times* was Donald Smyllie, brother of Bertie and father of the flamboyant Pat, a young man as colourful as his father. Donald Smyllie had served in the Chindits in Burma during the war, commanding a detachment of Gurkhas. Though the soul of kindness in his personal relations, he loved to tell bloodthirsty stories of his wartime adventures and those of his men, who sneaked through the jungle at night to cut the throats of Japanese soldiers. There is a famous scene in the movie *The Bridge on the River Kwai*, in which the Japanese lock a British officer, a prisoner of war, in a tin hut to bake in the sun. Smyllie commented: 'Oh, we did the same—only we wouldn't do it to officers!'

On leave in Calcutta, he was surprised to run into his brother Walker and find him wearing a British uniform. For Walker Smyllie in his youth had forsaken his family's unionism and joined the IRA. There is a story— alas, almost certainly apocryphal—about an encounter between him and Field Marshal Bernard Montgomery, who came like himself from an Irish unionist background. The story goes that Montgomery was inspecting a victory parade. He was the kind of general who liked to check unimportant details. Among the ribbons on Smyllie's chest he spotted one coloured black and tan, an Irish decoration signifying that the wearer had fought in the 'Troubles'. When asked to explain, Smyllie said: 'I got that for driving the British out of Ireland.'

On another leave, in Dublin, Donald Smyllie and a couple of other officers plotted an unarmed raid on the German diplomatic mission. Luckily he told his brother Bertie, who alerted the authorities. The raid was aborted and the affair hushed up.

On the *Irish Times*, his working methods were surely unique. He spent much of the evening in the Pearl Bar in the company of Michael Devine, the 'copy taster', whose role was to assess the value of each story that arrived on the subs' desk and pass them on. The rather sparse home stories from the newsdesk, and the mountains of material from the news agencies, would have been collected by a copy boy for his perusal. Devine was a thorough professional who worked, necessarily, at great speed. On their return from the pub, Smyllie would call out his requirements for suitable items to fill the pre-arranged slots, giving the type size and the lengths. When Devine handed over each item, Smyllie would roll the copy paper into a sort of dart, similar to schoolboys' paper aeroplanes, and fling it, with unerring aim, at one of the sub-editors, whose function it would be to process it in minutes—when he might have needed half an hour or more to get it into decent shape for publication.

Although I was Alan Montgomery's man, and he and Donald Smyllie did not like each other, I quickly developed, not just a good working relationship with my new boss but a real affection: this notwithstanding the wide gulf between our political attitudes. Not only did Donald share his brother Bertie's unionist prejudices and flaunt them, he expressed his racial views in a manner that had already become 'politically incorrect' in the 1960s. Scanning a piece of copy about events in Southern Africa, he said one night: 'I'm glad to see they spell White with a capital w.' A colleague, Arthur Reynolds, pointed out gleefully: 'They also spell Black with a capital B.' I hear that nowadays some computers (gadgets of which none of us had ever heard) refuse to accept the word black in any context. There should be some limit to political correctness.

I was the recipient of many paper missiles, and of material of greater import. I became what in the old Fleet Street they called 'the splash sub', handling the lead stories. This was not as glamorous as it may sound. Not many sensational political or crime stories came our way, and we often led on nothing sexier than the weather, if we got anything more out of the ordinary than freezing fog. Even more frequently we fell back on foreign stories. I swear that we led five nights in a row on the Algerian war, and during the wars in South-East Asia that both preceded and accompanied the Vietnam debacle I must have become a world expert on Cambodian princes, their family relationships and their politics.

Like so many people in this tale, Donald Smyllie died young. He was succeeded by Noel Fee, whose career had started on a newspaper in Longford. His editor sent him to interview a bishop, who began their conversation by remarking amiably: 'I see you are a Protestant.' Amazed that the bishop apparently could tell his religion by looking at him, he asked: 'How do you know?' 'Because you didn't kiss my ring.'

He suffered all his life from severe ill-health, constantly in and out of hospital or at least, during relatively minor bouts, unable to work. In one hospital, his condition was so extreme that the nurses thought he had died. They wheeled him off to the area reserved for such cases. When the porters came to collect the body, they found that he was still alive. In the end he lived past seventy, but hardly by his own efforts. He was a chain-smoker, so badly addicted that he would light a cigarette in the middle of a coughing spasm.

He also liked whiskey, but would seldom visit the pub during his working hours. He felt that he had lost so much time through illness that he had to make up for it by dedication when fit enough. Gageby said of him that he was the only man on the paper who knew exactly where every item appeared, even the smallest and most obscure. That was an exaggeration, but not too far from the truth. He enforced the rules on style, grammar and so forth with great strictness. I admired him and emulated him. We became intimate friends, the more so after I was promoted to deputy chief sub. The promotion, however, was something of a poisoned chalice, in two strikingly different ways.

Fee worried about me. He foresaw that I would one day find myself in line for the succession to Gageby, and he somehow knew that although my relationship with Gageby appeared excellent on the surface it would end in tears. In point of fact such a lofty ambition had not crossed my mind. I thought I saw, as many others did, two men of my own generation, Fergus Pyle and Andrew Whittaker, both Protestants, being 'groomed' for the job. If I thought about the succession, I must have supposed that I could serve either of them happily, perhaps as a deputy editor, but in those days I hardly thought about the matter at all. Fee, however, thought about it, and warned Moira that my career would end in disappointment, knowing that she would pass the warning on to me. I have often wondered how he knew.

His frequent absences forced me to take on the role of chief sub far more often than a deputy normally would. When I substituted for him, I would typically start at 4 p.m. and stay until copies of the first edition ran off the presses about 1 a.m. I would then discuss changes for the city edition with the colleagues whose duty it would be to see to them. On such occasions (not just a night or two running, but perhaps weeks on end) I seldom left the office before 2 a.m.

This regime was arduous, and tough on family and social life, but bearable for a healthy young man. Life grew more difficult for three months in 1966.

I had asked Gageby for a pay rise. Instead, he found me a lucrative part-time job as editor, and occasional presenter, of a nightly TV news programme called Late Extra. I believe that he did so less as a favour to me—though I was grateful for it—than to two of the top RTÉ executives, one of whom was probably a member of his dining club. (Gageby made much of his dislike of social life, but he made an exception for Murphy's Club, founded as a meeting place for eminent men by the accountant Russell Murphy, an elegant man-about-town who after his death was exposed for having stolen large amounts of money from clients who included Gay Byrne and Hugh Leonard.) The deal was as advantageous for them as for me. And if good came of it, and I believe it did, I have never felt I had any reason to resent it.

These far-sighted men had bigger fish to fry. They were planning a transformation in RTÉ current affairs coverage, the process which first gave us *Division*, a programme based on Dáil proceedings, and then the various programmes screened several nights a week, the predecessors of the present *Primetime* (which has upheld the standards then set, of quality and independence). In addition came the Irish-language *Féach*, so compelling that people with hardly any command of the language felt it obligatory to watch. One of the presenters was Breandán Ó hEithir, who would become doubly famous as a broadcaster and a novelist. He wrote *Lig Sinn i gCathú* (*Lead Us into Temptation*), a picaresque novel in a style reminiscent of Pádraig Ó Conaire. There emerged a generation of brilliant producers who included Muiris Mac Conghail, Eoghan Harris, Lelia Doolan—who, however, soon left and went into the film industry—and Brian Farrell and Olivia O'Leary, presenters beyond compare. And David Thornley.

Meanwhile, my programme filled a gap and helped modestly to pave the way. It was useful to the great folk in RTÉ in more ways than one, since I was expendable and anything I did was 'deniable'. And it made only the tiniest dent in the station's budget. We had no facilities of our own for editing film and videotape: such editing as we managed to access was obtained by the diplomatic skills of Joe Fahy, seconded from the newsroom as my deputy. Apart from 'talking heads', we relied mainly on cartoons, maps and other artwork.

Matters were complicated by my insistence that, first, we should base our work on the news of the day, and secondly, we should address serious issues. I thought, for example, that we should acknowledge that such a place as China existed. To convey this was difficult for media organisations with vastly greater resources, since information from China, to say nothing of illustration, was hard to come by. At the time, an obscure power struggle was going on between Mao Tse-tung and a general called Lin Piao, who died, like so many other inconvenient people, in a mysterious plane crash. When we tried to convey to our viewers that a contest for control of the Communist party was raging in China, our American producer, Don Lenox, was outraged. 'Mao and Pow!' he cried.

We also carried film of the American bombings of North Vietnam. Like all left-liberals, I was fiercely anti-American on the issue of the war. I soon found that my opinions were not universally shared by the RTÉ staff. Old hands in the newsroom, some with US or Canadian experience, vehemently supported the Americans and thought the bombings would bring the communists to their knees. These people of course were not typical. Some were unpolitical; others among the journalists, who like myself had originated in the provinces, valued objectivity above all else. The newsroom staff generally seemed to have had little or no training for television. But who was I to complain, seeing that I had none at all? And from their ranks emerged superb current affairs broadcasters, like Mike Burns and Seán Duignan.

Some of the producers, meanwhile, gave me the impression that they had no interest in news and cared only for striking images. They tended, and many producers and overpaid 'celebrity' presenters still tend, to suffer from an unmistakable RTÉ syndrome, self-importance. This, however, seldom afflicts the very best, several of whom entered the station as trainees while I worked there. Seán Ó Mordha went on to produce world-class documentaries on artistic and literary subjects, notably Samuel Beckett, as well as an unsurpassed series on Irish history. Muiris Mac Conghail was a political animal as well as a brave and imaginative producer. He developed a remarkable relationship with David Thornley, nurturing his genius as an interviewer. One of Thornley's most gripping interviews was with John A. Costello. He asked the former Taoiseach about his subservience to the church in the Mother and Child affair. Costello, by then an old man, almost leapt out of his seat as he proclaimed that he would never fail to obey the church on questions of faith and morals.

Mac Conghail for his part went on to become press secretary for the Fine Gael–Labour coalition government of 1973–77, and later a college lecturer in communications. He never achieved his greatest ambition, to be director-general of RTÉ. Had he got the job, his outstanding ability might have been a handicap instead of an advantage. Irish society was too small and inward-looking to accommodate free spirits. For myself, I was thrilled by this new (to Ireland) and exciting medium, but I could never have borne the constraints inseparable from working full-time for a state broadcasting service.

After my three-month contract expired, I continued as deputy chief sub in the *Irish Times*, but not for long. I was promoted to foreign editor. 'Foreign editor of the *Irish Times!*' It sounds impressive. The reality was rather different.

The foreign editor was not much more than a glorified deputy chief sub, and the work consisted mainly of assessing and sub-editing agency copy. I had only one full-time assistant: Peter Froestrup, a Norwegian by birth, a lovable but sad man haunted, as he said himself, by the Scandinavian 'black dog' of depression.

He died aged forty-six. I spoke at his funeral. I said that as an unbeliever he had not expected immortality for himself but he would live on in the memory of his friends and his lovely children. (The eldest was Mariella, who in adult life became a television star in London.) More than three decades later, I attended another very sad funeral, that of the splendid reporter and fine human being Mary Holland. In the cemetery Caroline Walsh, literary editor of the *Irish Times*, told me that she had lately met one of the Froestrup children, by now an adult, who had said that they always remembered my comforting words. You can imagine my gratification.

Bruce Williamson worked with me for a short time. I came to know him very well and to form a profound affection for him, not unlike my feelings for Peter Froestrup. Both of them differed enormously from myself in their attitude to life. Froestrup as I have said suffered from depression. Williamson was a pessimist, about himself and the human race. In his youth he had published poetry and attracted the attention of highbrow critics. In middle life he continued to write, but published nothing. He engaged in terrible drinking bouts in Bowe's pub, frequented by *Irish Times* journalists after the Pearl closed down. There he would order quadruple gins and swallow them without any sign of pleasure; no wonder, since they gave him none. He told me: 'I don't like the taste, dear boy. I drink to get drunk.' He was said to keep a bottle of gin in his desk, but I never saw any bottles. The drawers were full of uneaten biscuits and wine gums, signifying the schoolboy tastes which had never left him. When Gageby took him to lunch in a restaurant renowned for game, the only dish he cared for was the pudding.

He had had a difficult life since his impulsive resignation, finding freelance work hard to come by. His troubles may have been compounded by an erroneous belief among potential employers that he had ample private means, derived from a family-owned tannery in Belfast. In fact the business was not doing well, but his fortunes improved dramatically when the land, in the centre of the city, was sold and a large shopping centre built on the site. T.B. McDowell gave him useful help at the time of the transaction. Since I will have disobliging things to say about McDowell, I am all the happier to record this act of kindness.

Williamson came back to the paper shortly after Gageby's appointment. He spent part of his time on the foreign desk writing editorials: elegant, liberal, imbued with old-era *Irish Times* values, but to my way of thinking much too pro-American, pro-British (he had been educated partly in England) and above all pro-Israeli. For all his deep humanity and courtly manners, he simply did not believe that a Palestinian life was worth the same as an Israeli life.

Soon his position was regularised. He returned to the editor's office, first as a leader writer, eventually as deputy editor, much the same job as he had held under Newman. However, his relationship with Gageby did not remotely resemble his close friendship with Newman. He disliked and feared Gageby, and could not bring himself to believe that the journalists' regard for himself as an *Irish Times* icon made him unsackable. It has been said that Gageby persuaded him to give up drink, but that is simply mistaken.

As a deputy editor, he usually had charge of the paper at night. In his absences, he was sometimes replaced by the literary editor, Terence de Vere White. Gageby explained to me that he wanted White there as 'a senior presence', but the presence of this delightful and erudite man counted for very little because he knew nothing about newspapers. Indeed, he was not even well suited to the job of literary editor, because he was too sensitive for the rough-and-tumble of the bitchy Dublin intellectual world. He wrote several fine novels, but they would have been better if he had expended more sweat and pain on them: good writing came too easy to him.

He gloomed about himself. He told me that at the age of forty he had considered himself a failure in life. I chanced to mention this to Alexis FitzGerald (trusted political adviser to Garret FitzGerald, but no relation) and said that it struck me as unreasonable considering that by that age he had published some well-regarded books. FitzGerald replied, rather crossly, that by the same age Terence de Vere White had become his partner in McCann FitzGerald, one of the most successful solicitors' firms in Dublin.

When Bruce Williamson moved into the editor's office I was obliged to look around for casual sub-editors. Of those who worked for me on that basis, by far the best was Padraic Fallon. He was one of several brilliant brothers, among them the arts and literary critic Brian Fallon, husband of Marion FitzGerald, who had resigned along with Newman and Williamson.

Padraic Fallon was then a Trinity student and had rooms in the college. One afternoon, desperate for assistance and unable to persuade Noel Fee to assign anyone to me, I went round to the college and almost literally pulled him out of bed. He agreed to come in to work for a few hours. That was enough for me. An hour of his work was worth three of anyone else's. After graduating he went to London and grew very rich.

The features editor was Donal O'Donovan. In his youth he had joined the team in Newman's office, the first Catholic journalist to work in the inner sanctum. There he was initiated into the drinking culture, at a time when the editor's office, as previously under Bertie Smyllie, was fuelled by whiskey. I liked him enormously, for he was a man of great charm, though reckless of journalistic proprieties.

After he left the paper he worked as a press officer (in later times they would call it a corporate affairs manager, or some such title) for the Bank of Ireland. He wrote an autobiography which must be unique among the confessions of Irish journalists. He admitted his alcoholism, praising Gageby for helping him to dry out. Sensationally, he recorded that he had secretly worked for the Stasi, the notorious East German secret police in the communist era. I find it hard to imagine that they could have made much use of him. His own political views were about as far from communism as one could imagine. He commissioned articles from an organisation called Forum World Features, several of which he passed on to me for publication. They read like propaganda for the US Central Intelligence Agency. In the end, I refused to carry them. Many years later, Forum World Features was exposed as a CIA 'front'.

He met a young man called Vincent Browne, an activist in student politics, and commissioned him to write about an international student conference in Budapest. While he was there, the Soviet Union invaded Czechoslovakia and overthrew the reformist government. Browne, with characteristic dash and initiative, got across the border and into Prague, where he made contact with student activists or former activists who naturally supported the attempts to reform the communist system and opposed the invasion. He somehow obtained access to what was said to be the only telex machine operating in the city, and succeeded in sending despatches to Dublin.

In later times he became famous for a late-night radio programme featuring reconstructions of evidence to the tribunals inquiring into corruption. But to my mind he deserves greater fame for a much earlier piece of work, the Berry Diaries which he published as editor of *Magill* magazine. These were an invaluable contribution to our knowledge of the Arms Crisis of 1970, of which I will have much more to say below.

———

Vincent Browne and I were, in our different ways, minor participants in the political frenzies of the 1960s. He was one of the 'Young Tigers' who admired Garret FitzGerald and Declan Costello, author of the document *The Just Society* which on the surface at least turned Fine Gael from a deeply conservative party into a reformist one—though not a social democratic party, notwithstanding FitzGerald's efforts in that direction.

FitzGerald thought he had found a way to break the Fianna Fáil stranglehold on the political system: a merger of Fine Gael and Labour under the title Social Democratic Party. The Labour Party establishment took the idea seriously. At a joint meeting of the parliamentary party and the administrative council (national executive) the proposal was defeated by only one vote. FitzGerald in his memoirs quotes me as having given him this information. I remember telling him, but have no recollection of the date.

Could it have worked? I doubted it then, and I doubt it now. There will always be some kind of Labour party, and there will always be some kind of conservative party. But it might have brought about the realignment of Irish politics of which people have talked in vain for the last four decades.

At the time, I passionately opposed the notion. Like many others on the left, I hoped to force an alliance between Fianna Fáil and Fine Gael, leaving opposition—and, in time, government—to a vastly expanded Labour. This was far less realistic than FitzGerald's proposal, and I blush to think of the follies into which it led me. But I was still relatively young, and naïve. I was influenced in part by what looked like world-wide stirrings towards peaceful revolution both in the communist and capitalist worlds. Like-minded people drew a parallel in 1968 between Dubcek's 'Prague Spring' and the 'Student Revolution' in Paris. We have seen what happened to the first. As to the second, I asked Andrew Whittaker, then the *Irish Times* correspondent in Paris, to send me a few of the pamphlets pouring off the presses there. I was disappointed. Instead of analysis and serious proposals, I found fake philosophy and absurd slogans. But I was slow to learn the lesson.

In the mid-sixties I became closely involved with Labour. Michael McInerney, the political correspondent of the paper, told me of his enchantment with the party's new general secretary, Brendan Halligan. I met Halligan and was immensely impressed with his intellect and his commitment. In my little spare time, I did a lot of backroom work for him. I helped to write a notorious speech delivered by the party leader, Brendan Corish, in which he rejected the idea of coalescing with Fine Gael should the two parties between them achieve a Dáil majority after the next general election. It included the infamous line 'the seventies will be socialist.' Dublin wags immediately turned it round: 'The socialists will be seventy.' How right they were!

Another influence was the civil rights movement in Northern Ireland. Efforts to bring about a united Ireland, or to secure equal rights for Catholics within the North, either by force or persuasion, had failed miserably. Then a new force, with Dr Conn McCluskey and his wife Patricia as the pioneers, burst on to the political scene. It emulated the civil rights movement in the United States, adopted the non-violent philosophy of Dr Martin Luther King, and took 'We Shall Overcome' as its anthem. It seemed to enthusiasts like myself that this, too, was part of a world-wide movement towards peaceful revolution, and I saw the Irish Labour Party as the improbable instrument for its achievement.

Others took very different views. The IRA and Sinn Féin, led by Cathal Goulding, were busy reinventing themselves as left-wing campaigners instead of incompetent terrorists. 'Left-wing' covers a multitude. In the North, they infiltrated the Northern Ireland Civil Rights Association. In the Republic, they campaigned, not always peacefully, against foreign ownership of industry. Their internal organisation was unabashedly Stalinist. One of their leaders, when asked to explain the term democratic centralism, replied: 'Democratic centralism means that you bleedin' do what I bleedin' say.'

Farther still to the left, a few dyed-in-the-wool revolutionaries would see the emergence of the Provisional IRA and Provisional Sinn Féin in 1970 as the means of overturning the old society in the North, the Republic and Britain. They dreamed that a revolt in 'Britain's oldest colony', Ireland, would bring an end to the British empire. The empire was dead already, replaced by the United States. I would take a keen interest in their views and methods, although I regarded both as nonsensical. I told them that they might succeed in creating chaos, though that was unlikely. But what would come after? The most frequent and most truthful answer was 'I don't know.'

For a little while, it looked as if Labour might have found a way. We adopted a set of left-wing policies and rejected coalition with any conservative party, which in effect meant Fine Gael. Much more to the point, Halligan set about recruiting celebrity candidates for the 1969 general election. These were not just celebrities but people of real intellect and ability. They included Conor Cruise O'Brien, David Thornley and Justin Keating, son of the painter Seán Keating, a veterinary surgeon by trade and a television star by virtue of his incomparable presentation of an educational series for farmers. All were excellent speakers in their varying ways: O'Brien with his academic and declaratory style, Thornley with his heart on his sleeve, Keating with a gentle though compelling manner more suited to the conversational tone of television than to the public platform. The different approaches of the first two were well summed up at an election rally in O'Connell Street. O'Brien began his speech with the words 'the creative force of the human spirit', to which he attributed the birth of the Northern civil rights movement. Thornley said that 'we're laying ourselves on the line.'

Of course they were not laying themselves on the line in any dramatic sense, because none of them would starve or be shot if they failed in politics; and neither was I when the electoral bug bit me. Thankfully the infection did not go deep or last long, but it hurt.

Since I was then thirty-five years old and a dedicated student of politics, I cannot plausibly plead innocence or inexperience. But I went ahead and secured a nomination in Dublin Central. This queer-shaped constituency did not remotely resemble the latter-day Dublin Central, Bertie Ahern's fiefdom. It was the creation of a Fianna Fáil local government minister, Kevin Boland, in the days when governments could draw boundaries as they pleased without reference to an independent commission. It encompassed a substantial area in the south inner city and the nearby inner suburbs, along with a small section of the northside, the territory of Major Vivion de Valera. There were four Labour candidates, of whom the chief was the future party leader Frank Cluskey. He was a man of considerable charm and intelligence, with a quick wit, a marvellous raconteur, and I liked and admired him. He did not return my feelings, since he disliked anyone who fell in his reckoning into the category of 'middle-class intellectual'. In his campaigning he relied heavily on the support of the butchers' branch of the Federated Workers' Union of Ireland. He did little work in the constituency himself, partly because of his fondness for drink and partly because about the same time he was also campaigning, unsuccessfully, for the job of deputy secretary of the union, which in his view took precedence over Dáil politics.

In addition to what help I could get from the local Labour Party members, I enlisted a good many family and personal friends, among them Moira when she could spare time from minding two small children, my cousin Dympna Hughes, and two close friends from the *Irish Times*: Austin Coffey, a printer, and Dick Walsh, of whom I will have more to write in these pages. Although he was an intimate of Cathal Goulding and other leaders of what would shortly become the 'Official' Sinn Féin and IRA, Dick Walsh came out night after night to canvass votes for me.

I enjoyed the campaign enormously. The weather was beautiful. I already knew the south inner city well, having been a member of the Liberties Association, and I liked the salty humour of the people. On one hot afternoon, I canvassed a block of flats in James's Street. A dozen women were sitting in the courtyard in the sun. One of them assumed the role of spokeswoman for the group. She complained about the rapacity of Dáil deputies, who had given themselves a salary increase to something like £20 or £25 a week. I said that if elected I would give up my newspaper job, which paid better. 'Well then,' she said, 'you're only a fuckin' oul' eejit.'

In Blackpitts—then a slum, since gentrified—I came across two pretty young women sitting on chairs on the footpath. They were sisters, one of them visiting from Rialto where she lived with her husband and children. She was worried about the Labour candidates, because she had heard a priest preach a sermon in which he denounced us as communists. Her sister took a more complacent view: 'Sure the Catholic church itself is gone all arseways.'

The sermon was by no means unique. The Taoiseach, Jack Lynch, devoted much of his campaign to a tour of convents in various parts of the country, delivering the spoken or unspoken message to the nuns—and through them to children and parents—that only a Fianna Fáil vote could ward off the wild Labour revolutionaries. Conor Cruise O'Brien unwittingly helped him with an unwise remark when he said that we should close our embassy in Portugal and open one in Cuba. 'Cuban communism' took its place in the Fianna Fáil armoury, along with such fanciful allegations as that Labour planned land nationalisation. A bigger weapon was Lynch's personality. He had very nice manners and reminded voters of the friendly bank manager or the man from the St Vincent de Paul Society. The economy was flourishing. And voters, especially Fine Gael voters, were perturbed by Labour's anti-coalition policy. On polling day Labour fared disastrously. Fianna Fáil returned to office with an overall Dáil majority.

During the first half of the three-week campaign, I had felt that I was making reasonable progress. Then several things happened which made me realise that my situation was hopeless. Cluskey sobered up. An operation was mounted to canvass the area a second time and instruct Labour voters that the correct way to mark their ballot papers was Cluskey 1, Downey 2. This operation had as its chief target, not myself but another candidate, Jimmy Mooney, viewed by Cluskey's people as a more formidable rival. After the election Mooney ran into a woman who said: 'Mr Mooney, I gave you four votes.' She had been told to mark the Labour candidates 1, 2, 3, 4, and falsely assumed that that meant stating a preference for Mooney instead of the other way round.

One evening in the constituency headquarters Dick Walsh and I found ourselves surrounded by butchers. Someone needed a knife to open a parcel of posters, but nobody could find one. 'A roomful of butchers,' I said, 'and not a knife among you!' Outside, Walsh overcame a fit of giggles to tell me: 'The knives are all in your back.'

They were, but I never held it against Cluskey. Much later, when he stood against Michael O'Leary for the leadership of the Labour Party, I wrote editorials in the *Irish Times* supporting him—greatly to the surprise of at least one Labour deputy, who had assumed that I would feel vindictive and carry my feelings into my work. O'Leary, who knew better, accosted me angrily: 'I know you wrote that stuff.'

O'Leary, a frequenter of the Pearl Bar and a close friend of Donal Foley, was both sociable and highly intelligent but quite unsuited to politics. When Cluskey lost his Dáil seat during the convulsions of the early 1980s, he succeeded him as party leader, but went on to make a fatal mistake. He asked the 1982 party conference to give him carte blanche to enter a coalition with Fine Gael if the occasion arose. The delegates, under

Cluskey's prompting and for other reasons, turned him down. O'Leary then defected overnight to Fine Gael. His career never recovered.

In the 1969 election I polled a humiliating 895 first-preference votes, along with thousands of Cluskey's useless second preferences. I have always been profoundly grateful that I did so badly. Had I obtained a couple of thousand first preferences, my performance would have been regarded as a marker and I would have come under pressure to remain in contention for a Dáil seat at a future election. Even with my terrible record, I did come under a little pressure later to stand for election to the Dublin city council—some of it, ironically, from Michael Mullen, general secretary of the Transport Union, whom I suspected of involvement in the operation to steal my votes in 1969. But the electoral bug had not bitten deep, and the following year I parted company with the Labour Party gladly and on good terms when Gageby and McDowell offered me a new job, London editor of the *Irish Times*. I saw this role as incompatible with membership of a political party, and here I may as well set out my views on journalists' participation in party politics.

I felt that I had done nothing unprofessional in standing for election while I was foreign editor, since that position had little or no connection with domestic politics. Being London editor was entirely different, since the work involved covering Anglo-Irish relations. Others could do as their own consciences dictated. McInerney had been a fervent communist but had left the party in one of the many crises that disillusioned idealists: in his case, probably the invasion of Hungary in 1956. He joined Labour and remained a starry-eyed socialist, dedicated first to Noel Browne and then to Conor Cruise O'Brien. As political correspondent of the *Irish Times*, he became notorious for assuming that large numbers of Dáil members shared his own opinions. When he wrote about 'a Labour view', he usually meant his own view. And he did not stop there. He fantasised about the imminent conversion of other parties to socialism. But he had sufficient sense of humour to tell a story against himself. When interviewing Seán Lemass, he asked him: 'Who are the left wing of Fianna Fáil?' Lemass, exasperated, said: 'Michael, for years you've been writing this rubbish about the left wing of Fianna Fáil. There is no left wing in Fianna Fáil. I'm the left wing of Fianna Fáil!'

John Horgan, who proved his worth with his magnificent coverage of the second Vatican Council in the early sixties, was one of eight or nine people whom at various times I would come to regard, along with myself, as worthy contenders for the editorship of the *Irish Times*. None of them still worked for the paper when my own career crisis arrived in 1986. Horgan stood successfully as an independent candidate and afterwards a Labour candidate, first for the Senate, then for the Dáil. After a good deal of logic-chopping, McDowell decided that it was all right for him to sit in the Dáil as an independent but that he took a step too far when he joined Labour.

When the IRA and Sinn Féin split into two wings in 1970, almost all the 'republicans' among the *Irish Times* journalists went with the misnamed 'Official' faction. At least half a dozen were members of Official Sinn Féin; others were sympathisers. To my knowledge, only one or two inclined towards the Provisionals, contrary to the widespread canard that the media were full of Provo sympathisers. On the wilder shores, there were of course a couple of Trotskyists, possibly influenced more by their hatred of Stalinism than by communist ideology, but no Maoists. The Maoists of the time, by the way, embraced the 'two nations' theory and demanded 'national rights' for the Northern Protestants. The Soviet leaders, by contrast, wanted a united Irish 'workers' and small farmers' republic'. They patronised the Officials, soon to become known as the Stickies, in preference to the minuscule Irish communist party, and supplied them with funds. By then, the Stickies had moved from revolutionism to Stalinism and from there to constitutional politics and to what their former comrades considered an acceptance of the 'two nations' theory. Eventually they split, inevitably, between the parliamentary party and the central committee, called themselves Democratic Left, and carried out a reverse takeover of the Labour Party. I could never have borne this party-lining—I found Labour more than enough—but all but one of my Sticky friends remained loyal to the organisation throughout these manoeuvres.

That was their choice, and they did not have to accept my view of the constraints on journalists' involvement in politics. This, however, does not apply to the two or three who were actual members of the IRA; and the position of Dick Walsh was, to say the least, anomalous. He was so close to the 'Official' chiefs that he was able to show me a transcript of the court-martial (in absentia) of Seamus Costello, a noted defector. Costello was sentenced to death, and the sentence was carried out, long after the Official IRA had announced the cessation of violent activities North and South. The organisation tried to attribute the murder to a dissident group, but indubitably the Official IRA 'executed' Costello.

Much as I liked Dick Walsh and loved his company, I could not think it proper that he could combine such intimacy with a job as political correspondent of the *Irish Times*. It amazed me that so few people appeared to know his record, of which he made little secret, and that speakers at his funeral praised what they called his dedication to parliamentary democracy.

Fianna Fáil ministers, who always know a great many secrets, raised the subject with me from time to time. They were genuinely angry and puzzled, but they had grossly inflated ideas about the influence of the Stickies, and more so the imaginary Provos, in the *Irish Times* and RTÉ. In the *Irish Times*, the Stickies carried out their journalistic duties conscientiously. In RTÉ, the perception was largely manufactured by a Sticky faction which carried out a campaign of bullying and defamation against people who had no Provo connections or sympathies but who might wish to put the nationalist case. One of their targets was Mary McAleese, afterwards President of Ireland.

––––

In many ways, the *Irish Times* of the 1960s epitomised the spirit of the age. It sat on a tripod composed of these elements: the perception that it had retained the standards of its past while shaking off the less desirable parts of its unionist and 'West British' background; Gageby's overwhelming personality combined with his integrity and his eccentric but attractive political views, and its enthusiastic campaigning for a new and more liberal Ireland. All these came together in a way that gave it a unique status in Irish journalism and something of an international reputation. Along with the exceptional talents of the journalists, they made it almost, though not quite, a great newspaper. They also made it, for most of us, a joy to work in Westmoreland Street.

Gageby, like so many men of his kind, was full of paradoxes. He could be both ruthless and intemperate. He had little conception of moderation or of the gravity with which, as the great Francis Bacon advised, those 'in great place' should issue rebukes. Contributors to *Bright, Brilliant Days* have described how he terrorised editorial conferences, making the faint-hearted look dumbly at the floor while he ranted about real or imaginary errors. Sometimes his reprimands were justified, more often they derived from mere ill-temper. Occasionally his complaints were simply invented, as when he asked why some story had not appeared in that day's edition of the paper although a glance through the pages would, as he knew perfectly well, have shown that it had in fact been published.

Yet nobody was more often or more thoroughly forgiven for liverishness and unfairness. Forgiveness, and admiration, derived less from his frequent kindness to staff who were ill or in various kinds of trouble than from the simple facts that the staff trusted him to make decisions advantageous to the paper, as he usually did, and that—along with most readers, especially new readers—they strongly approved of the direction in which he was taking the paper.

Although Alec Newman had worked long and closely with Bertie Smyllie and been ineradicably influenced by him, he was no unionist but a staunch nationalist. Yet neither he nor Alan Montgomery had succeeded in dispelling the West British image that had persisted during Bertie Smyllie's reign. This now changed drastically. There could no longer be any doubting that the editor of the *Irish Times* shared the aspirations, not to say the prejudices, of the population, and in particular the most influential, intelligent and enterprising elements of the population. Most of all, there could be no doubt about his commitment to an independent, united, non-sectarian Ireland. He constantly invoked the name of Theobald Wolfe Tone, who had called on 'Catholic, Protestant and Dissenter' to unite and accept a common identity. And there certainly was no doubt about how he viewed his own identity and allegiance.

His robust nationalist views would soon lead him into strange paths, and several of his best injunctions to the public would be misunderstood or ignored. When Northern Ireland exploded in 1969, with murderous attacks on Catholic areas of Belfast led by elements of the unionist security forces, that same public saw him as 'on our side'. He was, to the extent that he hated unionism. He insisted that no such person existed as a moderate or liberal unionist. He deplored the discrimination against Catholics that had characterised half a century of unionist domination of the North. But he deplored, in addition, the common reaction in the Republic, support for 'our people'. Who, he asked, were our people? Were the Protestants not our people too? If not, what did we mean by a united Ireland? No united Ireland worth having could be achieved by a Catholic victory in a sectarian civil war. He asked good questions, which in time would evoke answers little to his taste.

Closer to home, the paper took what appeared, somewhat misleadingly, a turn to the left. It put itself in the forefront of the campaigns for divorce and contraception and the general thrust of what came to be known as the Liberal Agenda. This, however, did not greatly differentiate it from what had gone before. What made it massively different in the sixties was Gageby's nationalism, along with the grasp of the Zeitgeist which is permanently and rightly associated with the name of Donal Foley.

Foley, Gageby's inspired appointment, has gone down in legend as one of the great news editors. This is both more and less than the true case. As a news editor properly speaking, he was no better than most and considerably inferior to some. His genius lay in two fields. First, his choice of writers. In that regard he had his faults, since he tended to value stylish and provocative writers above 'straight news' reporters, give them a very loose rein, and thereby encourage one of the besetting sins of the *Irish Times*, self-indulgence. But the best of them were terrific: not just stylists, but investigative reporters who turned over many stones to expose the faults of our society, which haunt us still in the disclosures of institutional sex abuse.

Secondly, Foley broadened the horizons of the paper as well as the coverage. Under his guidance Eileen O'Brien, Mary Maher and Nell McCafferty wrote about a class hitherto ignored, the poor. He employed numerous female reporters who enthusiastically supported, and sometimes led, the women's rights movement. Himself a liberal Catholic like John Horgan, he campaigned for ecumenism and Catholic church reform. At an early stage he spotted the revival of traditional music and gave it its proper place in the conspectus of Irish culture. And he insisted that the paper should pay far more attention to Gaelic games, which had always been popular but in the sixties became something more: they became fashionable. Like Gageby himself, Foley lacked attention to detail, but he had superb instincts.

Gageby, oddly, was not entirely in sympathy with the new shape of the organ which, under him, would become almost but not quite a great newspaper.

In the first place, he had no feeling for design and production. By contrast with the dashing innovations carried out by the *Guardian* or the London *Independent*, or the clever compromises in the *Daily Telegraph* under the editorship of Max Hastings, the *Irish Times* never undertook a truly new layout. It would enter the twenty-first century with excellent design in some sections but with its news pages crammed with dull, poorly written and presented stories under headlines in unexciting typefaces.

After holidays in France, he would bring home copies of French provincial newspapers and invite night editors and chief sub-editors to copy their hideous layouts. He had little visual sense. He preferred scenic photographs, which frequently dominated the front pages, to news pictures. He had little or no interest in presenting lead stories in such a style as to indicate their importance.

He assumed that our readers never read any other newspapers or, if they did, that they considered nothing to be of consequence unless they saw it in the *Irish Times*. He thought nothing of publishing items that had appeared, almost word for word, in rival publications two or three days earlier. He ignored my pleas that we should find ways of 'updating' such stories to give them an appearance of freshness. Yet such was the prestige the paper attained under his reign that from time to time the *Sunday Tribune* and RTÉ, for example, would credit the *Irish Times* with exclusively publishing some story which had in fact appeared in other dailies.

More to the present point, he had little interest in the causes for which Foley and his staff campaigned. Like his acolyte John Healy, he preferred to celebrate the progress the country made under the Fianna Fáil modernisers. The fact of the progress was unquestionable, and Gageby was undoubtedly right in his enthusiasm for one epochal development, the introduction of free secondary education by Donogh O'Malley. But both Gageby and Healy went overboard in that instance. They would have done better to accept that Ireland had lagged behind shockingly, that without the reform we would have had no chance of turning ourselves into a modern economy, and that we still had a very long way to go. Instead, they continued to wave an increasingly tattered flag for years after O'Malley's early death, and Healy seized—or manufactured—countless opportunities to refer to 'O'Malley's mini-buses' taking children to school. These vehicles are mostly buses of normal size, and they are not O'Malley's buses, they are the taxpayers' buses.

On rare occasions Gageby permitted his exasperation with the emphasis on social conscience to break out. He once said to me angrily: 'Those women Mary Maher writes about—they're LOSERS!' But for the most part he permitted the left-liberal ethos free rein in editorials and throughout the publication, and contented himself with deploying Healy as a counterweight.

This did not mean extolling the glories of capitalism, but something bordering on the indescribable, almost the irrational. Healy developed a theory based on the work of the anthropologist Claude Levi-Strauss. It ignored liberal democracy and held that the Fianna Fáil Party constituted 'a moral community' which in turn was derived from, or at least analogous to, the 'peasant society' whose values (self-help tempered by voluntary joint action at, for instance, harvest times) had survived modernisation and urbanisation. It would have done nicely for a once-off ironic comparison, but as a description of Irish politics and society in the 1960s and subsequent decades it was nonsense. Equally nonsensical were his rants about the depopulation of the West of Ireland. He never tried to advance any serious alternative to the flight from the land, and he did not risk the unpopularity he would have attracted by supporting the one true choice. If we had chosen the path of nominating growth centres and providing the necessary infrastructure, the market would have done the rest. In the event, one centre, Galway, did grow to several times its original size without any help from the government. Among the predictable consequences were the destruction of an enchanting small city's ambience and pollution which made the water undrinkable throughout the summer of 2007.

Healy maintained that the public sector contributed nothing to the economy and constantly denounced the 'permanent socialist government', meaning the civil service. He praised 'nation builders', predominantly entrepreneurs (very thin on the ground in his time) but also, paradoxically, including the chiefs of the few successful state-owned industries. This gave the paper little solid ground from which to identify and condemn government policies which propped up failing publicly-owned industries at vast expense, and the inconsistencies were glaring. Both Gageby and Healy maintained that a newspaper did not have to be consistent. I disagree.

Gageby held views much more quirky than his nationalism. Newman had disliked the Irish system based on 'civil war politics', dominated by the two successor-parties of those who had fought each other in 1922–23. He argued that we should have a choice between right and left: not a practical proposition, but intellectually more respectable than Gageby's opinions. Dick Walsh said, with some plausibility, that Gageby wanted the country run by a Francoist *movimiento nacional*. In private conversation, Gageby said (correctly) that Fianna Fáil and the Ulster Unionist Party had a lot in common, and (incorrectly) that a united Ireland would be governed by a Fianna Fáil–UUP axis. That would have horrified me, and I fancy that it would have horrified Thomas Davis. Later he modified his views and took to the idea of 'an all-Ireland SDLP'. After his death we got a sort of echo of that in the proposition that Fianna Fáil should contest elections in the North in an alliance with the SDLP. I have never known whether to take that seriously, but if it happened it would be an alliance between a cat and a canary.

Both Gageby and Healy supported the European unity project, and Ireland's participation in it, with great fervour combined with a total absence of rigorous analysis, especially on the question of defence. Gageby seemed to find no difficulty in maintaining, like the Fianna Fáil Party, that membership of the Community (now the European Union) had no defence implications, indeed no political implications, and that we could cling on to our 'traditional neutrality', since redefined as refusal to join any military alliances. Weirdly, he advanced as an argument for membership of the Community the fact that the egregious Seán MacBride supported it. I doubt that many *Irish Times* readers wanted to take MacBride for a model.

I have to confess that at the time I retained a sentimental attachment to the idea of neutrality. It did not survive the crash course in the international facts of life from which I benefited in London, but I disliked Edward Heath's proposal for an Anglo–French nuclear axis and for many years I was dubious about Irish participation in a defence alliance reliant on nuclear weapons. After my eventual conversion to reality, I got into trouble with Gageby, who called the official Irish line, that neutrality consisted merely of a refusal to join military alliances, 'honourable'.

But Gageby had brought with him from Burgh Quay some of the Irish Press group's great virtues as well as its faults. In judging the importance of stories, he could let his enthusiasm on the one hand or his disdain on the other run away with him, but he clung to the first principles of journalism. When a big story broke he conveyed his own excitement to the staff. Everybody who worked on the news desk knew that if something sensational happened Gageby must be informed at once, dragged back to the office if necessary from a dinner party or a trip with his wife to the theatre. It baffled him that some journalists did not share his enthusiasm for news. Once he said to me, in puzzlement, that an offending reporter 'doesn't seem to have normal human curiosity.' He valued hard work and professionalism. And although he was sparing of his praise for reporters, and even more sparing in praise for sub-editors, he had a shrewd idea of every individual's capability.

For those reasons, the *Irish Times* during his two reigns, and especially in the 1960s, was for most of us a wonderful place to work. The days were fraught, but they were, to borrow two words from Andrew Whittaker, bright and brilliant.

I was surrounded by people whom I liked and who were the best of company, in the office and outside it. Most were intelligent, some were eccentric, all were comrades. In periods of relaxation, like the interval between the end of work on the first edition and the second orgy of activity that followed the arrival of the printed copies of the paper, we engaged in poker games and lively debates on all imaginable subjects. Religious argument of a very odd kind was frequent. The main arguments centred on the views of Frank Cairns, one of the very few members of the *Evening Mail* staff who had made a successful transition to the *Irish Times*. He was a member of a fundamentalist sect and had once preached the Bible on the corner of O'Connell Street and Abbey Street. He held that he had been 'saved' and was certain of salvation. The rest of us, Catholics, Protestants and atheists, would all assuredly go to Hell. He dismissed the view of the Jehovah's Witnesses, who, he complained, believed that the 'saved' would number 144,000 persons. That figure, in his opinion, was much too high.

For those of us whose religion, or lack of religion, permitted indulgence in liquid and solid mind-altering substances, the favourite location was Bowe's pub in Fleet Street after it replaced the Pearl as the *Irish Times* 'house' resort. Foley held court there, often beyond the legal licensing hours. He was joined by writers and television people and by the women he had employed. At the official closing time the proprietor, Tommy McRedmond, would dim the lights and stop serving drink until the ordinary customers had left, then resume serving those whom he considered the elite. The lights remained dimmed.

Next door, over a bookmaker's shop, was the *Irish Times* Club. For some of the uninitiated, the title suggested leather armchairs, deep carpets and bookshelves. The reality was otherwise. In order to gain entry, it was necessary to press a bell three times. In due course the steward, Charlie Long, a former sergeant in the Dublin Metropolitan Police, would appear at the window and throw down the dirty and battered matchbox which contained the key to the front door. The next manoeuvre involved climbing several flights of rickety stairs which I always feared would collapse under me. The club itself occupied two dingy rooms, one dominated by a pool table. The quality of the pints of Guinness served depended on Charlie Long's whim. So did closing time, between 4.30 a.m. and 5 a.m., heralded by the steward's loud call: 'No moor dhrink noo!'

But the company made up for the surroundings. Three stalwarts of the *Irish Press*, Michael Wolsey, John Spain and Seán Ó hEalaí, lamented over their pints the dire financial troubles of their paper, which made it next to impossible for them to compete with the *Irish Independent*. Their *Indo* rivals were represented by Vinny Doyle, Vinny Mahon, Michael Brophy, Gerry O'Regan and Niall Hanly; Hanly's promising career, sadly, was cut short when he was killed in a plane crash. Members often brought in distinguished visitors. Peter Lennon (*Guardian* writer, film director and brother of my friend Tony Lennon, the *Irish Times* librarian) took Peter Ustinov along one murky night. Ustinov, possibly the most sophisticated man on the planet, looked on in disbelief as Lennon scrabbled for the matchbox in the filthy gutter.

Another frequenter of the place was the much-loved sportswriter and trade union activist Seán Kilfeather, a man of great goodness and humour but one who constantly misjudged his own capacity for alcoholic intake. Up to a certain stage—impossible for him or anyone else to guess in advance—he was splendid, witty company; then the tipping point came and he became truculent, turning on people whom he disliked, usually with good reason, for pomposity and similar faults. One night he was expelled for expressing his opinion of another member in terms both witty and abusive. The steward who had succeeded Charlie Long escorted him down the stairs, expressing his apologies at every step. As they reached the door he added: 'And everybody agrees with what you said, Mr Kilfeather.'

On another occasion, I found myself called on, late at night, to bail him out of Store Street Garda station. He had quarrelled with a bus conductor and, to emphasise his point, lain down in front of the bus on O'Connell Bridge. By the time I arrived, he was not in a cell but in a 'day room', looking glum and fairly sober. I addressed the desk sergeant in my humblest and most persuasive tones, as one does in such circumstances, and begged him to let the prisoner go. He said that unfortunately they had already charged him and he would have to appear in court in the morning. I signed his bail, guaranteeing that I would pay some trifling sum if he failed to answer it, and off we went.

By then, Kilfeather had fallen prey to the feeling (I know it well) that he had not had quite enough to drink. He insisted that we should repair to the club. Weakly pleading 'just one pint, Seán', I gave in. We rang the bell, climbed the stairs and joined two of his colleagues from the sports department at a table. He then proceeded to pursue a grievance with the sports editor, of whose genesis I knew nothing. Somehow I extricated him and drove him home. He did not turn up in court in the morning, but the Gardaí dropped the charges anyway. They never came after me for the bail money.

The *Irish Times* Club is no more. It was already an anachronism in my time. But it was fun while it lasted.

| 1970: THE IRISH QUESTION

In the mid-sixties, Gageby sent Fergus Pyle to Belfast to cover the Stormont parliament, and devoted an enormous amount of space to Pyle's voluminous reports. In times to come, the paper would have more sensational matters to report, and the work would be done by a series of superb journalists like Conor O'Clery, Fionnuala O Connor and my great friend David McKittrick. Once I found myself standing beside McKittrick's mother at the launch of one of his books. I said: 'Your son is the best reporter in Ireland.' She replied: 'You told me that before, but you were drunk at the time.' I said: 'I remember. It was at his wedding reception, and I wasn't drunk.'

Gageby also deployed Healy to beat the drum for the more eccentric aspects of his own notions about how to report the North.

Every year, the paper carried lavish coverage of the Orange Order's Twelfth of July celebrations. It was full of contradictions. On the one hand, it acidly reported speeches by stupid bigots in which they ranted about 'enemies', meaning Catholics, and pictured themselves as the last bulwark against Rome, the Scarlet Woman, the Whore of Babylon. On the other hand, it portrayed the ordinary Orangemen with their banners, their drums and their soft drinks as fine fellows, good neighbours, the salt of the earth, who needed only a little enlightenment to make them understand their affinity with ourselves. Healy took these absurdities to greater heights, as when he described an Orangeman with his belly hanging over his waistband, thereby resembling an overfed Mayo farmer, as if this were somehow a good thing.

Notwithstanding his hatred of unionists, Gageby took a fancy to the 'reforming' Stormont prime minister, Terence O'Neill, and hugely exaggerated the extent of initiatives which amounted to little more than a message to O'Neill's fellow-Protestants that they should treat Catholics as fellow-citizens. Any concrete reforms brought in by O'Neill, and by his successors James Chichester-Clark and Brian Faulkner, were dictated, in the main, by the British Labour government led by Harold Wilson. All of them came too slowly and grudgingly, and all of them met with ferocious opposition from the right wing of the Ulster Unionist Party. O'Neill for his part tried to fight his enemies in his government and party by appealing over their heads to the moderate elements of the Protestant population. He called an election for the Stormont parliament early in 1969. The results were unfavourable, and he resigned soon after.

Earlier, Gageby had enthused about the meetings between O'Neill and Seán Lemass, followed by further meetings with Lemass's successor, Jack Lynch. He held, with some justice, that they signalled a new and better era in North–South relations, but he over-estimated O'Neill's ability to build on them and in particular to persuade his people to acknowledge the desirability either of North–South co-operation or of according Catholics the rights of equal citizens. He praised O'Neill's (imaginary) political skills and enlisted Healy in this cause. In one of his articles, Healy grotesquely described O'Neill as 'a panther'. He went to his Antrim constituency and fantasised about old-time republicans coming down from the hills to support the unionist premier.

Flesh-and-blood old-timers—and new generations—would soon take the opposite course. When loyalists led by elements of the Stormont security forces attacked Catholic areas of Belfast in August 1969, the inhabitants found themselves defenceless. The IRA, in so far as they then existed at all in Belfast, had no guns. Out of these events were born Provisional Sinn Féin and the Provisional IRA. At first their leadership was dominated by 'Southerners', but in time these would be replaced by younger, tougher men from Belfast and Derry who would fight a fierce, bloody and cruel guerrilla war, who would profit from every mistake made by the unionists and the British, and who, when they turned to politics, would extract every last ounce of concessions with equal ruthlessness.

Wilson and his ministers responded to the events in Belfast and the 'Battle of the Bogside' in Derry by deploying troops on the streets of these cities and elsewhere. They disarmed the Royal Ulster Constabulary and disbanded the sectarian militia, the 'B Specials,' replacing them with the Ulster Defence Regiment. They saw the troop deployment as a temporary measure to tide them over until they could restore something approaching normal conditions. Meanwhile, they assured Dublin and the Northern Catholic population that their forces would put down violence emanating from either the Catholic or the Protestant side.

In May 1970 I interviewed Roy Hattersley, then a middle-ranking defence minister in Harold Wilson's government. He seemed amazed that anyone should doubt Whitehall's intention to take an even-handed approach, or fear that British troops would have to stay in Northern Ireland for years, not months. He also said that the reforms then in train had been 'required' of the Stormont regime by the British government. To his surprise and mine, this statement of the plain facts of life caused such anxiety in Downing Street that he was summoned there, in the middle of the night, from the Birmingham constituency where he was fighting an election campaign. In the end, Wilson decided that no public statement was needed to soothe unionist feelings.

When the British troops arrived in Northern Ireland, they came equipped for a war, not a police operation. An Irish military observer in Derry was amazed to see the heavy guns and armoured vehicles which they discharged on the quayside. The British generals correctly supposed that they would soon be fighting a war. They were correct, too, in supposing that their enemies would be nationalists, not loyalists. But like their political chiefs they had no idea how powerful and resourceful those enemies would be, or how long the conflict would continue.

In the Republic, these events were viewed with a mixture of horror, apprehension and glee. Horror at the sight of Catholics being murdered or burned out of their houses, thousands of refugees crossing the border, far greater numbers moving to safer areas of Belfast in the biggest population movement in Western Europe since the second world war. Apprehension at the likely spreading of the conflict to the Republic in the context of an inflamed public opinion and passionate demands for intervention in support of the endangered Catholics. And glee, not just in the predictable quarters but in some of the highest levels of politics and society, inspired by the belief that an opportunity now presented itself to tackle our 'unfinished business' with Britain and unite Ireland by force of arms.

This belief was ridiculous, and secret Military Intelligence reports to the cabinet showed just how mistaken it was. These reports, and the proceedings of an interdepartmental committee set up to examine Northern Ireland, have become available for public view in recent years under the thirty-year rule. They show that we had at best 5,500 effective troops, a trifle by comparison with the forces available to the British, the Stormont security forces, and the irregulars who would fight on the loyalist side. To seize and hold the whole territory of Northern Ireland would require 60,000 troops, fully trained and equipped, with perhaps as many more to maintain essential services: a stark impossibility. In the event of military incursions into the North, followed by all-out civil war, thousands of people would be killed and hundreds of thousands displaced from their homes. There would be loyalist incursions into the Republic, aimed at destroying vital installations (at least one attempt of this kind was in fact mounted). The economy in both parts of Ireland would be devastated. The fighting would end with a ceasefire in place, followed by the formal repartition of the island on more manageable boundaries. Such few Catholics as remained in the North would suffer far worse repression from an extremist Protestant regime than ever before. The Republic would have a refugee crisis with which it did not have the resources to cope. And guerrilla organisations, in effect the embryo Provisional IRA, might seize and rule chunks of territory.

The Garda Síochána, in their response to these assessments, raised a most alarming possibility, that subversives might take over the seats of the government, parliament and RTÉ. They therefore proposed that the government should raise its eyes from the North and devote all available resources to its own protection.

There was one more, fanciful and dangerous, idea which attracted more attention than it deserved in high quarters. This was that we could move troops into Newry and/or into the Derry Bogside, thereby creating an international incident, and seek United Nations intervention which might take the form of a UN peacekeeping force and temporary rule of Northern Ireland under a UN mandate. Apart altogether from the overwhelming practical defects of the proposal, and apart from the outrageous breach of our international obligations which it would involve, it would have been certain to come up against a British veto at the UN Security Council.

As the unhappy leader of a government and a country in turmoil, Jack Lynch went on television and made the situation worse with what became notorious as his 'stand idly by' speech.

Apart from his meetings with Terence O'Neill, Lynch had never taken the smallest interest in the North. A little anecdote may illustrate that. Not long before the conflagration of August 1969, he received a letter from John Hume, who had begun to emerge as the future leader of moderate nationalism. In it, Hume set out his ideas for progress based on civil rights and non-violence, leading ultimately to Irish unity. Almost forty years later, I found Lynch's reply in the National Archives. In it, he thanked Hume and said that he had found the letter most enlightening. When I mentioned this at a dinner party hosted by a retired senior civil servant, my host and another eminent retired official laughed, slapped their thighs and said to each other: 'Bertie O'Dowd!' O'Dowd had been Lynch's private secretary at the time. They assumed that he had composed the reply himself and that his boss did not read it carefully, if at all, before approving it.

In August 1969 Lynch had no way of refusing to address a distasteful subject. He responded with a combination of diplomatic moves, soothing words and posturing: 'rattling his toy sabre', as one English commentator put it. He sent his Foreign Minister, Dr P.J. Hillery, to New York to find out what if anything could be achieved at the United Nations. The answer of course was nothing, but Hillery at least avoided embarrassment by his own and his officials' diplomatic skills and with help from the friendly British ambassador, Lord Caradon. Meanwhile, to placate feeling among the public and especially within the Fianna Fáil Party, Lynch sent troops to the border, set up field hospitals, and provided accommodation for refugees.

It will be interesting to see if documentation appears at some time in the future to clarify the instructions and indoctrination those troops received. I have spoken to officers and enlisted men who believed they were on the border to prepare for an invasion. I regard that as confirmation of Lynch's and others' deplorable attitude to the armed forces, which within a few months would contribute to engendering a crisis of historic dimensions.

As to soothing words, those he used in his television address were not taken as soothing in the least. When Lynch arrived in the RTÉ studios, he was in a state of extreme nervous agitation. He flabbergasted an RTÉ executive (Desmond Fisher, whom we have met before) by asking him if he thought we should invade Northern Ireland. He made numerous changes to his script and telephone calls to his wife Máirín. The original script contained the phrase 'we cannot stand idly by and see people injured or worse.' In the version as delivered, the word 'idly' was omitted. Much has been made of this, but I cannot see that it has any significance. At any rate, the address has always been known as the 'stand idly by speech'.

Lynch knew the depth and danger of feeling in his party and his cabinet, but he failed to distinguish between the level-headed people and the extremists. He trusted nobody except his wife. An exasperated Hillery exclaimed to friends: 'He doesn't even trust ME!' The great majority of

Lynch's cabinet were both sensible and loyal—notably George Colley, whom he had defeated in a vote for the party leadership in 1966. Brian Lenihan senior, who in his later years boasted, truthfully, that he had loyally served every Taoiseach in his political career, came under unjustified suspicion, and was spied on by the Special Branch, because of his friendship with dissident ministers.

Of these dissidents, the chief in the coming months would appear in retrospect to be the finance minister, Haughey. This was a mistaken view. The most extreme hawks were Kevin Boland (who, however, was not influential because his views were considered too eccentric) and, supremely, Neil Blaney.

Blaney turned up in the Bogside during the August fighting, pressing large-denomination banknotes into the hands of Trotskyist revolutionaries who had nothing in common with him except a desire to provoke civil war. He believed that a civil war would not be disastrous, that it would end quickly, and that the unionists would see that they could have a satisfactory future in a united Ireland. How intelligent men could dismiss the apocalyptic assessment to which they had access as cabinet ministers, and indeed, everything that was clear to ordinary common sense, is perhaps best left to the imagination.

In the meantime, he made inflammatory speeches which Lynch affected not to know about. One morning the Taoiseach, on his way into his office, was greeted by an official who mentioned 'the latest speech by the minister for agriculture'. He took his pipe out of his mouth and replied: 'Oh! Has he said something?' Blaney's importance lay less in his cabinet position than in the influence he exerted, then and later, over Haughey, who thought him the embodiment of nationalism, his own mentor and his conduit to the 'green' wing of Fianna Fáil.

————

The British were disappointed by the 'stand idly by' address, but mollified by a conciliatory speech which Lynch made the following month in Tralee. He made several other moves, one of which had long-lasting significance: the appointment of two fine foreign affairs officials, Eamonn Gallagher and Seán Ronan, to draw up a document indicating new and more fruitful—and, above all, pragmatic—developments in Northern policy. Other moves were less commendable.

He set up a cabinet committee composed of Blaney and Haughey along with two men whom even Lynch acknowledged as loyalists, Joe Brennan and Pádraig Faulkner. The committee died in its cradle when Blaney and Haughey did not turn up for their first business meeting. Brennan and Faulkner, though naturally chagrined, appear to have taken no action whatever, even to reproach the delinquents or complain to the Taoiseach. The incident was a most extraordinary example of the distrust and suspicion that prevailed within the cabinet and the party.

The Dáil voted £100,000, then a substantial sum of money, for 'relief of distress' in the North. Haughey was given sole charge of the fund. Most of the money was misappropriated, diverted to the illegal purchase and attempted importation of arms.

The Arms Crisis of 1970 had its roots here, and in the conspiracy with the IRA (still the Marxist IRA under Goulding's leadership) and the Northern Catholic citizens' defence committees. Lynch's defenders claim that he knew nothing about the conspiracy until the spring of 1970. This is immensely difficult to believe. The more extensive establishment version, which holds that both he and his defence minister, James Gibbons, were ignorant of developments, is impossible to believe.

From as early as September 1969, rumours abounded of contacts between the IRA and Fianna Fáil ministers. I have direct personal knowledge of the manoeuvrings of the time, because an emissary from Goulding sought me out. He must have thought that I had some influence in the Labour Party or the *Irish Times* (where in fact as foreign editor I had no input whatever into domestic coverage or policy). His object was to assure me that the rumours were untrue. I knew him for an honourable man, committed to bringing the IRA on to the political path, and it is possible that he himself may have been misled. I did not believe him. Instead, I wondered then and have wondered since how the Taoiseach could fail to know what I, in my relatively humble and decidedly peripheral position, knew; what the proverbial 'dogs in the street' barked. Of course he knew. The entire cabinet knew, or at least suspected, though their degrees of knowledge varied; politicians can be quite skilful at ensuring that they do not know dangerous or embarrassing things. The defence and justice ministers, in particular, knew a great deal, but they did not know how Lynch wanted them to react.

That same month, a conference was held at McKee Barracks to make preparations for a meeting with representatives of the citizens' defence committees in Bailieborough, County Cavan, in October. Among those

James McGowan, the author's maternal grandfather, with his wife Nell and their thirteen children, 1917.

Inky schoolboy, 1948.

Back to the roots: the author with his father in Dromahair, 1960.

Wedding day, London, 1963.

Making a farewell presentation to Stephen Hilliard (*right*) who left the Irish Times to become a Church of Ireland clergyman. He was later killed by an intruder in his rectory in Rathdrum, Co. Wicklow. *Left to right*: Seamus Martin (partly obscured), Seán Ó Tuathail, Niall Kiely, Frank McDonald (partly obscured).

The old Pearl Bar.
(© *Fantasyjackpalance.com*)

The *Irish Times* carries the news of John F. Kennedy's assassination, 1963. (© *Irish Times*)

Former offices of the Irish Times in D'Olier Street, Dublin. (© *Irish Times*)

Captain James Kelly.
(© *Captainkelly.org*)

Charles J. Haughey after his acquittal in the Arms Trial, 1970. (© *Irish Times*)

A protester leaves the Contraception Train holding a banned contraceptive, 1971. (© *Irish Times*)

Bernadette Devlin in Derry during the Battle of the Bogside, 1969. (© *Getty*)

The French oil tanker *Betelgeuse* explodes in Bantry Bay, 1979. Fifty people were killed. (© *Getty*)

Pope John Paul II visits Ireland, 1979. (© *Irish Times*)

The wreckage of the Stardust Ballroom, burnt down with great loss of life, 1981. (© *Irish Times*)

Rioters overturning a burning lorry to make a barricade, Belfast, 1981. (© *Getty*)

John Hume addresses the New Ireland Forum in Dublin Castle, 1984. (© *Irish Times*)

Hours after surviving an IRA assassination attempt, Margaret Thatcher makes a triumphant speech at the Conservative Party conference in Brighton, 1984. (© *Corbis*)

Ronald Reagan visits the land of his ancestors, 1984. (© *Corbis*)

Former offices of the Irish Independent in Abbey Street, Dublin. (© *Collins Photos*)

A 78-year-old admirer tries to greet Charles J. Haughey as he leaves a tribunal hearing in Dublin Castle. (© *Photocall*)

Bertie Ahern leaves the Mahon tribunal for the last time after giving evidence. (© *Photocall*)

Departed friends: Breandán Ó hEithir, Seán Mac Reamoin, Benedict Kiely.

(© *RTE Stills Library*)

(© *Irish Times*)

(© *Irish Times*)

Anti-Lisbon poster, 2008. (© *Irish Times*)

Symbol of the boom: the Irish Financial Services Centre. (© *Collins Photos*)

The headquarters of Anglo Irish Bank in Dublin. (© *Press Association Images Ltd*)

Symbols of the bust: uncompleted houses in Longford. (© *Photocall*)

who attended were Haughey, Gibbons, Colonel Michael Hefferon, director of Military Intelligence, and Captain James Kelly, one of four or five Intelligence officers operating within Northern Ireland. Kelly had strong political views and was under Blaney's influence. Hefferon was a very much older officer, and of a very different kind.

He had served in the army for nearly forty years, fourteen of them as aide-de-camp to President Seán T. Ó Ceallaigh and seven as Intelligence chief. He kept his political views, if any, strictly to himself. He reported weekly to Gibbons, whom he regarded as a friend. Both were witty and well-read men, and Hefferon had not yet begun to entertain suspicions of his minister. He assumed that Gibbons, like himself, was dedicated to the proprieties of the service.

He had a less easy relationship with another man dedicated to state security. Peter Berry, the long-serving secretary of the Department of Justice, wanted to take control of all intelligence services, including the military. To Berry's annoyance, Hefferon quietly vetoed the idea.

With equal discretion, and still keeping himself out of the public's knowledge, Hefferon intervened in two dangerous affairs. At the beginning of the Troubles, men from Derry were illegally inducted into the armed forces and given instructions in handling arms at Fort Dunree in Donegal, close to the border. Hefferon ordered the practice stopped. Then, early in 1970, he learned that 500 rifles had been sent to Dundalk Barracks, at Blaney's instigation, for despatch across the border. The countermanding order was issued by Lynch, but not before Hefferon learned of the incident and intervened. His alarm was intensified by the knowledge that the rifles were stamped with numbers and could be traced back to their source.

The full story of his role in these events may not be known until the publication of his private papers, which are in the Military Archives. The location of his official papers is unknown to me, and I am not certain that they have survived. At the time of the first 'arms trial' he was denied access to them (Micheál Ó Móráin, the minister for justice forced to resign by Lynch, was similarly treated.) They may have been destroyed.

Hefferon grew increasingly worried about Kelly's activities in the North and his close relations with Gibbons. In January 1970 Kelly told him: 'I have decided to throw my lot in with the Northerners.' Hefferon: 'You can't do that and wear the Irish Army uniform. Think about it. You have a wife and five young children.' A few days later Kelly came back and said he was determined on resignation. Hefferon took the papers to Gibbons, who was at first dismayed but then said that Haughey might 'fix him up with something'. He suggested a job as a pig-smuggling prevention officer. This may have been intended as irony.

A few weeks later, in early February 1970, the government issued a directive to the defence forces ordering them to prepare for incursions into Northern Ireland. For decades the existence of the directive was disputed, much to the chagrin of Kelly, who insisted that at all times he had acted in accordance with orders and with government policy and who published two books on the subject. At last the document turned up in the National Archives under the thirty-year rule. Kelly himself found it, and claimed it as vindication.

At the time, the directive was given *orally* to Hefferon and the Chief of Staff, General Seán Mac Eoin. On leaving their meeting with Gibbons, Mac Eoin told Hefferon: 'I am going to write all this stuff down. I advise you to do the same.'

By now, Hefferon had begun to acknowledge to himself that he had suspicions of the minister on two counts. First, he worried about Gibbons's plans, in conjunction with Haughey, for his junior officer. They seemed to envisage Kelly, in or out of uniform, in or out of the government service, continuing his mysterious activities in the North. Secondly, he suspected that Gibbons was not passing on the contents of his briefings to Lynch. But the February 1970 directive arose from a collective cabinet decision. And indeed a decision had been taken to prepare for military intervention in Northern Ireland, but only in the event of 'Doomsday', a complete breakdown of law and order accompanied by mass murders and displacement of Catholics.

This, then, seems a good point at which to ask the question which has provoked so much debate and dissension ever since. How much did Lynch know, and when?

In at least one sense, the answer is unequivocal. Peter Berry informed him about the conspiracy to import arms as early as October 1969. At the time, Berry was seriously ill in hospital. His message may not have been well conveyed, and Lynch when he visited him may have had some grounds for thinking that he was raving. Indubitably Berry was a conspiracy theorist who thought he saw subversives under every bed, but one might have thought that any Taoiseach would be alarmed by, and take action on, a warning from the key official responsible for state security. He could have personally questioned Mac Eoin, or Hefferon, or the head of the Special Branch, or all three. He did none of these things. In fact, he did not meet Mac Eoin until the following July.

After much deliberation, Berry decided that he could not trust the Taoiseach. He therefore, contrary to all protocol, approached President de Valera, who did not press him for details but told him that he must inform the Taoiseach. He did so in April 1970, but still Lynch did not act. Finally the Taoiseach's hand was forced by the Fine Gael leader, Liam Cosgrave, who had received a sensational letter from a highly-placed person in the Special Branch. (It is still a matter of speculation whether the Special Branch got their information from their own sources or from the British; it is certainly highly probable that the British informed them.) Lynch then, having no option, moved swiftly. He demanded the resignations of Blaney and Haughey. When they refused, he sacked them. He demanded and received the resignation of the minister for justice, Ó Móráin (a neat way of passing on the blame to the justice department and unfair to Ó Móráin, wrongly linked by the rumour mill to the conspiracy). Kevin Boland resigned voluntarily and quixotically. He had played no part in these events. The British ambassador reported to Whitehall that Boland, whatever his eccentricities, was the only one among the Fianna Fáil politicians who had come out of the affair with any honour.

When Lynch met Cosgrave and accepted the inevitability of disclosure, he assured the Fine Gael leader that Gibbons had played no part in the conspiracy, and Cosgrave did not use his name in the statement he made to the Dáil on the affair. Lynch's motivation here is obviously interlinked with the issue of how much he himself knew, but it is still open to question. Indubitably the dismissal of the Defence Minister, had Lynch been forced to take such an action, would have made a desperate crisis even worse and deepened the unavoidable split in the Fianna Fáil Party and the country. In fairness to Lynch, he may have wished to protect Gibbons and the army for national reasons, not merely party reasons.

However, the facts dictate a stark choice, familiar to political leaders in a crisis, between the unpalatable and the disastrous. Either Gibbons had fulfilled his plain duty of informing the Taoiseach, or he had not. If the first, Lynch was guilty of breathtaking recklessness and gross negligence. If the second, he should have dismissed Gibbons. In later life, Lynch whinged to his friends that Gibbons had 'let me down'. Yet he promoted him and used him as a weapon to humiliate Haughey; and as I have mentioned above, what became the establishment version holds that both he and Gibbons acted properly.

Lynch also determined that Blaney and Haughey, and their associates, must stand trial charged with conspiracy to import arms. It has been speculated that he did so at the insistence of the British, and that is a distinct possibility. Brian Lenihan argued with him against this course of action, correctly foreseeing a calamitous outcome, but Lynch was adamant. Blaney, Haughey, Captain James Kelly, John Kelly, described as 'a Belfast republican', and Albert Luykx, a Dutch businessman resident in Ireland, were indicted. A district court found that there was no case for Blaney to answer. Haughey, the two Kellys and Luykx were returned for trial to the Central Criminal Court.

It is necessary to remember that there were two trials. The first was aborted. The second resulted in the acquittal of all four defendants. In the following passages it will be necessary for me to make a distinction between the two trials; otherwise I will refer to the second in the usual way, as simply the Arms Trial.

Throughout all this period the country was in an uproar which manifested itself in turbulent scenes at different times inside and outside the courthouse, in the Dáil and in the streets. After the dismissal of the ministers, the Dáil had held an all-night debate in which Fianna Fáil deputies named 'the unity of the party'—not the country—as the first priority, and opposition deputies, particularly in the Labour Party, expressed a belief that the purpose of the attempted arms importation was a *coup d'état.* Those who held the latter view were simply wrong: the arms were for the North.

Naturally the prosecution and the defendants sought and obtained the services of the best and brightest lawyers, among them a future Supreme Court judge, Niall McCarthy SC. Lynch might usefully have taken this point on board before proceeding. The prosecution needed in effect to achieve something notoriously difficult: to prove a negative, namely that the defendants had not acted in accordance with government policy. This applied with special force to James Kelly. Unless the prosecution could show that he acted contrary to his orders, their case against him would fall apart. Their chief witnesses would be Gibbons and Hefferon.

Gibbons was a bad witness, the kind certain to alienate juries with a combination of two-clever-by-half and evasion. At one stage he was forced to admit that he had 'vestigial knowledge' of the conspiracy. Hefferon, by then in retirement, prepared for his own ordeal by sitting in a church for three hours, agonising over his position. He was not an exceptionally religious man, but he was a soldier. He resolved to tell the truth and stand the consequences.

The prosecution found his evidence at the first trial so disappointing that they decided—or someone decided for them—not to call him at the second trial. However, the judge called him, and he told the same story. In the meantime, his witness statement was heavily 'doctored', a pointless exercise as it proved, since the jury heard his evidence anyway.

When the verdict, finding all four defendants not guilty, was announced, the mob of Haughey supporters outside the court went wild. Haughey himself showed signs of temporary derangement, perhaps owing not only to excess of joy but to the lingering effects of a riding accident. He addressed his 'fellow patriots', a hyperbolic phrase at the best of times and particularly inapt coming from someone whose defence had been that he knew nothing about the attempted arms importation. He called on Lynch to consider his position. Lynch replied by arranging for almost the entire Fianna Fáil parliamentary party to cheer him at Dublin Airport when he returned from a visit to the United States. He then called two votes of confidence in the Dáil, one in the government, one in individual ministers. Blaney revolted, lost the Fianna Fáil whip, left the party—he liked to say that the party left him, not the other way round—and set up his own 'independent Fianna Fáil' organisation. Haughey swallowed the humiliation, voted with the government, and began to travel the long, hard road to his ultimate comeback.

Before trying to summarise some of the issues raised by, or surrounding, the Arms Trial, I must briefly address two subjects, one which has caused much controversy and one which has special *Irish Times* relevance.

Did the Lynch government as a whole, or ministers acting with the sanction of the government, conspire in the attempted arms importation or facilitate the emergence of the Provisional IRA and a three-decade terrorist campaign? Did it see the Provisionals as a desirable counterweight to the Marxist Official IRA? The answer to both questions is no, but with some qualifications. Blaney openly boasted that he had helped in the birth of the Provos. To plan for military intervention in the event of Doomsday was perfectly sensible and absolutely necessary, but the manner in which the directive of February 1970 was issued was grotesque and illustrated the confusion and panic of the times. The two most relevant officers got an oral version, while the proof lay in the National Archives for all to see once the state papers of the period came into the public domain.

Hefferon throughout the rest of his life was ostracised by former brother-officers. He was deeply hurt, but believed that he would ultimately be vindicated.

Long before I met any members of his family (but after several conversations with James Kelly and after reading the two books he wrote about the affair) I came to the conclusion that Hefferon had been treated abominably and that Lynch and Gibbons in the interest of minding their own backs had encouraged the belief to take root that both Hefferon and Kelly had failed in their duty and allied themselves with the enemies of the state. Kelly, whose naïve political opinions unfitted him for the role of an Intelligence officer operating in the North, might be said to have exceeded his duty, and unquestionably his decision to 'throw his lot in with the Northerners' was incompatible with his wearing an army uniform. But in his subsequent writings he made a persuasive case that he had every reason to believe that he acted at all times under orders. As to Hefferon, he may have considered moving Kelly to other duties at a much earlier date. If so, however, he would have had to take into account the relationship between Kelly and Gibbons—and his ignorance of precisely what that relationship was.

After the captain's arrest, Gibbons dropped a hint full of meaning to Hefferon: 'Kelly wasn't reporting very much.' Hefferon merely replied that 'Captain Kelly never refused to report at any time he was asked.'

It is easy to scapegoat and sideline soldiers, and it has happened in every age. But it angers me to think that politicians reacted to the third greatest crisis in the history of the state—the others being the civil war and the second world war—by casting the blame on men of honour. And if it angers me, it infuriated Gageby, who was, as we have seen, himself a former Intelligence officer. In time to come, his fury would induce him to develop a strange theory, that a government must stand by its security forces in all circumstances. This of course is grotesque in the case of gross misconduct or threats to state security. But I have always suspected that his hatred of Lynch had more to do with political prejudice than with concern for the proprieties.

Lynch has received lavish praise, not to say adulation, for taking the country safely through the crisis. In my opinion it is at best inflated. I have devoted much time, thought and research to the questions, did he know, and how much did he know, and when did he learn. On the evidence, the likeliest answer is that—leaving aside Berry's attempt to enlighten him—Gibbons kept him informed. It is possible, though less likely, that Gibbons either did not pass on his information to Lynch or ceased at some stage to inform him. In either case, that does not indicate that the Defence Minister was subservient to Haughey, still less that he was part of the conspiracy; he may have concluded that Lynch did not want to hear bad and embarrassing news. He may also have assumed that the Taoiseach had kept himself informed through his own sources, through the Special Branch, or through Berry personally, a very reasonable assumption.

As to the question whether the government considered the Provos as a counterweight to the Marxist Official IRA, there undoubtedly were many Fianna Fáil (and some Fine Gael) supporters who saw little wrong with an insurrection in the North so long as the violence did not spill over the border. John Healy made fun of them in the *Irish Times*, painting an improbable picture of upper-middle-class dinner parties in Foxrock at which everybody called everybody else 'darling' and praised the Provos because they did not resemble the dreadful people in the Republic who wanted a communist revolution. More to the point, the government as a whole and the dissidents (Boland excepted) had this much in common, that they wanted to contain the troubles to the North. Unlike Berry, they cannot have entertained any real fears of revolution in the Republic although, if the IRA split weakened the Goulding faction, which it did, that was a bonus.

When Lynch set about reconstructing his government, he realised what he should have known much earlier, that he could repose complete trust in ministers like Colley and Hillery. I do not believe that he ever came to trust Lenihan, who was completely loyal but who differed radically from his Taoiseach in every aspect of life, from his fondness for late-night socialising to his unusual habit of reading books.

Hillery at this time performed a most important service for Lynch. At the Fianna Fáil ard-fheis of 1971 a large proportion of the delegates noisily expressed their dislike of Lynch's conciliatory line on Northern Ireland by supporting and cheering Kevin Boland. Hillery from the platform made his voice heard over the hullabaloo. 'You can have Boland,' he told them, 'but you can't have Fianna Fáil.' That cooled their nationalist fervour. They chose the party and the material advantages that went with it.

For all their complexities, the Arms Trial and the events surrounding it can be summed up in quite simple terms.

Two government ministers, Blaney and Haughey, conspired with other persons to import arms illegally. They intended the consignment for use in Northern Ireland, not for a *coup d'état*. Blaney openly boasted that he had helped in the foundation of the Provisional IRA.

In court, Haughey denied any involvement. He thereby perjured himself. The judge told the jury that there was a direct conflict of evidence between him and Gibbons. The fact that Haughey lied did not necessarily mean that Gibbons was telling the truth.

John Kelly did not give evidence at the Arms Trial because he did not want to subject himself to cross-examination. He made an unsworn statement in which he did not deny his part in the affair. Nobody doubted his sincerity.

Albert Luykx was close to Blaney and a go-between with an arms dealer in Hamburg.

Captain James Kelly believed that he was acting under orders. He saw the government directive of February 1970 as vindication, and he had grounds for pointing to it as an indication of government policy. However, this does not prove that intervention in the North was government policy months earlier when he attended the notorious Bailieborough meeting with known subversives, including Cathal Goulding.

Kevin Boland and Micheál Ó Móráin had nothing to do with the plot. The pretext for Lynch's insistence on Ó Móráin's resignation was that the Minister for Justice had not kept the Taoiseach informed. Ó Móráin most likely knew that Berry had tried to tell Lynch and, when no action followed, decided to let events take their course. He almost certainly did not know of the desperation that led an eminent public servant to approach the President and prompted one or more senior Special Branch officers to write to the leader of the opposition.

Either Gibbons passed on the contents of his Intelligence briefings to the Taoiseach or he did not. If he did, Lynch's inaction was breathtaking. But even if he did not, Lynch's negligence was outrageous.

Aside from the aborted arms importation involving the Arms Trial defendants, we have to look at an earlier incident, the despatch of rifles to Dundalk in February 1970, authorised by Gibbons at Blaney's persuasion. Lynch has been praised for ordering them sent back to Dublin. It may be that more credit belongs to Hefferon. Either Lynch knew how the incident had come about, or he deliberately blinded himself to Blaney's involvement and Gibbons's foolishness.

Nevertheless, it has to be said that for all his manoeuvrings and vacillations he succeeded in the entirely worthy objective of maintaining civil order in the Republic. As Michael McInerney put it, 'Dev kept us out of the war. Lynch kept us out of the North.' And *raison d'état* is a powerful argument.

John Healy dubbed Lynch 'Honest Jack'. He meant it ironically, but the tag lived on as a compliment. He also held that Lynch had set a cunning trap for tigers, in which Gibbons served as the bait, the donkey. Gibbons, who never lost his good opinion of himself, was most annoyed. It may not have been a million miles from the truth. The most favourable explanation of Lynch's behaviour is that, as some argued, he bided his time and gave the conspirators enough rope to hang themselves. But that exhausts my stock of mixed metaphors.

———

During the three years from 1970 to 1973, my involvement in the paper's Northern coverage became intense. After Gageby, in consultation with McDowell, appointed me London editor, I took up the job in August 1970. Before that, I had a little 'dry run' when I wrote a few pieces from London, Birmingham and elsewhere in the run-up to the election of June 1970. Like almost everybody else, I got it wrong.

The country was prosperous, the mood relaxed. The Wilson government appeared to have come through numerous crises well enough, if not with any great credit. Wilson, still deceptively young and vigorous, looked a more attractive proposition than the Conservative leader, Edward Heath, a poor campaigner and an awkward television performer. The opinion polls were so favourable to Labour that it was easy to underestimate the lasting effect on the public of two outstanding failures, the forced devaluation of sterling in 1967 and the vetoing by James Callaghan of an attempt by Barbara Castle to restrict the powers of the trade unions. The Tories promised to complete her unfinished work, but they were not widely believed. The unions were regarded as a fact of life, much like the weather.

However, the polls were telling a tale that I should have read more carefully. As the campaign progressed, the Labour lead fell and fell again. On election day, the only poll to get the result exactly right appeared in the London *Standard*. It gave a Tory lead of two per cent. Beside the story appeared a piece by the paper's long-serving political editor, Robert Carvel. He told his readers that the poll had it wrong: Labour would win. When the election returns came in, a radio interviewer asked him if he would now 'consider his position'. He was not amused.

Spokesmen for the new government assured anyone who would listen

that there would be no change in Northern policy on either the political
or the military front. They apparently did not know that the outgoing
government had had in mind a drastic change. Wilson and Callaghan
(who as Home Secretary had been the cabinet member responsible for
Northern Ireland) had prepared a bill to abolish the Stormont
government and parliament and impose direct Whitehall rule. They
thought they would retain office after the election and could then proceed.
In the event, their loss of office was followed by a fatal delay, marked by
serious British errors.

Since I intend to discuss these and other grave errors in some detail, it is
only fair to say that very few of them derived from prejudice, irresponsibility
or lack of good will. Long afterwards, as the North moved towards the
settlement of 2007, I mused over the turbulent history of the preceding forty
years with David McKittrick. He said: 'You know, all in all, the Brits haven't
done too badly.' I replied: 'You know, David, I've been thinking the same
thing myself.' Coming from the likes of us, that counts as high praise.

In the summer of 1970, however, the British made a shocking
misjudgment. The army imposed a three-day curfew on the Catholic Falls
area of Belfast. Three people were killed. Stormont ministers rode into the
Falls on military armoured vehicles. The population of the area took the
incident as a declaration of war.

When I started work in London in August, I had almost no contacts
except for those I inherited from my predecessor, Andrew Whittaker.
Those I did make early in my tenure—Tories as well as the Labour MPs
who backed the civil rights movement and favoured a united Ireland—all
echoed the Heath government's line. Like myself, they underestimated the
effects of the Falls curfew.

At first I had no idea that the Northern question would not only
dominate my term as London editor but that I would find myself involved
in the coverage, in one way and another, for more than half a lifetime. I
assumed that in addition to Anglo-Irish relations I would chiefly cover
British domestic politics, concentrating on the two great issues that
preoccupied the new Prime Minister, Heath, and the rest of the political
world: Europe and the economy, the latter linked with trade union reform.
But it did not take me long to realise that I occupied an exceptionally
privileged position. The British political establishment were about to learn
that the 'Irish Question', which had split parties and brought down
governments in the nineteenth and early twentieth centuries, had raised its
head again.

In December 1921, when their leaders wrongly thought that David Lloyd George had found the answer, Winston Churchill had asked: 'Whence does this mysterious power of Ireland come? It is a small, poor, sparsely populated island, lapped about by British sea power ... How is it that she sways our councils, shakes our parties and infects us with bitterness, convulses our passions and deranges our action? How is it that she has forced generation after generation to stop the whole traffic of the British empire in order to debate her domestic affairs?' Half a century on, the curtain had risen on the latest act of the drama. I had a seat in the front row of the dress circle.

I set about making contacts and observing the political scene at close quarters. To this end, I took advantage of the fact that the 'season' began, at it still does, with the TUC conference and the party conferences. My chief interest lay in the Tories as the party of government, and I knew they would be hard to penetrate. But first I went to beautiful Brighton to become acquainted with the TUC.

My first encounters, like all subsequent encounters, were discouraging. My sympathies lay with the downtrodden, but no amount of sympathy could blind me to the perception that the lovely fellows who stayed in the same hotel were rapidly losing touch with the real world and unlikely to regain contact. They were major officials of minor unions and minor officials of major unions. They resented the way in which Wilson had manipulated the main union leaders, but had enough sense to expect that they and their ill-paid members would fare worse under Heath. Like their friends on the left wing (and not only on the left wing) of the Labour Party, they passionately opposed British entry into the European Economic Community and dreamed of establishing some kind of socialist state in a basically conservative country. Meanwhile, they drank warm beer and sang Irish rebel songs—badly. Much as I liked them, I thought them hopelessly out of touch, especially on the European question.

I had not expected to come across much to interest me at the next conference, the Liberal assembly in Eastbourne. In the event, I found it fascinating. For the first time in my life, I heard Lloyd George well spoken of as the man who had pulled off 'the Irish settlement' in 1920–22. I thought the defects of that settlement were fairly obvious. But I was impressed by the standard of the speeches. One of the tiny handful of Liberal MPs denounced the ridiculous capers of the Young Liberals, who under the leadership of Peter Hain had taken up positions to the left of Labour. He warned them that if they continued with their antics they would get a change all right, but 'it will not be the New Left. It will be the Old Right.' As it turned out, we would in due course get a touch, or more than a touch, of the New Right as well. As for Hain, he eventually joined Labour and became, of all things, Secretary of State for Northern Ireland.

Richard Moore, a friend of Whittaker and political secretary to the party leader, Jeremy Thorpe, took me to see Thorpe in his suite in a very grand hotel. He received us clad in a silk dressing gown, in a room with extraordinarily dim lighting. I remember the dressing gown and the lighting all the more plainly because he had little of consequence to say. He may have been preoccupied with his complicated personal affairs. I happened by chance to know that he was one of what the tabloids called 'a homosexual ring' at a time when male homosexual acts were illegal in Ireland and had only recently been legalised in Britain; another was a prominent Irish politician. His choice of other friends was less wise. Some years later, he was sensationally tried and acquitted on a charge of attempting to murder one of them. Nevertheless, he was a canny politician who with better luck might have brought about a Tory-Liberal coalition in 1974.

At the Tory conference in Blackpool, I began to cultivate the Young Conservatives, an organisation famous for pretty girls and right-wing opinions. The pretty girls were real, but not the right-wing opinions, because the Young Tories were in a liberal phase. I got on well with them because they shared my pro-Europe views, and partly through them I made friends in the months and years that followed with influential and well-informed members of parliament.

Labour met, also in Blackpool, the week before the Conservative event. They sadly lacked direction, leadership and unity. I had yet to learn how hopelessly divided they were, not just between left and right but between the soft and hard ('loony') left and within the centrist or right-wing factions. There was a world of difference between the chief intellectuals, epitomised by Roy Jenkins, Anthony Crosland, Denis Healey and my new acquaintance Roy Hattersley, on the one hand, and on the other the bulk of the foot soldiers, usually union-sponsored and usually anti-Europe. Commonly, the miners' union, still a power in the land, and other unions would give loyal servants nominations for safe Labour seats when they had passed their prime. It was called their 'gold watch'. Those who handed out this patronage did not choose their best people.

The constituency organisations were often dominated by the various left-wing factions. Their delegates, when called upon to speak, denounced the leadership as right-wing and unimaginative. They firmly believed that they could have won the election with more radical candidates and policies. More harmful than this erroneous belief was the sheer hatred that characterised relations between the factions and turned all Labour conferences in this period into bearpits. The brilliant *Guardian* writer Ian Aitken, himself a member of the left-wing Tribune Group, said to me: 'God ordained that the Tories should meet the week after Labour.' He meant that the irritation with Labour follies felt by such as ourselves would dissipate as soon as we saw the Conservative right wing in full voice, yelling for the return of hanging and flogging and for the waging of the class war.

On these points the Tories were themselves divided. Sensible people knew that hanging and flogging would not return and that longer jail sentences would fill the prisons without decreasing the crime rate, and they supported trade union legislation as something necessary for the good of the country. But conference delegates were far more passionate, and far less rational, than either their leaders or the generality of Tory voters.

I had little interest in these people: too little, perhaps, for I did not realise how much trouble they would give Heath on the European issue or that he would have to take their strong pro-unionist views into account, at least to some extent, when, much against his will, he would find himself obliged to address the Northern Ireland question. In the two wonderful environments in which I would revel for the next three years, I saw my main task as making authoritative contacts as close as possible to the centre of power.

――――

These environments, a few minutes' Tube travel apart, were Fleet Street and Westminster. My office was in *The Times* building in Blackfriars: a modern building, not the original *Times* headquarters where some of the world's greatest editors had presided and where the oddities of the staff prompted Lord Northcliffe, when he owned the paper, to dub them the Black Friars. 'The Black Friars,' he said, 'think that news, like wine, improves with age.' Of the countless Blackfriars stories, perhaps the most famous comes from the nineteenth century. It is at least partly true. Editorial writers of the period occupied a room equipped with paper, ink, quill pens and a jug of claret. They took their time over their work and their wine. A newly employed writer took too much. As the deadline neared, the editor and the chief printer fretted about whether to hurry him up. At last they entered the room and found him asleep over his empty claret jug. They went to see how much of his work might be usable. He had written only one word, 'notwithstanding.'

In my time other newspapers besides the *Irish Times* rented offices there. I made friends with the Australians, always among my favourite nationalities, and with Bob Reston, correspondent of the *Los Angeles Times* and son of the famous James 'Scotty' Reston. Bob Reston had worked in Washington and Moscow and thought London a backwater, whereas to me it was of colossal importance.

Physically the quarter—now, alas, completely abandoned by the media—was an urban delight. There are several fine buildings, notably St Bride's Church and the headquarters then occupied by the *Daily Telegraph*, the *Daily Express* and Reuters. All around are little squares and alleys, overwhelmed, like the street itself, with history. The Bell pub was once the living quarters of the men who built St Paul's Cathedral for Christopher Wren. Samuel Johnson drank in the Cheshire Cheese and John Dryden frequented the Lamb and Flag, not far away in Covent Garden. The near-legendary columnists who worked in the street a little before my time mostly preferred El Vino's. Vincent Mulchrone of the *Daily Mail* was said to have started every day with a triple drink: a glass of water, a quarter-bottle of champagne, and a Fernet Branca as a curative. When Winston Churchill's body was lying in state in Westminster Hall, selected journalists were allowed in for a look at the catafalque. Mulchrone checked his watch in El Vino's, finished his drink and said: 'All right, lads, one quick trip around Winston and back to the pub.'

In the seventies, the drinking was still on a heroic scale, but the pub most frequented by the Irish journalists, the King and Keys, was more decorous than most. One of its most celebrated and most faithful customers was T.E. (Peter) Utley of the *Daily Telegraph*, a High Tory and a man of great style and intellect. He was blind and always had a secretary to mind him. The secretary's duties, however, did not appear to extend to attempting the impossible task of keeping his clothes clear of cigarette ash. Utley in hot argument with a cigarette in his fingers, the ash growing longer and certain to fall over his clothes, was a sight to behold.

The *Telegraph* people usually occupied the front of the pub, the Irish the back, but we frequently mingled and had many heated but civil debates. Among the Irish were Gery Lawless and my old friend Aidan Hennigan, both very good company. Lawless had been interned on the Curragh during the IRA 'border campaign'. In a celebrated case, he brought an action against the Irish state in the European Court of Human Rights. Seán MacBride represented him. He lost his case, but he established the right of citizens as well as governments to litigate in the Human Rights Court. In the early seventies he was a Trotskyist who looked forward to the Irish revolution, and he was obsessed with the activities of the security services. He exaggerated their role in political events, but he certainly had abundant sources of information. Later he would become a Labour member of one of the London borough councils, wholly out of sympathy with the 'Loony Left'.

Con Howard, press counsellor at the Irish embassy, was another mainstay of the pub. His successors would include outstanding officials who rose to higher rank, like John McColgan, Dáithí Ó Ceallaigh, and Dermot Gallagher, a future secretary of the foreign affairs department. But Howard had a rare genius for making contacts—and for turning them into close friends. One was the future Chancellor of the Exchequer Denis Healey, who had possibly the finest intellect in the British Labour Party. Howard would go on to make similarly impressive contacts in Washington. In the early seventies he addressed himself to a quixotic effort to convert the Conservative Party to the Irish nationalist cause. He reported to Iveagh House on a conversation with Lady Hartwell, daughter of Lord Birkenhead and wife of Lord Hartwell, proprietor of the *Telegraph*. She was considered a person of enormous influence. She asked him if we really wanted to take on board 'those screaming women in the Shankill Road'. A pertinent question.

——

At Westminster, drink flowed as freely as in Fleet Street. Among the numerous bars in the Palace of Westminster, journalists had a choice of three. Their own was part of a complex which included various offices, a cafeteria, a restaurant and a library. Annie's Bar (since closed, a victim of the age of political correctness) was exclusive to MPs, former MPs, lobby correspondents and parliamentary sketch writers. By a strange anomaly, the chief Irish journalists were members of the lobby, as also of the foreign correspondents' association and the organisation representing London editors of British regional newspapers. The Strangers' Bar was the haunt of union-sponsored Labour members. In theory only MPs were permitted to buy drinks there, but the rule was often ignored. On top of all this, one could drink on the terrace in the summer and relish the unprintable stories told by the SDLP leader, Gerry Fitt. In the intervals between yarns, he liked to hold up his glass ('gin and tonic, no ice') and shout to the people travelling up and down the Thames on pleasure boats: 'It's all free, you know!' It was not free, but heavily subsidised.

All the drinking, lunching, dining and attendance at receptions had a serious purpose. I worked extremely hard, and I used the lobby system to considerable effect. Its chief advantage was not access to the members' lobby, though that was useful: it was access to the daily briefings by officials and weekly briefings by the leader of the opposition, Wilson, and the leader of the House of Commons, Willie Whitelaw.

Whitelaw held the extraordinary title of Lord President; other weird titles, still in use, include Chancellor of the Duchy of Lancaster and Lord Privy Seal. Asked to explain the latter, Churchill had once replied, unhelpfully: 'He is neither a lord, nor a privy, nor a seal.' The truthful answer is that the holders of these titles perform whatever duties the prime minister chooses to assign to them in the House of Commons or the House of Lords. They may be as obscure as the titles, or persons of consequence in the government or their parties. Whitelaw was a person of enormous consequence: one of Heath's very few intimate friends, a supreme political operator skilled in Commons backstairs dealings, a conciliator, the custodian of many secrets, and a man of great political intelligence. On one grand occasion in Windsor Castle the Irish ambassador, Dr Donal O'Sullivan, met Harold Wilson, who said: 'I saw you talking to Willie Whitelaw. A nice man. A pity he's so stupid.' Whitelaw was far from stupid. I soon came to know him well and to admire him.

I also came quickly to find that politicians of all shades knew as much about the journalists with whom they mingled as the journalists themselves. They were, rightly, much less concerned about the lobby correspondents' political opinions than their integrity and objectivity, and they had no trouble spotting bias or outright corruption. Parliaments, like more mundane organisations, depend heavily on trust and character. In the House of Commons, centrists might be admired for their policies and intelligence but disliked for arrogance or snootiness. Some on the Tory far right might be equally held in high regard for their integrity, others were singularly unpleasant characters suspected of dodgy financial or sexual activities. A few of the extreme Labour left-wingers were crypto (or not so crypto) communists with close contacts with the Soviet Union and the embassies of its satellite countries. The 'loony left' and the Trotskyists who in later years would give Neil Kinnock so much grief had not yet made much mark.

I was dismayed to learn how much petty corruption existed, though I had only one direct experience. An intermediary offered me an annual retainer equivalent to 40 per cent of my then salary to supply his principal with information gained through my position as a lobby correspondent. He refused to name the principal. I declined his offer politely. I don't know how many others may have accepted such offers.

A couple of my colleagues told me they knew I was 'all right' when they saw me chatting with Northern MPs across the spectrum from Ian Paisley to Bernadette Devlin. Paisley was a mystery to them—and to me. Would this mob orator learn the art of normal politics at Westminster, or would he revert in the usual way to type? Would he ever renounce religious bigotry? I could not answer the first question. I had a better idea about the second after some intriguing conversations on the terrace. At one point he asked me if the retirement of John Charles McQuaid as archbishop of Dublin and his succession by Dermot Ryan would signal a new liberalism in the Catholic church in Ireland. I told him it would not. I knew that the church would fight the Liberal Agenda every inch of the way. Perhaps it is not fanciful to suggest that the question showed that Paisley even then was not a fundamentalist but an opportunist, someone open to accommodation once he had cleared the unionist establishment out of the way, as he finally did—in old age, though, after he had lost the tremendous vigour of his youth and middle years. But it would certainly be fanciful to claim that I could foresee the emergence of this rabble-rouser in his brief but dramatic manifestation as the benign 'father of his people' when he took office in alliance with Sinn Féin in the Northern executive in 2007. That would have needed the gift of prophecy.

Most of the 'official' Ulster Unionist MPs, whether troglodytes or moderates, seemed to have few contacts outside the Conservative right wing. They were remarkably ill-informed and had little understanding of their own humble place in the United Kingdom political conspectus.

Among the points they did not appear to understand was that the needs of Whitehall would always prevail over their own prejudices. Like so many other individuals and governments, they took too little account of the depth and power of the 'traditional governing class', both politicians and officials. This class would survive, though bloodied, through the radicalism of Margaret Thatcher in the following decade when she pulled off the marvellous trick of fighting wars on two fronts, against the aristocracy and against the unions, and winning both. In the early seventies Heath preached radicalism but did not practise it. He appointed members or sympathisers of the 'old gang' to his cabinet: Whitelaw, James Prior, the former prime minister Sir Alec Douglas-Home. These were clever and worldly men, quite unlike the unreconstructed rustic squires who populated much of the Tory benches in both houses of parliament. They held a sophisticated view of their country's interests, above all in the economic and military spheres. Few of those among them who ever looked seriously into the Irish question had any objection to a sovereign united Ireland, provided British interests were safeguarded. A man in the same mould, Peter Brooke, would sum up a complex question when, as Secretary of State for Northern Ireland in 1990, he said that Britain 'no longer' had any selfish strategic or economic interest in Northern Ireland. Profoundly true. What Britain once had, it no longer had.

The Tory moderates supported Heath in the negotiations to join the European Community. This drew me towards them, as also towards the Labour pro-Europeans. At the time, my contacts on the Labour 'soft left', almost without exception, opposed British entry. One day Ian Aitken said to me and my friend Kevin McNamara MP: 'You cardinals (his term for Catholics) are all pro-Europe.' We burst out laughing. McNamara, a fervent Catholic, was anti whereas I, a sceptic in matters of religion, had quickly been identified as pro.

The president of the Association of European Journalists' British section told me that he had heard reports to this effect, and wondered how I reconciled it with my known left-wing views. That was typical of British misconceptions which persist to this day, even in pro-European newspapers like the *Guardian* and the *Observer*. I joined the AEJ and ate many pleasant lunches in the St James's Club, a dusty but magnificent survival from another era, with aged waiters and excellent food and wine. Spirits, to my recollection, were served at only one lunch. Our guest was Sir Christopher Soames, the British ambassador to France. His bulk and the colour of his face indicated his tastes, but his mind was as sharp as a razor. He talked volubly, with knowledge and insight, about French foreign policy. At length his voice failed him, and to revive him a glass of brandy was called for. It cured him instantly.

Contacts of another kind were to be found in the Irish Club in Eaton

Square. Gerry Fitt lived there when in London. So did Stan Orme, a left-wing Labour MP, later a junior minister in Northern Ireland. Irish building contractors, having worked an eighteen-hour day and swollen their already vast bank accounts, congregated there late at night. They pressed banknotes into the hand of this advocate of the Irish cause. 'Don't they realise,' he asked me, 'that they and I are on opposite sides?'

Dublin politicians made frequent visits. It was easy, and useful, to get to know them in the club, at the embassy and in private houses. But the politicians I knew and liked best were the chief thinkers of the SDLP, John Hume and Austin Currie, whose intellects matched their honesty and their hatred of violence. I considered Hume the greatest Irishman of his generation. However, I thought then, and still think, that he had far too little knowledge of, or feeling for, British political history or the particularities of the British system of governance, and that when he became a member of parliament he should have tried harder to ignore the flummery, see the value of the centuries-old conventions, and enjoy the theatre of the set pieces. He much preferred Strasbourg. But the European Parliament, though worthy, is boring. The House of Commons on its good days is exciting.

My main mentors among the lobby correspondents were Ian Aitken and Andrew Shepard, then with the Manchester *Evening News*, later with RTÉ in Dublin. At the time, the RTÉ correspondent was a most remarkable character, John O'Sullivan, who went on to write speeches for Margaret Thatcher, to work for the Heritage Foundation in the United States, to edit the *National Review*, and to reach the top in United Press International. He passionately believed in all the tenets of the New Right in a period when they had not yet become fashionable. He was pro-unionist and anti-Europe. He derided the U-turns performed by Heath when the Prime Minister made accommodations with the unions and bailed out lame-duck industries. He was a proto-Thatcherite and proto-Friedmanite. Even more, he was a disciple of Ayn Rand, with her doctrine of 'creative destruction'.

O'Sullivan's eyes shone—literally—when he extolled the glories of the free market. He saw the market, under the guidance of Adam Smith's 'invisible hand', as perfect. Although I had begun to harbour doubts about state ownership and control of industry, I thought the uncontrolled market very far from perfect. It might be if everybody had equal information and equal opportunity, but that has never happened and will never happen. And anyone who thinks an uncontrolled market is desirable, to say nothing of perfect, need only look at the credit crunch which hit the whole world in 2007, spurred by the madness of 'sub-prime' mortgages, which means lending money to people who cannot possibly pay the interest. That calamitous practice grew up while the American central bank, the us Federal Reserve, was presided over by another disciple of Ayn Rand, Alan Greenspan. At the same time, the use of bizarre financial instruments, described as 'pixie-dust' by *Time* magazine, became more and more common and made control of the system close to impossible. The result was the world financial and economic crisis of 2008.

Back in the early 1970s, I pointed out to O'Sullivan that in one respect we could never have totally free trade in all commodities. Since tradeable commodities include human beings, we would have to reintroduce slavery. Of course he furiously rejected this argument, and I was enormously amused when the journalist and economist Paul Tansey, a great friend of mine and the husband of Olivia O'Leary, attended a course of lectures in the London School of Economics by Milton Friedman himself. The sage told his students, with a twinkle, that we could not have completely free markets because that would mean bringing back slavery. Since then, alas, we have witnessed the growth of two abominable forms of slavery, child labour in the developing world and the trafficking of women and children in Europe for prostitution and much worse.

His ideas have been put into practice by the Bush administration in the United States. We know the results, in terms of both domestic and foreign policy. They do not show that we should reject the capitalist system—there is nothing to replace it. They do show the folly of unregulated markets.

Before and after Thatcher's accession to power, O'Sullivan would form part of a group who took part in policy discussions as well as writing speeches. Their approach to any policy issue was to ask, how do we create a market in such and such a service or commodity? This gave birth to such absurdities as water privatisation. The New Right reminded me of nobody so much as the old-time Trotskyites and other extreme left-wingers, who could never leave well enough alone.

But at the same time he was the best of company. Unlike Lady Thatcher, he had a sense of humour. When leader of the opposition, she lived in Chelsea. She would go through draft after draft with her team, sometimes until long after midnight. Her devoted husband, Denis, was always on hand. Late one night he called a break and took the speechwriters round the block for a walk. He told them: 'I don't know how you fellows stick it.'

At the risk of harming chronology, I cannot resist two more anecdotes on the theme of her lack of humour. After she defeated Whitelaw in the leadership race that followed Heath's resignation, Whitelaw remained ostentatiously loyal and so invaluable to her that she said 'every prime minister needs a Willie.' She could not understand why this provoked her cabinet ministers to laughter. They laughed again a few minutes after Michael Heseltine stormed out of a cabinet meeting. She had broken the ensuing horrified silence by saying that they had better turn to something non-controversial and invited Tom King to brief them on Northern Ireland.

But her working habits saved her life. She was at her desk late at night in her suite in the Grand Hotel in Brighton when an IRA bomb almost blew up her entire cabinet. Had she been in her bedroom a few feet away, she would have been killed or seriously injured, like several of her colleagues.

———

The Old Right and the New Right combined with the Silly Left and the unenlightened elements of the Labour right wing to oppose British entry into the EEC. Heath had had a tough time negotiating in Brussels. He now had an equally tough time in the House of Commons, where he did not command a majority on the issue and would have to proceed with the utmost skill and ruthlessness to get the necessary legislation through.

He began the process with a debate which lasted no less than six days. Curiously, there was little objection to this excessive devotion of time to one subject, however important. Everybody had a say, including the Tory backwoodsmen who considered the project an act of treason—and the Ulster Unionists, who could seldom hope, and seldom tried, for an audience on any question but Northern Ireland. One day, I approached Stanley McMaster, MP for Belfast East, on his way to the Chamber and asked him how he intended to vote. He replied: 'I can't say until I've spoken.' In the end, he voted Aye on one clause of the bill, No on another, and abstained on a third.

That was not as odd as it might seem. The debate on the central question was followed by far lengthier debates in the course of which MPs went through the legislation line by line. Many of the clauses were contentious for one reason or another, and it was quite reasonable for members to take differing views of the various clauses. The government's majority was always under threat. The Conservative whips used all of their black arts to persuade, bully or, in all probability, blackmail backbenchers to vote with the government. But their biggest weapon was their alliance with the pro-Europe wing of Labour. It extended to constant meetings at which both sides totted up the numbers and went so far as to decide how many and which Labour MPs should vote yes on specific clauses or abstain. Of course the anti-Europe majority suspected and resented the operation. Wilson, obsessed with party unity, was unable to prevent the widening divisions between the Labour factions. After his return to office, he would be forced to hold a ridiculous referendum on whether Britain should remain in the EEC, and to allow not just backbenchers but cabinet members to take opposing sides.

It was impossible to avoid coming into contact with the sheer hatred the issue engendered. One day I arranged to have a quiet chat with a staunch Labour pro-European, Sir Geoffrey de Freitas, in Annie's Bar. Another Labour MP, Dennis Skinner, came in and sat a little distance away. De Freitas was one of the Sephardic Jewish aristocracy. Skinner, who would become famous as the 'Beast of Bolsover' (his constituency) was a brilliant parliamentarian, but his manners left something to be desired. He heckled de Freitas so loudly and offensively that in the end de Freitas slammed down his glass on the bar, smashing it, and walked out. The next day he sent me an unnecessary note of apology.

Hatred between factions, and bad manners, were not confined to the Labour side. I was invited to a party given by the right-wing Monday Club in a haunt of Tory grandees, the Carlton Club. As I entered, Sir Edward Boyle, formerly a liberal education secretary detested by right-wingers for trying to reform a system which heavily subsidised the middle classes, walked across the lobby. Loutish Monday Club members, who were only there on sufferance, booed him. Inside, I made for a corner of the bar to order a drink. A stout middle-aged man who looked somewhat like Toad of Toad Hall was standing nearby. He said: 'I don't think much of this lot.' I waited for him to tell me why. He explained that they would not support his curious campaign in a curious cause, the abolition of an equally curious phenomenon, the endorsement by members of the royal family of various goods and services. The genesis of the campaign, he said, was that he had had one of his cars serviced in a garage with such a warrant and the garage had done the job disastrously. He had also brought an unsuccessful court action. I remarked sympathetically that litigation was expensive. 'Yes,' he said, 'I often sue and I usually lose. But I don't mind. I have plenty of money.' It occurred to me that although I would never wish to be cast away on a desert island with members of the club, at least they had enough sense not to support Mr Toad's daft campaigns.

Back in the real world Heath was discovering, to his undisguised chagrin, that he was going to have to take on board a third issue in addition to the economy and Europe. And I was discovering some of the defects of the lobby system.

If you trust your contacts and they trust you—specifically, if they know you will never reveal your sources—you get wide and privileged access to 'non-attributable' information. But officials as well as politicians abused the system, and would abuse it more blatantly in later times. Often it gave rise to fairly minor irritation, as when a minister would tell the lobby as a whole, or an individual, something non-attributably, thereby preventing us from quoting him directly, and then repeat it for the public on television. An infinitely more serious abuse arose when they misled the lobby, knowing that correspondents could not say where the information came from. Heath came to speak to us in person and told us that the European question was so momentous that other countries would expect the British government to impose a 'three-line whip' (a direct order carrying sanctions if disobeyed) on Conservative MPs. Reports appeared to the effect that this was the government's intention. The opposite was the truth. Heath planned to allow a free vote, which would have the dual effect of obscuring the inevitable backbench Tory rebellion and embarrassing Labour. The inaccuracy of the reports reflected on the journalists who wrote them, myself included, not on the Prime Minister, to whom the blame properly belonged.

I was out of temper with the government for much more solid reasons than any pique an incident like that could cause. I deplored its lack of willingness to focus on the Northern Ireland problem, which was getting out of control at the political level and on the streets. James Chichester-Clark, who had succeeded O'Neill as Stormont prime minister, did not last long. He resigned, and Brian Faulkner took his place. Faulkner was regarded by Catholics as an Orange bigot. His subsequent career would prove otherwise, but not before both he and the British government would make epochal mistakes.

By 1972 at latest, the Provisional IRA had become the most ruthless, most inventive and best organised terrorist organisation in Europe. They invented the car bomb and the horrific proxy bombings in which they forced men to drive vehicles loaded with explosives into military posts.

They murdered parents in front of their children and teachers in front of their pupils. They abducted and killed people whom they deemed, rightly or wrongly, informers, and buried their bodies in remote locations. Some of the bodies have never been found. But a list of their crimes and cruelties, and those of the loyalist terrorists, would take up a book much longer than this; and indeed it has filled the pages of many books, of which the most outstanding is *Lost Lives* by David McKittrick and his collaborators.

———

The British, as so often, responded to the political and security crises with a mixture of conciliation and repression, and with a hopeless sense of timing. Their military men had made a bad mistake when they permitted Stormont ministers to ride through the Falls on armoured vehicles in 1970. In August 1971 Faulkner made a worse mistake when, with Heath's approval, he introduced internment without trial, a disastrous move.

We can never know if it might have worked under the right conditions. These would have had to include the simultaneous introduction of internment in the Republic, and in the North the arrest of the right people, including loyalist terrorists. But Lynch's government was too weak for the first option, and the British army and the RUC botched the operation itself. They used out-of-date lists, in some cases arresting fathers instead of sons or men who had no connection at all with terrorists. The Northern leaderships of both the Provisional IRA and the Official IRA were almost untouched, as were all the loyalists. Then reports emerged, and proved true, that detainees had been tortured by the British army. The Irish government brought an action in the European Human Rights Commission, and subsequently in the Human Rights Court, which dragged on for several years, a grave irritant in Anglo-Irish relations. At last the court ruled, wrongly in my opinion, that the detainees had not been subjected to torture but to 'inhuman and degrading treatment'. When is torture not torture? Meanwhile, the Provisional IRA exploited the injustice to step up violence to new levels and to tighten their grip on the Catholic communities in the cities and in border areas like South Armagh.

Heath realised that he must move quickly to re-establish control. He began to contemplate abolishing the Stormont government and parliament and imposing direct British rule. I reported to this effect in the autumn. About the same time, a similar report, but clearly based on different sources, appeared in the *Financial Times*. Asked about my story at a lobby briefing, Heath's press secretary, Donald Maitland, described it as 'bunkum'. I don't recall him saying anything about the *Financial Times*.

At the time, after a year in London, I had developed so many well-informed contacts that I was able, then and in the following two years, to write several exclusive stories. The direct rule one was the scoop that attracted most attention, but some of the others were almost equally important. For example, I reported that James Callaghan was preparing to come out, as he soon afterwards did, with a proposal to withdraw British troops from Northern Ireland. This would not have led, as the deluded advocates of withdrawal in the 'Troops Out Movement' thought, to a united Ireland. It would have brought about civil war.

Full-scale civil war seemed to come closer when a dreadful event occurred in Derry on Bloody Sunday, in January 1972. Paratroopers opened fire on people taking part in a banned civil rights march, killing thirteen men; a fourteenth died of his injuries.

I was at home in Beckenham when the news began to come through from Derry. I went at once to the Irish Club, where I knew that people would gather and assess the developments and the likely, terrible consequences. From there, I made several telephone calls to Northern Ireland. One was to Lord Brockway, the renowned campaigner against colonialism, who had taken part, along with Bernadette Devlin, in the banned march. He gave me an account which I filed to the *Irish Times*. It was contradicted almost at once by Lord Carrington, then defence secretary.

We still do not know the full truth. Unfortunately, by the end of 2008 the inquiry into Bloody Sunday headed by Lord Saville had not yet reported.

In the summer of 1972, on a visit to Derry, I tried to ascertain some of the facts at first hand. I walked through the Bogside and Creggan with Dermot Mullane of the *Irish Times* and Robert Fox of the BBC. We met leaders of the Official IRA in the Bogside Inn and of the Provisional IRA, including Martin McGuinness, in the gasworks, which they had seized and occupied. The Stickies said that they had had 'a gunman' at the scene but he had not used his weapon. The Provos said that four of them had observed the outbreak of shooting from the upper window of a nearby house, then quietly got into their car and drove away.

These reminiscences cannot add much to the sum of human

knowledge, but they are relevant to the crucial questions, who fired first and who, at what level, was responsible for the massacre. The immediate and predictable reaction of the British government was to claim that their troops acted only after being fired on. That is improbable in the extreme. The second question is more important.

Northern Catholics reacted to the massacre with even greater fury than that provoked by the Falls curfew. As in the Falls case, the Catholics saw the British government as having declared war on them. There was a flood of Provisional IRA recruitment. The anger spread over the border. Lynch recalled his ambassador from London: a good example of being in the right and putting oneself in the wrong. The British embassy in Dublin was burned down. Lynch's critics said mockingly that he was happy that the attackers had not turned their attention to the nearby government and parliament buildings, heavily guarded by the Special Branch. One of those who took part in the petrol-bombing of the embassy told me that at least one Special Branch member had joined them—in a moment of madness, not because his political superiors wanted it.

I do not believe that Lynch took any pleasure in seeing Leinster House and Government Buildings spared at the price of the embassy. Nor do I believe that the Heath government ordered or condoned the Derry massacre. On the contrary, the news horrified ministers and officials almost as much as they did the 'friends of Ireland' in Eaton Square on that awful day. Their reaction came close to panic. In the immediate aftermath, it centred on their fears of what might happen at a similar march in Newry two weeks later. Luckily, the Newry march went off without incident, but the question remained: Did the soldiers in Derry run amok, or did their commanders order the massacre 'to teach the Catholics a lesson'? I believe there can be no reasonable doubt that the action was deliberate and that the orders came from close to the highest level in the British command. This raises numerous other disturbing issues: the nature of the senior officers' indoctrination and personal prejudices, their degree of freedom of action, and the anomalous situation in which Stormont officially had responsibility for security whereas the British could not cede control of the army to a subordinate authority.

The day after the massacre, Bernadette Devlin crossed the floor of the House of Commons and physically attacked the cabinet member responsible for Northern affairs, Reginald Maudling. Maudling, notoriously, had expressed his own view of Northern Ireland when, after visiting Belfast, he entered his plane and said: 'What a bloody awful country. Bring me a large Scotch.' In the Commons, he gave the government line on Derry, whereupon the MP for Mid-Ulster rushed across the floor of the chamber and struck him several times in the face. She did him no physical damage, since she was a tiny person and he was a large and portly man. Several Tory MPs milled about, uncertain whether they should try to restrain her or what other action they might take. Another very large man, Hugh Delargy, a Labour MP and a campaigner for Irish unity, waded in with his arms flailing. He hit one of the Conservative whips, Oscar Murton, a blow on the side of the head. The Tories thought that he was trying to come to their aid and that the blow was accidental. Not so. A few minutes later Delargy and I made our way together to Annie's Bar. As he walked along, he was thanked by Murton and other Conservatives. Delargy knew that I knew better.

Heath admitted publicly that Bloody Sunday had shocked him and his ministers and hastened the actions which he now took after delaying since the previous autumn. In March 1972 he summoned Faulkner to London and presented him with what amounted to an impossible choice: hand over all security powers to Whitehall, or face direct rule. Faulkner could not accept the first, because it would have undermined him fatally. Heath therefore 'prorogued' (a typical British euphemism) the Stormont parliament, threw the Ulster Unionist government out of office, and proceeded to govern Northern Ireland directly, with Willie Whitelaw, as secretary of state, wielding extensive powers.

Faulkner took it badly. Along with Paisley and other hardliners, he appeared at an enormous rally at Stormont and made a most intemperate speech which worsened his already disastrous relationship with Heath. It looked for a time as if this relationship was irreparable, but the most perceptive observers took a deeper and a better view. Gerald Barry of RTÉ placed a bet that within one year Faulkner would hold the same job from which Heath had dismissed him, or the equivalent job. Barry won his bet.

He won it because Heath and those closest to him, most of all Whitelaw, took little time to conclude that they had to do business with Faulkner, for two reasons: his undeniable and rare ability as a practising politician, and their belief that he could reach an accommodation with nationalists and make it stick. Whitelaw's people pointed me in his direction, and I met him several times in Belfast for pleasant and fruitful chats. I was impressed. I never saw any sign of anti-Catholic bigotry, but rather a sincere desire to do his best for justice and stability and to establish good relations with Dublin.

I also had several meetings with Whitelaw and his chief press secretary, Keith McDowall, together or separately. My relationship with them was smoothed by their appreciation of my knowledge of British political history, but there was a much more obvious factor. It was greatly in Whitelaw's interest that the most influential newspaper in Ireland should support his work. He knew my own sympathies, which of course lay with him. McDowall was less sure about Gageby. In the hope of improving relations, Whitelaw invited Gageby and myself, along with McDowall, to lunch in Buck's Club, an establishment inner sanctum in St James's.

If they hoped to impress Gageby, they failed. It surprised me that although he was of course perfectly civil, he was visibly uncomfortable. When Whitelaw outlined his plans, he made little response. The great man tried a trick often used by politicians, asking journalists their opinion. He asked us when he should hold the 'border poll', a plebiscite on the issue of Irish unity designed to placate the unionists, who were certain to win, and thereby, as he hoped, clear this issue out of the way before getting down to the hard work of bringing about power-sharing. Gageby replied that he should not hold the plebiscite at all, and I agreed. When we left, he asked me if I knew the location of an upmarket shop selling sports goods in St James's; apparently he thought he might buy a new fishing rod. I had no idea, but I suppose that after we parted he found the shop and decided that his trip had not been wasted.

Whitelaw and McDowall may or may not have known that, by now, someone else was influencing Gageby to a far greater extent than either of them. Gageby had taken part in civil rights marches in the early days of the movement and developed a deep admiration for John Hume. I shared this admiration, which soon blossomed into a personal friendship with Hume and his wife Pat, close enough for them to invite me to stay with them in their house in Derry in the summer of 1972. This was the same visit on which I heard the Sticky and Provo versions of the events of Bloody Sunday.

I found myself in a very different ambience when Hume took me drinking in a club frequented by Catholic businessmen. They admired him as much as I did, but they held an opposing position on how to solve the national question: let us have a united Ireland, and 'let the Protestants go back to Scotland if they don't like it.' Hume, often wrongly thought to lack a sense of humour, was amused. He felt I had had a learning experience.

I slept so soundly that I did not know until the morning that during the night the Provisional IRA had attacked the military-police post on the far side of the garden fence and that the ensuing gun battle had woken up everybody else in the neighbourhood. This blessing of rest would stay with me into middle age: I would sleep through the hurricane that hit the south-east of England in 1987. Alas, though, it would ultimately desert me. Old men sleep fitfully, and consumption of alcoholic drink makes matters worse.

––––

The British, and all of us, had lost a lot through the inaction that followed the 1970 election. Now, when they did move, they moved too fast.

Heath wanted to clear the Northern Ireland question off his agenda. He also wanted to bring Whitelaw home as soon as possible, in a capacity in which the great conciliator could reach an accommodation with the trade unions. The ominous rumblings in this quarter threatened the government's hopes of tackling the economic issues in the context of entry to the European Economic Community, which would be costly for Britain and would involve drastic changes in the trading system. In addition, the North was a drain on British military resources at a time when Heath longed for new defence initiatives in Europe. On this last point, he has been described as 'the most anti-American prime minister', but that is unfair. It is not necessarily anti-American to wish to make Europe an independent military power. Heath underestimated the difficulties—still not overcome—of matching European economic power with political, much less military might. He had scored a historic triumph with British entry, and he wanted to build on it.

Whitelaw went to Belfast determined on a dual policy, essentially the same policy decided on by the SDLP thinkers led by Hume: an internal settlement which would set up a new government at Stormont with nationalist members included as of right, and a major role for Dublin, also as of right. He thought he could 'park' the issue of Irish unity with the border poll, which was certain to result in a huge majority for maintaining the North's status as part of the United Kingdom. But he did not intend it to diminish Dublin's influence or exclude the possibility, at some remote date, of a united Ireland. His words and actions so clearly reflected this as to distress the unionists' Tory friends, notably Enoch Powell. The unionists themselves, for the most part, were slow to see the full import—unlike Powell with his penetrating mind—or to see that Whitehall had found, in

Brian Faulkner, a man to work with.

Throughout that spring and summer, while Provisional IRA violence reached new heights, Whitelaw worked on his constitutional plans. They appeared in print in the form of a Green Paper in the autumn.

Before the publication, I met him by arrangement in the Imperial Hotel in Blackpool, where the Conservative conference was in progress. The scene was rather surreal. The guests, all Tory conference representatives, had deserted the hotel for an important economic debate in the Winter Gardens. Apart from the two of us and some hovering waiters and security men, the large lobby was empty. We sat, and he talked. He outlined in detail, without notes, the provisions of the Green Paper. Close though I had been to developments, I was surprised at how accurately they matched the wishes of the SDLP and the Irish government. In particular, they provided for a North–South Council of Ireland 'with executive powers', in essence the SDLP formula for an embryo united Ireland.

It was another scoop, but in order to conceal my source I waited until I arrived back in London before filing my story. It entertained me to discover afterwards that neither Keith McDowall nor, apparently, any other official of the Northern Ireland Office, had guessed the source.

After the publication of the document, I spoke to the leader of the Ulster Unionist MPs, Captain L.P.S. Orr. He saw nothing to alarm him in the phrase 'executive powers'. Things would change radically once the measures foreshadowed in the paper began to come into operation.

The subsequent legislation provided for the election of a Stormont assembly and the formation of a three-party executive; the Council of Ireland would come later. Late one night while the legislation was going through the House of Commons, Ian Aitken and I were drinking in the Strangers' Bar with Dr John Gilbert, one of the Labour intellectuals. An important Tory backbencher, known to have Heath's ear, came in. Someone offered him a drink. He declined, saying that he only wanted to buy some cigars. We told him that we were discussing the new system of governance for Northern Ireland. He commented: 'The man who flew the plane to Nagasaki went in the wrong direction. He should have gone to Belfast.' As he walked out, Aitken assumed an expression of awe and said: 'There speaks the voice of the Prime Minister.' The incident illustrated Heath's exasperation. The story is recounted in my book *Them and Us* and also in Aitken's biography (with Mark Garnett) of Willie Whitelaw.

Possibly a more important insight into British thinking, at every level of the establishment, was revealed by a sensational and notorious development. That summer, Whitelaw brought leaders of the Provisional IRA to London for talks. One of them was their chief of staff, Seán Mac Stíofáin, English-born and to the Northern Provos 'a Southerner'. A much younger and much more impressive man, Gerry Adams, was taken out of the Long Kesh internment camp to fly to London: an indication of things to come, when the Northerners, led by Adams, would displace the Southerners.

Arguments raged on the question whether Whitelaw was willing to make a deal with the Provos, sidelining the Dublin government and the Northern constitutional parties. One of his officials told me: 'We only wanted to let the dog see the rabbit.' Others thought they saw much more in the talks. Lynch was furious, but London–Dublin relations, of whose importance Whitelaw was always conscious, were quickly if not fully repaired.

Garnett and Aitken quote a British army officer who said the military should be behind anything that would bring peace to 'this infernal country', an echo of Maudling's 'bloody awful country'. When Whitelaw succeeded in bringing about a short-lived ceasefire, the only tangible fruit of the Provo talks, William Deedes told me that he viewed David O'Connell, another Provo leader, as 'the new Michael Collins'. Deedes was a former cabinet minister who would shortly become editor of the *Daily Telegraph* and would continue to work as a journalist until his death aged ninety-four. In early life he had been the model, though he denied it, for William Boot in Evelyn Waugh's inimitable lampoon of journalism, *Scoop*. I was quite shocked to hear him say it, but in a sense he was proved right in 2007 when Sinn Féin entered government in Northern Ireland in alliance with Ian Paisley's Democratic Unionist Party. At the time, it certainly helped to prove British willingness to negotiate with terrorists.

On my visits to Belfast, I discussed the prospects with Faulkner. He ignored the implications of Whitelaw's talks with the Provisional IRA and maintained a hopeful, indeed excessively optimistic, attitude. He found some grounds for optimism when his party performed tolerably well in the election for the new assembly, but said that when it came to the formation of an executive he had to ensure that 'unionists must never be in the minority.'

In the protracted negotiations to agree on the composition of the executive (Unionists, SDLP and the 'non-sectarian' Alliance Party) the Ulster Unionist Party got a bare majority. The outcome of the talks had never been in any serious doubt. On the day that the parties reached agreement, I went to see one of the SDLP's founders, Paddy Devlin, in his house in Andersonstown. He told me that the deal was clinched.

He prepared for his journey to Stormont by cleaning out his revolver. Most Northern politicians carried guns; Hume was a rare exception. Gerry Fitt carried a tiny weapon, about three inches long. Waving it, he fended off an IRA-inspired mob who invaded his house in North Belfast. I don't suppose he ever had any firearms training. Clearly Devlin had had none. When he emptied the chamber of his large revolver, the bullets flew about, in a room with a blazing fire a few feet from his desk. In the 1940s, he had been a member of the IRA. Their successors in the 1970s handled weapons too well.

Finally, a conference of the three executive parties was held at Sunningdale in Berkshire in December 1973. Agreement on the Council of Ireland had to be reached before the executive could take office on 1 January 1974. Ian Paisley's DUP were not invited. When British ministers discussed the invitations, Heath opposed an invitation, saying in his barrack-room manner that 'if Paisley goes, it will only be to fuck it up.' In fact, Paisley would certainly have refused an invitation. It would be a long time before he would sit in any palace or conference centre instead of holding placards of protest outside.

Conferences are often doomed to failure. The Sunningdale conference was doomed to illusory success.

A few days before it convened, I had a telephone conversation with Faulkner. He said that his 'bottom-line' demands were recognition and extradition. The first meant recognition by Dublin of Northern Ireland's status as part of the United Kingdom. The second meant an end to the Republic's refusal to extradite persons suspected of what were deemed 'political offences'. I told him that he would certainly not get both and would be lucky to get even partial satisfaction on either. He said that in that event he would refuse to come to an agreement.

The conduct of the conference suffered from the absence of the wily Whitelaw. Heath had moved him back to London in the vain hope of conciliating the unions, and a decent but inexperienced man, Francis Pym, had succeeded him as Northern Ireland Secretary. It suffered more from the determination of Dublin and the SDLP to make the maximum gains. But most of all it suffered from the Prime Minister's arrogance and his eagerness to make a quick deal and move on to other issues. When Faulkner baulked, Heath flew into Sunningdale and, it is fair to say, bullied him into making precisely the concessions which a few days earlier he had regarded as fatal.

After three days and two wakeful nights, agreement was announced at press conferences held by the Irish government, the British government and the Northern executive-elect respectively. I attended one, Conor O'Clery the second, Renagh Holohan the third. Afterwards O'Clery wrote an excellent blow-by-blow account in the *Irish Times* of the three days of talks. I did not try to identify his sources. I could make a good guess.

Faulkner, as predicted, failed on both counts. The extradition question was finessed with an agreement to set up a joint commission of jurists which would lead to 'extra-territorial jurisdiction': in other words, persons suspected of terrorist offences could be tried in the Republic for crimes committed in Britain or Northern Ireland and vice versa. Dublin held that extradition for politically motivated offences would contravene the Irish constitution, being contrary to international law and practice. If this was truly the case then, it is no longer so. At the time, the British implemented extra-territorial jurisdiction only patchily and reluctantly. In the end, the ban on extradition for political offences was removed.

'Recognition', too, was finessed with a joint Paragraph Five in which the positions of the two governments were set out side by side in the communiqué. Northern Ireland's existing constitutional standing was asserted, but it was stated that if at any time a majority there voted to join with the Republic the British government would not stand in the way. Paragraph Five would give rise to a furore in the Republic which almost equalled the anger in the North provoked by the agreement on the Council of Ireland.

Owing to communications difficulties, and confusion and misunderstanding at home, it was very late before I could file the main story. Part of the delay was caused by the necessity to explain Paragraph Five to Gageby, who was extremely disturbed at what appeared to him an abandonment of the Republic's claim to the territory of Northern Ireland. I said that it was in fact a gain for nationalism, embodied in the fact that the two statements in the paragraph appeared side by side. I thought I had persuaded him.

At last I sat down to file. By now it was so late that I did not have time to put anything on paper—even an introduction—and had to rely entirely on my notes. Luckily the person at the other end of the phone, who typed the copy, was fast and accurate. The call must have lasted at least an hour. Olivia O'Leary kept up my morale, if not my mental sharpness, by ferrying me glasses of brandy from the bar. Brandy is not good for the liver. It may or may not be good for the brain.

When I finished filing, I made for the bar, where I met John Hume. I mentioned Gageby's anxieties and said that I had reassured him. To my surprise, Hume at once became extremely agitated. He rushed to the telephone to tell Gageby that his doubts were misplaced and that the support of the *Irish Times* for the Sunningdale Agreement was vital. Indeed it was, and Gageby would continue to take the line Hume wanted through the turbulence of the coming months. But in the end it would lead him into unwise paths.

Chapter 7

1973: NORTHERN CONVULSIONS

By the time of the Sunningdale conference, I had taken up yet another job. I had served three years in London. The term was not set in stone, and I could—and should—have obtained an extension. But although Moira would have preferred to stay in London, I was anxious to get the children settled in Irish schools because I did not wish to have to disrupt their education at a later stage. I had therefore pressed Gageby for some months to name the next role he envisaged for me. There was more than a hint of Washington, a dazzling idea but unappealing for family reasons. There was almost a firm offer of appointment as political correspondent on the retirement of Michael McInerney, but nobody should know better than I what such promises are worth. I believe Gageby had promised the job to Dick Walsh as well. McDowell was involved in the appointment, and was represented at the discussions by Ken Gray, by now his representative on the editorial floor. After a good deal of irritating and distrustful talk Walsh and I were jointly accorded the title, mocked by Walsh's wife, Ruth Kelly, as 'half a political correspondent'. He would concentrate on domestic politics, myself on the North and Anglo-Irish relations. I would have to make the best of it.

The best was not very good. We had to sell our house in Beckenham on a depressed market and buy a house in Monkstown on a rising market. Partly because of this, but chiefly because of the low *Irish Times* salaries, our finances did not recover, in so far as they ever did, for a long time. Our entire life savings—not very wisely invested—went on the children's university education and ran out before our younger daughter, Vanessa, finished her forestry course in University College Dublin.

I was distressed to find two of my dearest friends in poor shape. David Thornley was doubly unhappy, in the European Parliament and as a Dáil backbencher supporting a government with which he was out of sympathy, the Fine Gael–Labour coalition which came to power in 1973. His political career had come to a dead end. Meanwhile, the lovable Brendan Scott, a pillar of the left and of the anti-apartheid movement, was dying of cancer. Even on his deathbed, he fretted about Thornley. He said that his old friend had listened to the blandishments of ministers who held out improbable prospects of office to keep him 'on side' and entertained hopes that they might deliver, although 'he knows it for the lie it is.'

The wider scene, the apparent success of the Anglo-Irish rapprochement notwithstanding, did not induce much lightening of mood. In the autumn of 1973, I went to Strasbourg to cover one instalment of the 'torture case' against the British government. The proceedings were in private, and the officials of the Human Rights Court and Commission were profoundly unhelpful. In a melancholy frame of mind, I repaired to the lovely little park nearby, the Orangerie. In the park is a restaurant with tables outside. I cheered up when I saw Raymond Smith, one of the most colourful reporters of his generation, sitting in the autumn sunshine. He greeted me and called to the waiter, in his inimitable broken French: 'Garçon, bring me une autre bottle de Alsatian wine!'

That night, and every night of our stay, he introduced me and other Irish journalists to the culinary delights of the city. His own familiarity with them was such as to make him critical of first courses and apt to propose an unusual practice, finding a second restaurant in which to eat the next. When we resisted, he insisted on the first night that we should at least move to an agreeable little place he knew for coffee and brandy. He should have said 'if we can find it.' The River Ill flows through Strasbourg in four channels, crossed by numerous bridges, and Smith's imperfect sense of direction had us wandering around the city for about an hour. At last we settled on a café full of shift workers in boiler suits who glared at us resentfully for encroaching on their territory.

Unable to squeeze any information out of the Human Rights Commission officials, I resorted to phoning a contact in London. The issue between the Irish and British governments was whether the Irish would accept a compromise 'friendly settlement' or continue to pursue the case. My man informed me that the Irish were holding out, and I filed a story to this effect. Some sub-editor inserted the word 'not' in the sentence in which I had written that Dublin was pursuing the case relentlessly. Uproar followed. The Irish officials in Strasbourg assumed that I had written the story as it appeared and that I must have been misled by the

British. To get matters straightened out, Smith arranged a meeting with one of the Irish team in the Terminus Hotel. It should have taken place in a private room, but owing to Smith's impatience we all met in the lobby. We sat in the kind of armchairs seldom found anywhere but in hotel lobbies, the kind in which you sink into the cushions and find it next to impossible to hear anyone's conversation. None of us could hear anything but Smith, who gave us a briefing of sorts on the tram that took us back into the city centre.

After four days we all went home via Paris and London. But before leaving Strasbourg I cannot resist a couple of anecdotes.

Those of us on our first visit there had never seen prostitutes to compare with the local variety. They were beautiful women, dressed in the height of Paris fashion. When politicians from Northern Ireland began to frequent the fringes of the European Parliament there at a later date, one of them wondered how much they charged. A colleague replied without hesitation 'two hundred francs' or whatever the price was.

Of the countless Smith yarns—all of them true—perhaps the most famous is a question he posed to P.J. Hillery about a long-running dispute over fishing quotas: 'Is fish a dead duck?' I prefer the one about his biography of Garret FitzGerald, *Garret The Enigma*. Smith, who never spared words, used the working title *Garret FitzGerald The Mysterious Enigma*. He showed it to Aengus Fanning, afterwards editor of the *Sunday Independent*. Fanning said: 'Raymond, don't you think there's a redundant word there?' Smith took a look and struck out the word FitzGerald.

He loved to fantasise about his death and funeral. He planned to die during a Munster hurling final in Thurles. As his body was being carried out, word would go out through the devastated crowd of what a hero they had lost. At the funeral, an enormous limousine would draw up and the richest man in Ireland would get out, accompanied by a mysterious veiled woman in black who would move forward and place a single red rose on the coffin. Yes, we've all seen the movies, but only a privileged few have laughed until their ribs ached on listening to Smith's own description, embellished by his likening of the characters to real persons among his hearers. When he died before his time—in bed, not in a GAA stadium—he was mourned with great affection and the classic yarns were recalled.

———

Those of us who went home by way of Paris were 'bumped' off the last plane to London on a Saturday night and had to stay in a hotel. In the morning, hung over, breakfastless and suffering from lack of sleep, I bought two newspapers to read on the plane.

Both of them featured the Yom Kippur war and had begun to speculate on the likely effects throughout the Middle East and the world at large. It was my foretaste of the oil crisis which would soon hit everyone and in which one of the casualties would be the Fine Gael–Labour coalition under Liam Cosgrave.

This government had taken office with high hopes. The fervour of its supporters bordered on delirium. The ministers included FitzGerald, as well as two of the Labour stars of 1969, Conor Cruise O'Brien and Justin Keating. Michael McInerney called the coalition 'the government of all the talents'. Presumably he did not know that the original phrase 'ministry of all the talents' had been coined satirically, in reference to a long-forgotten British coalition government devoid of all the leading men of the time. Talented or otherwise, the Irish ministers of 1973–77 were unable to surmount the dreadful difficulties they would now encounter on two fronts, Northern Ireland and the world economic crisis.

Hardly had the new power-sharing executive taken office at Stormont than it began to reel under a series of blows which would soon prove fatal. Since all these developments are well known and millions of words have been written about them, I will concentrate on those of which I have direct personal experience and try to improve the perspective.

One event deserves more attention than it normally receives. One night, only a month or so after the formation of the executive, an *Irish Times* 'stringer' in Belfast, Bertie Sibbett, got wind of an important meeting to be held in the morning between Dublin and Northern ministers. I telephoned several contacts, including FitzGerald and O'Brien, and recruited other reporters in the hope of 'fleshing out' the story. We managed to cobble together a cursory report.

I assumed, and probably we all assumed, that the purpose of the meeting was to find ways of propping up Faulkner's already shaky position, on which the whole enterprise depended. Not a bit of it. It turned out that the ministers were there to discuss the operation of the executive powers to be exercised by the Council of Ireland. They went into fine— and ill-judged—detail. To implement the measures they proposed would have required the employment of at least 20,000 extra civil servants, a burdensome task and a grotesque expense. Moreover, the Dublin ministers, for all the talk of a united Ireland, were most reluctant to cede any of their own powers. Here was political misjudgment on a heroic scale.

In the meantime Heath, confronted with a miners' strike and a crisis in power supply which forced the imposition of a three-day week on industry, called a general election. He foolishly fought it on the question 'who governs?' The electorate answered: 'Not you.' Wilson came back as head of a minority Labour government. It was assumed, correctly, that he would soon call another election in the hope of achieving a solid House of Commons majority. That autumn, he would indeed improve his position but he and his successor James Callaghan would never have the firm majority they craved.

If the outcome in Britain was uncertain, the results in Northern Ireland were catastrophic. At the time, the North had twelve seats in the House of Commons. Faulkner did not win even one. Unionists of various stripes, all opposed to him, took eleven. The remaining seat went to Gerry Fitt. Faulkner had lost his legitimacy.

During the election campaign I spent an evening with Merlyn Rees in his Leeds constituency. In opposition, he had been one of my best-informed contacts. Both in opposition and in government, he was close to James Callaghan. Our closeness notwithstanding, I suspected that he and Callaghan, whom I greatly disliked, shared some of the residual anti-Catholic feeling still discernible in some British Labour quarters. Whether for this or for more tangible reasons, he disliked the SDLP and the Dublin ministers, none of whom he considered 'fit to run a corner shop'. He agonised over the plight of the Northern Protestant working class, virtually unrepresented except by organisations which stemmed from the loyalist terrorist groups.

He took me to an evangelical chapel where the candidates of the three main parties made short speeches during the service. The Tory and Liberal candidates were indifferent speakers. Rees, with his Welsh eloquence, outshone them. The service itself enchanted me. I had expected blood and thunder, hellfire and damnation. Instead, I found brotherly love and excellent singing.

From there we went to a Labour club in Hunslet, much to my pleasure since Hunslet is the *mise-en-scène* of a marvellous book by Richard Hoggart, *The Uses of Literacy*. Finally we ended up drinking in the Dragonara Hotel, where Rees agonised about his favourite subject, what he could do about 'the Prods' once Wilson appointed him, as everybody expected, Northern Ireland Secretary.

We would find out all too soon what the Protestant working class would do for itself and to everybody else. In May the Ulster Workers' Council, largely a 'front' for the terrorist Ulster Volunteer Force, mounted a general strike. Elements of the middle class joined in. Fuel supplies were controlled by the UWC, who handed out petrol vouchers. Workers in the power stations and the sanitary services went on strike. Clearly public services were about to collapse. Before that could happen, the executive itself collapsed.

Among the many good accounts of these events, one of the most striking is that of the leading public servant Sir Kenneth Bloomfield. He does not blush to say that he shed tears for the end of a noble experiment. He records his bitterness when middle-class people took the UWC petrol vouchers and when farmers, heavily subsidised by British public money, blocked roads with their expensive tractors. Rees for his part said, both publicly and in private conversation with me, that those who constituted the backbones of both communities had 'gone back to the tribe.'

His own role has been the subject of much unfavourable comment. Certainly the public spectacle of his confessed helplessness was unedifying. But in my opinion Wilson must share the blame. Both of them were guilty of much more than inaction, and Wilson was guilty of much worse a little later. We may as well call it treachery.

In April, Cosgrave had met Wilson and Rees in London. They assured him that they would stand by Faulkner and the executive, come what might. I went to London to cover the meeting and stayed on for a day or two, in the course of which I met Rees and other contacts. Rees told me with exceptional forthrightness that the executive must stand or fall by its own efforts and that if unbearable pressure came on it, he and Wilson could do nothing. I reported this (without mentioning the source) and spoke to Gageby in the hope of moderating our excessively optimistic coverage. He refused to believe me. His own guru, John Hume, was among the optimists.

At the very least, Wilson and Rees were guilty of deception. On the substantive question of their ability to face down the strikers, they may deserve a kinder assessment. What can a democratic government in the late twentieth or early twenty-first century do when power workers refuse to generate electricity? It cannot take them out one by one and shoot them until someone agrees to go back to work. It can call in the army, but the army said—truthfully, it would appear—that they did not have the facilities or the expertise to do the job themselves. Moreover, the strike was not confined to power workers. It affected a range of public services, including sewerage works. In 1969 Irish Military Intelligence had estimated that it would take 60,000 men to maintain public services in the North in addition to 60,000 fighters. Even the resources of the British army would not have stretched to that in addition to fighting a small but powerful guerrilla force at a time when the IRA raised their cruelty, and the deathrate, to new levels.

This summation may have wider appeal at present than it did in May 1974. Then, the excuses made on the basis of British impotence were strongly challenged on both sides of the water. Privately, Whitelaw thought that the army could have moved into the power stations and kept them running with the help of technicians and middle management. However, it would have been next to impossible for the army, at whatever strength, to maintain any semblance of normal conditions in the face of an all-out Protestant insurrection. The generals certainly thought so, and they foresaw a casualty rate among their troops which a democratic government, especially a weak one like Wilson's, could not tolerate.

In Dublin, Cosgrave was furious. During the strike, he had said that the British army should hose demonstrators off the streets. Now he revived an old but impossible idea, that the British should withdraw from the North over a twenty-year period during which they would continue their subsidies. Quickly, however, he changed his line to even more severe condemnation of the IRA. He was also conscious of the diminution of his own government's standing when a major triumph, for which it had claimed due credit, ended in humiliation. Fianna Fáil, meanwhile, were solemn in public, but in private many of them were gleeful.

And Gageby berated me for the sins of 'your friends', the treacherous British Labour Party. Having warned him in advance of the coming calamity, I thought the criticism of myself singularly ill-directed.

———

The day before the executive fell, Conor O'Clery filed a story from Belfast forecasting the event. The deputy news editor on duty was unhappy with a report which would not please the editor. O'Clery insisted that he was right. He was then bullied by one of Gageby's lieutenants into changing the story, much to his discomfiture. He described the incident in his essay in *Bright, Brilliant Days*, and I mentioned it in my own essay in that work. He has speculated that Gageby wanted to stand by Hume to the bitter end.

The end was bitter indeed. On the morning of the debacle, the paper led with a weird headline which proclaimed COUNCIL OF IRELAND TO COME IN TWO STAGES. This referred to talks within the executive aimed at diluting and delaying the plans for the Council of Ireland and thereby placating the Protestant population. SDLP concessions on the point came too late, and earlier concessions would probably have made no difference, since the strikers wanted to destroy power-sharing, with or without an all-Ireland dimension. Inside, an editorial began with the words 'the executive is standing firm.' The whole affair was unworthy of a newspaper which prided itself on giving readers the truth. I might observe in passing that there is no point in employing people like myself and O'Clery if our superiors insist on printing the opposite of the facts which we have laboured to ascertain. The more knowledgable members of the staff were disturbed. Some went so far as to ask one another if Gageby was 'losing it'.

This colossal misjudgment, however, was overshadowed by an extraordinary deal made by McDowell with the approval of the other directors, who were also the holders of the voting shares. They were bought out—in effect, they bought themselves out—and the *Irish Times* became a trust. The operation was financed by a loan of £1.7 million, a lot of money in 1974, from the Bank of Ireland. The five directors shared it among themselves. Gageby retired as editor, and the Brussels correspondent, Fergus Pyle, succeeded him.

What was Gageby's true role in all this, what was his underlying relationship with McDowell, and what were his future plans? Let us look at the evidence.

In the first place, he collaborated with McDowell in persuading Pyle to take the job. Pyle's own position was characteristically confused. Although he knew, and everybody knew, that he had been groomed for the succession, he protested that he was not ready. He told me much later that Gageby summoned him to the south of France and put him under considerable pressure—this notwithstanding that Pyle had almost no executive experience but had made his name as Northern editor. Gageby must also have known that Pyle was one of the most disorganised people on the planet. That was reflected in his tousled hair and rumpled clothes, and would now be reflected in a more important way, in his chaotic attempts to run the paper.

For all Gageby's genuine belief in non-sectarianism, Pyle was selected essentially because he was a Protestant. Donal Foley, the leading candidate and the one favoured by the staff regardless of what, if any, religion they might profess, was a Catholic. When the deal was finalised, Gageby and McDowell met in the chairman's office, which was also the boardroom. (This room, accessed by a system of doors dubbed the 'airlock', was popularly known as the 'bunker'.) They sent for Foley in order to inform him. While he was descending the stairs, Gageby said: 'By the way, Tom, I told Donal that he would succeed me.' They then gave the stricken Foley a consolation prize, a seat on the board.

As to the value of Gageby's word, he made a similar promise at various times to myself and, to my certain knowledge, half a dozen other people. As to McDowell's intentions, he kept Gageby on for a while as a member of the newly formed trust, presumably as an indication of continuity, but then quietly got rid of him. There can be no doubt whatever that he wanted a radical change in editorial policy. As far back as 1969 the British ambassador, Sir Andrew Gilchrist, had reported that McDowell had confessed to him his embarrassment at the excessive nationalistic enthusiasm of Gageby, whom he described as 'a renegade or white nigger'. When this became public after thirty years, McDowell denied using the phrase. It is possible that Gilchrist paraphrased McDowell's remark, but British ambassadors do not normally embroider their despatches with misleading colour and in the actual despatch he put the words in quotation marks. In 1974 McDowell told Foley that he now had 'my young man' in place, ready for new departures. He conveyed a similar, though more guardedly expressed, message to a meeting (which I attended) of leading persons from the editorial and commercial sides of the company.

'White nigger' was a term used by American racists to describe whites who supported the black civil rights movement. Whether or not McDowell used it in a different context, it was he who sought the meeting with Gilchrist, at which he asked him if there was any way in which he could help. He told the ambassador that one or two other members of the *Irish Times* board shared his views and, like himself, would welcome guidance. I have no doubt that his intentions were good, but it is grotesque to imagine that the *Irish Times* should be influenced, contrary to the editor's opinions and his independence in editorial policy, by 'guidance' from the British Foreign Office.

However, I have equally no doubt about the seriousness of the operation in which McDowell engaged in 1969. John Martin's book, *The Irish Times: Past and Present*, published in April 2008, discusses the subject at some length. Martin believes that the initiative came from Harold Wilson personally after an approach by McDowell to 10 Downing Street.

He also believes, correctly in my opinion, that the reference to 'guidance', and the probable involvement of Intelligence as well as diplomatic contacts, were more important than the term 'white nigger'. McDowell held conversations with Irish as well as British officials, and some of the Irish civil servants assumed that he passed on information which he received from them. They assumed, in addition, that he was in touch with British Military Intelligence, something that would hardly be surprising in a former British legal officer who was a member of the Army and Navy Club in London. They exploited what they saw as his naïvety and told him what they thought the British wanted to hear.

McDowell had a holiday house in Northern Ireland, and was thought to use it to facilitate confidential meetings of politicians and others. If so, I would suppose that it was an entirely worthy and well-intentioned activity. I do not believe in any conspiracy theory which holds that any of this derived from a deep-seated plot to bring the Irish Republic back into the United Kingdom or to restore the Anglo-Irish ascendancy as the rulers of Ireland. Such theories do not take into account the reality of the British establishment's acceptance of Irish independence, or the flavour of its more sophisticated members for a united Ireland—provided that within a united Ireland British strategic interests and the rights of Northern unionists were safeguarded.

Nevertheless, it is an indisputable fact that under Pyle's reign between 1974 and 1977 the tone of the paper's Northern coverage, and of its editorials on the subject, changed palpably. Again indisputably, this contributed in large part to the calamitous decline in advertising and circulation. Financial as well as editorial realities had to come into the reckoning; and they would come into the reckoning with a vengeance in 1977.

But to me the most significant, and most puzzling, aspect of the strange relationship of McDowell and Gageby is what passed, or did not pass, between them, and between them and the trust members. How did McDowell handle complaints about editorial policy at meetings? In what terms did he convey his own anxieties to the editor? To what extent, if any, did he disclose to Gageby his own desires and his own activities? And how much did Gageby know, from his own observation and from outside sources? Almost certainly, a great deal. He may well have known details of the contacts, and he knew that, to put it mildly, his chairman and some other board members did not share his opinions. If the contents of the Gilchrist letter had become public at the time, readers would have lost all confidence in the paper and the position of the chairman or the editor, or both, could have become untenable. In the event, the public knew nothing and in the period 1969–74 there was no evident effect on the line pursued by the paper. I may say in addition that in 1970, when I was appointed London editor, McDowell gave me a briefing in which the only point of significance was that he wanted my work to be 'authoritative'. He made no attempt to steer me in any political direction, and he never suggested that I should meet any of his own contacts.

Apart from Gageby's financial gains, did he look forward to a long sabbatical, followed by his return, often discussed as the Second Coming? Did he foresee that Pyle would make a hash of the job and that McDowell, in desperation, would finally have to urge him to come back? I have never made up my mind about the speculation on this subject. I do not rule it out, but to believe it requires the attribution to Gageby of a degree of deviousness that might have shocked Niccolo Machiavelli. Much simpler people have mixed motivations.

Fergus Pyle must have been one of the worst editors ever to preside over any considerable newspaper. He laboured from the beginning under several handicaps. At first, he enjoyed the good will of the staff but not their respect. Then he forfeited the good will. He had always been an amiable colleague, but now he showed himself petty, unreliable, a fatal mixture of tyranny and uncertainty—and a person who displayed bad manners of a weird kind.

The most senior members of the staff were dismayed by his habit of rushing down the stairs to the 'bunker' for consultations with McDowell. We assumed that he was getting instructions, and his standing was undermined. Long afterwards McDowell told me that the usual subject of their conversations was Pyle's contract, but the terms of a contract do not often require weekly discussion over a period of three years.

For whatever reason, he dithered for a year before strengthening his own team. At last he appointed myself and Dennis Kennedy as assistant editors: Donal Foley and Ken Gray each held the title of deputy editor. Kennedy, whose work was as crisp as Pyle's was wandering, had engaged in fierce arguments with Gageby on the Northern question. Legend had it that Gageby liked people to stand up to him—in Kennedy's case, that meant putting forward a unionist viewpoint, but also a sharp analysis of history and current events. Legend had it wrong: Gageby did not like to be contradicted. Kennedy now looked forward to greater objectivity and consistency. We got nothing of the kind.

Foley was sidelined. Only Williamson felt more comfortable in a scene from which Gageby was absent. For me, life became hellish. I had to steel myself daily to enter a location in which I did not know what follies I might have to face. Although we worked in adjacent offices with a communicating door, Pyle sent me instructions through his secretary. Sometimes he sent me written messages instead. One accused me of 'pique' after I wrote something uncomplimentary about the famous constitutional lawyer and stalwart of Fine Gael's conservative wing, John Maurice Kelly (evidently he did not know that I admired Kelly and had many lively chats with him). When he mislaid a gold pen, he turned the place upside down, enlisting the help of several people in the search, before finding it in front of him, in a pile of papers on his desk. He kicked up a tremendous row because an unimportant story had appeared in a rival newspaper, not ours. Someone showed him the story—in the previous day's *Irish Times*. He told me sheepishly that he did not always read the paper on the day of publication, and often confused one day's paper with another. I could not resist saying that I always knew what day of the week it was.

He did one splendid thing as editor, commissioning a series of articles which exposed the activities of the Garda 'heavy gang', a squad that beat confessions out of suspects. That was brave in an era in which a large proportion of *Irish Times* readers were willing to close their eyes to any abuses in the name of combating terrorism. But he spoiled it by agonising and panicking; for example, sending me to demand of the team of reporters on the story whether they had affidavits to back up their allegations instead of doing it himself. Of course they did not have affidavits.

One afternoon I read a printer's proof of the page on which the latest 'heavy gang' article would appear the following day. It was accompanied by a large picture of Gardaí attending the funeral of a murdered colleague. Not only was this in the worst of taste, but many of them were identifiable. Horrified, I showed it to him and urged him to ditch the picture. He said 'no, no, that's all right, let it go' and would not listen to any further argument. The next day, we were flooded with protests. He said to me: 'You shouldn't have let that picture into the paper.' When I recovered my breath, I said: 'But you told me to let it go.' He replied: 'You still shouldn't have done it.'

These and other incidents convinced me that I simply could not work for this impossible man. In desperation, I made tentative inquiries about moving out. I was influenced to a minor extent by a book David McKittrick gave me. *Up The Organisation*, by David Townsend, the immensely successful chief of the Avis car hire farm, contained a 'rate your boss' section consisting of ten questions, each on a ten-point scale. Townsend wrote that anyone who scored a boss under 50 should seek alternative employment. With the best will in the world I could not give Pyle more than 10 points out of 100.

I asked the director general of RTÉ, Oliver Maloney, if he could find me a job as an executive or a producer. He said he was interested and would try to see if he could get me into a 'holding orbit'. I got a somewhat similar answer from my old acquaintance Mickser Hand, by now editor of the *Sunday Independent*. Our talks centred less on my problems than on Hand's hilarious descriptions of his own travails. He said that a key member of his staff, whom he did not name, ignored his instructions and did whatever took his fancy. He could neither control this man nor sack him. 'Good Lord, Mick,' I said, 'what are you going to do?' He replied in his ripe Drogheda accent: 'Oi think Oi'll kill the fockaw!'

Maloney and Hand were the only two contacts who took me seriously. Others refused to believe that an assistant editor of the *Irish Times* could possibly wish to come down in the world by taking a job with another organisation. One was Conor O'Brien, a man now little remembered—undeservedly so, since he was a very fine journalist who had been at the centre of a remarkable incident a few years earlier.

O'Brien (not to be confused with Conor Cruise O'Brien) had succeeded Gageby as editor of the *Evening Press*. From there he moved to edit the *Sunday Independent*, where he commissioned Joe MacAnthony to investigate the Irish Hospitals' Sweepstakes. MacAnthony uncovered a web of unorthodox, sometimes illegal, dealings in Sweeps tickets involving criminal elements in the United States. He wrote his findings in the form of two articles, but when he showed them to his editor, O'Brien decided that he had better publish them as one piece. His rationale was that if he published the first article as submitted, the second would be suppressed.

How right he was! The consequences were sensational. The establishment—then much smaller and based on 'old money'—closed ranks. Advertising was withdrawn. The chairman of Independent Newspapers found himself ostracised at Leopardstown, where he was one of the stewards. Soon afterwards the company was sold at a knockdown price to Tony O'Reilly, one of Ireland's greatest rugby stars and a famously successful businessman.

O'Brien was moved from the *Sunday Independent* to an executive job in which, inter alia, he scrutinised applications for employment. I sent him an application for a job in the *Irish Independent* newsroom. He wrote back a letter expressing his surprise that I should be interested in such a humble appointment. He did not know that I had acted on the advice of Hand.

I don't know what might have ensued from the pursuit of either option, since I took neither any farther. Fergus Pyle lasted only three years, and all through his last year as editor it was obvious that his departure could not be long delayed. His personal quirks were as nothing compared with the editorial and commercial disasters during his reign. Circulation and advertising fell through the floor. Panic measures, like frequent substantial price increases, were introduced. These had the predictable effect of depressing the circulation even more. The staff grew restive, then mutinous. Meanwhile, executives on the commercial side took fright at the calamitous condition of the company's finances. There followed an upheaval comparable to that of the late 1950s and early 1960s.

It is pointless to speculate on what might have happened in better times: if the economy, hit by the oil crisis and misguided government policies, had not gone into recession; if stability had been restored in the North, giving some justification for the colossal expenditure of time and effort on the situation there and the fallout in the Republic. The simple fact remains that Fergus Pyle was unfitted to edit the paper. But it was chiefly the fallout from the dismal economic circumstances that created the final crisis.

————

The Cosgrave government lost the confidence of the business community—and the farmers, still very numerous and, as always, wielding more political influence than their numbers warranted—by introducing a wealth tax. This delighted a few political writers, myself among them, who naïvely thought it a useful move towards fairness in taxation. Pyle personally favoured it. Healy did not. He took part in a voluble campaign against it, reminiscent of one that he and Gageby had waged back in 1969. Then, Conor Cruise O'Brien had raised the issue of Charles J. Haughey's ostentatious wealth and questioned the source of his finances. Healy and Gageby denounced the 'politics of envy', and Healy made a misleading comparison with the profit gained by Justin Keating from the sale of some land on which the Dublin county council built houses.

Fine Gael ministers, however conservative their own views might be, were scrupulous in their attempts to implement the government programme agreed with Labour. The Finance Minister, Richie Ryan, unfairly dubbed 'Red Richie' and 'Richie Ruin', stood firm on the wealth tax. Fianna Fáil saw, and seized, an irresistible opportunity. On the committee stage of the bill to introduce the tax, they criticised the proposals line by line, pointedly and forcefully. This was a striking departure from their usual parliamentary form, since typically in government they relied heavily on the civil service and in opposition they seldom troubled to brief themselves. But there was a second departure, ominous for Lynch. Haughey insisted on coming back temporarily on to the front bench for the specific purpose of opposing the wealth tax.

Another internal party development troubled Lynch. Much against his wishes, Fianna Fáil adopted a Northern Ireland policy which called for phased British withdrawal. This ended Dáil bipartisanship, or what Lynch in his hair-splitting way called 'an agreed approach'. Fianna Fáil were not exclusively to blame: some coalition ministers had been less than bipartisan when they called attention to his contradictory statements on the subject and questioned his role in the Arms Crisis. That did them little good, because their line appealed only to coalition supporters (and not all of these) and it did not help any Fianna Fáil backbenchers who held moderate views. These backbenchers were already under intense pressure at the grassroots level.

Haughey, having survived the indignities inflicted on him by Lynch in the aftermath of the Arms Crisis, was making his way back by appealing to the grassroots over the heads of the parliamentary party and the party leadership. He took to the 'rubber chicken circuit', dining and drinking with Fianna Fáil activists around the country. It was a comic comedown from the grand Dublin and Paris restaurants where he was accustomed to dine on delicacies, and occasionally he found it hard to conceal his dislike for the fare on offer. He was incensed when he had to eat, if he could, the rubber chicken and over-cooked vegetables while a local deputy, sitting beside him, was served a luscious steak. But the operation worked for him. The audiences were enthusiastic. They swallowed his 'patriotic' line along with their food, and complained about the exclusion from the front bench of a man of his acknowledged ability. At last Lynch, conscious of the grassroots pressure, felt it necessary to bring him back on to the front bench and to appoint him to his cabinet when he returned to office in 1977.

Fianna Fáil complained about the coalition's helplessness following the collapse of the Sunningdale Agreement. They were not alone, but most of the criticism was misguided. Wilson as British Premier and Merlyn Rees as Northern Ireland Secretary were searching for a new internal policy. Their feeble efforts have been thoroughly described in various books, so I will not try to detail them here. Enough to say that they failed, and meanwhile support swelled in Britain for a rapid troop withdrawal.

Withdrawal was the last thing the Irish government wanted. The interdepartmental committee considering the question believed that 'phased' would quickly turn into 'precipitate' withdrawal, with all its appalling consequences. These were outlined in apocalyptic warnings by Conor Cruise O'Brien, similar to those in the Intelligence reports of 1969. But British official papers, like the Irish reports secret then and public now, have disclosed something even worse.

By 1975 Harold Wilson, though not yet sixty years old, had begun to suffer from premature senility. Whether for that reason or because of the tendency to treachery and opportunism that had caused the right wing of the Labour Party to detest him, he now reversed his previous attitude to Irish affairs.

In opposition between 1970 and 1974, he had been a strong advocate of Irish unity. He had produced elaborate proposals, a 'twelve-point plan' and a 'fifteen-point plan', both designed to lead to a united Ireland. But after the fall of the power-sharing executive and the inevitable failure of the unionist-dominated constitutional convention set up by Rees as a holding operation, Wilson turned to favouring British military withdrawal—not with a view to uniting Ireland but to handing over control of the North to an extreme form of unionism. It centred on giving Northern Ireland 'commonwealth status': in effect independence, an option urged at the time by the violent loyalist organisations. In the circumstances then prevailing, elections within an independent entity would have produced an even more anti-Catholic and exclusive government than those that had held power under the old Stormont system. There would be 'guarantees' for Catholics, but obviously they would be worthless. Nationalists, seeing themselves as betrayed, would support the Provisional IRA almost unanimously. The local security forces, exclusively Protestant and containing hundreds of former loyalist terrorists, would regard their hands as having been freed and take the most extreme measures. All the apocalyptic forecasts would come true: thousands of deaths, a mass exodus of Catholics, repartition, economic collapse, destabilisation of the Republic.

To their great credit, the Dublin coalition ministers derided by Rees were well informed and in a position to oppose this crazy move. Doubtless their information came partly from Intelligence sources, but it must have come chiefly from the superb officials in the diplomatic service—by now greatly augmented—and from their own contacts in the British establishment.

The Foreign Minister, Garret FitzGerald, disclosed long afterwards that he had urged Callaghan to oppose Wilson's plans in cabinet. Callaghan was a useful ally, but FitzGerald's action cannot have been the key reason why the shameful idea was shelved. Wilson had set up a committee of top civil servants to consider the proposition. They took the common-sense view that it could only bring disaster, and not only for Ireland. It would cause outrage in the United States and in the European Community, in which Britain and Ireland were now partners, and Britain's standing in the world would be diminished.

Nevertheless it stands on the coalition's record, and on FitzGerald's record in particular, that the government knew the appalling reality and did whatever lay in its power to prevent the worst from happening. It is also clear from the proceedings of the concurrent interdepartmental committee, since made public, that Irish officials from several departments were equally able to make accurate and unpalatable assessments. And it illustrates the unhappy situation of the Cosgrave government, facing at one and the same time an economic crisis and a security crisis. Its reactions to the latter would have deep and long-lasting repercussions.

———

In the summer of 1976, Christopher Ewart-Biggs was appointed British ambassador to Ireland. He was exceptionally well informed about the situation in Northern Ireland, not only from the customary briefings he received at the time of the appointment but because of his close contacts with the security services and his friendship with Roy Hattersley, who by then had emerged as one of the most considerable of the younger figures in the British Labour Party. I met the new ambassador at a reception given by one of the embassy officials to welcome him to Dublin. We talked at some length about the possibilities—slight enough—of initiatives to restore some life to the stagnant Northern political scene.

A few days later he was murdered by the Provisional IRA when a bomb exploded in a culvert under the road outside his residence, Glencairn, at the moment his car was passing over it. The atrocity occurred within sight of the entrance to the Glencairn estate. Clearly the attackers must have taken up a position nearby from which they could see the car and could know when to set off the bomb.

To lose an ambassador to terrorism is shocking enough. To botch the investigation into the murder was unforgivable. But the Garda Síochána did botch the investigation—in addition to having failed to look to the security arrangements close to Glencairn. The government was deeply embarrassed, and the British were furious. They sent a high-ranking official, Sir Richard Sykes, to Dublin to make his own inquiries. He did not brook vague answers to his questions, but subjected the officials he met to a fierce inquisition. Sykes was later murdered by the IRA in the Netherlands, where he had moved as ambassador.

Frustrated and outmanoeuvred on the ground, the Irish government reached for a feeble instrument but the nearest to hand, the statute book. The state of emergency declared during the second world war and never repealed was now abolished and a new emergency declared. An emergency powers bill was prepared, debated in the Oireachtas and approved, but not passed into law because the President refused to sign it before referring it to the Supreme Court for a judgment on its constitutionality.

The President was Cearbhall Ó Dálaigh, who had come to office without an electoral contest after the sudden death of President Erskine Childers. When Childers died, Fine Gael and Labour did not dare to run a candidate of their own because they knew they could not win a presidential election. They therefore left the field clear for Fianna Fáil. Their grudging acceptance of Ó Dálaigh did not make for the good relations that Merrion Street and Áras an Úachtaráin should enjoy, and matters were not helped by the personality contrasts between the voluble President and the taciturn Cosgrave.

Ó Dálaigh had been a Fianna Fáil attorney general and afterwards Chief Justice. In the latter role, he had been a 'judicial activist', something that does not please constitutional lawyers. These by their nature were conservative. They were also better lawyers than Ó Dálaigh, who was at once pedantic and imaginative—too imaginative for their liking. He was erudite, but much too fond of displaying his erudition. He sprinkled his speeches with phrases in Irish, French, or whatever language seemed to him to express his meaning better, although his thoughts could be perfectly well expressed in English. His courtesy and outgoing nature did not compensate for these quirks. In short, he was a pain in the neck.

Nevertheless, the government should have taken pains to treat him with the respect a President deserves. He got no respect when he referred the emergency provisions bill to the Supreme Court.

Under the constitution, the President has the power to refer a bill to the Supreme Court for a judgment on its constitutionality. He does not have to consult the government or parliament on the question. He has to consult the advisory Council of State, but the decision is his alone. Ó Dálaigh referred the emergency legislation to the court. The judges ruled that it conformed with the terms of the constitution.

His action provoked an unprecedented public outburst from the Fine Gael Defence Minister, Paddy Donegan. Donegan questioned the President's commitment to law and order and called him 'a thundering disgrace'. To make matters worse, he addressed these remarks to an audience of military officers. The President is commander in chief of the defence forces.

Ó Dálaigh refused to accept an apology from Donegan and demanded that he resign his office. Donegan offered his resignation to Cosgrave, who rejected it. Ó Dálaigh then resigned the presidency. The ensuing furore was made all the hotter by the fact that Fine Gael prided themselves on their commitment to the proprieties. I was one of many who asked whether they were now the 'slightly constitutional party', an infamous phrase first used by Seán Lemass in reference to Fianna Fáil. The *Irish Times* published floods of letters criticising Donegan and supporting Ó Dálaigh's action, and took a vehement editorial stand against the minister. Unfortunately, Fergus Pyle's enthusiasm for the controversy took him too far. In one of the editorials, he described the President as the guardian of the constitution. John M. Kelly, the leading authority on the subject, pounced, pointing out that the Supreme Court is the guardian of the constitution.

Pyle, however, was a minor character in the drama, which was now played out on the party-political stage. Ó Dálaigh had to be replaced. By whom? If the coalition had not dared to contest a presidential election after the death of Childers, their position following the Ó Dálaigh–Donegan affair was infinitely weaker. They made a feeble effort to persuade Fianna Fáil to agree on a non-controversial candidate and thereby avoid an election. When they failed, they had no option but to surrender and allow the candidate put forward by Lynch to become President.

This was P.J. Hillery, the man who had helped to pull the Fianna Fáil Party together after the Arms Crisis. By now he was a vice-president of the European Commission. He was happy in Brussels, and most reluctant to come home to a powerless position, as full of tedium as of honour. At Lynch's urging, he accepted the distasteful cup in the national interest. For once, the phrase was not a cover for expediency but the simple truth. For the next seven years, he bore with the tedium in order to restore calm. He then accepted a second seven-year term. He quipped privately that his reward for good behaviour had been to have his 'sentence' increased by seven years.

Cosgrave for his part reacted to the humiliation not only with his customary fortitude and taciturnity but, apparently, with optimism. He still thought he could win a general election a year later. He called the election in the summer of 1977. After the dissolution of the Dáil, the government commissioned an opinion poll, a rarity in those days. Jack Jones, the head of the market research company, introduced his outline of the results to the cabinet with the cheerful comment that the findings indicated certain and devastating defeat. That came as a shock, for a very simple reason.

After the formation of the Fine Gael–Labour coalition in 1973, I had had a conversation with John Hume in which he said that he would judge the performance of the new government, in large part, on whether it set up an independent commission to determine the Dáil constituency boundaries. He asked me my opinion. I said that the government could not resist the temptation to have 'one last go' at drawing the boundaries in such a way as to benefit the governing parties. So it proved. The Local Government Minister, James Tully of the Labour Party, produced the 'Tullymander', under which it appeared impossible for the government to lose. Most forecasts of the election result, my own included, were based on analysis, constituency by constituency, which appeared to bear this out. We did not take sufficient account of the consideration that a sharp electoral 'swing' would have the opposite effect, giving Fianna Fáil a large Dáil majority instead of the normal close result. The findings of the government's poll were concealed, but had we known them we would not have believed them. The *Irish Times* commissioned their own poll, which forecast a Fianna Fáil first-preference vote of 52 per cent, enough for a whopping majority regardless of the constituency boundaries. None of us thought this remotely possible. Pyle suppressed the story, not because of political prejudice but because he too disbelieved the poll findings. It is possible to construct an argument that a newspaper which publishes unlikely and contradictory forecasts (as has often happened) damages its credibility, but he should have stood by the old and excellent advice, Print it! Publish and be damned.

The actual result was 50.6 per cent for Fianna Fáil and a twenty-seat Dáil majority. It has often been attributed to the package of bribes they offered to the electorate, including the abolition of the wealth tax, car tax and domestic rates (property tax) and help for 'first-time buyers' of houses, a shibboleth which in combination with other silly ideas would contribute to driving up house prices beyond all reasonable limits. But wiser heads knew from the beginning that 'style of government' had an equally strong effect on the voters. The Donegan–Ó Dálaigh affair was only one illustration, if the most spectacular, of a style that the voters deeply disliked.

As to the bribes to the electorate, members of the coterie that Lynch had drawn around him after the Arms Crisis maintained for decades that they were not cynical measures but designed to stimulate the economy. But it is always easy for politicians to persuade themselves that they do expedient things from the highest motives. It is unquestionably the case that Lynch was deeply worried about Haughey's growing influence and wanted to shore up his own popularity. In the event, he succeeded too well. Hardly had the votes been counted than he said the excessively large Fianna Fáil majority would create problems for himself because it would bring complacency and the danger of backbench revolts. He knew that his triumph was hollow and that the 'rubber chicken circuit' had done its work. The real winner was Haughey. He had openly derided the Santa Claus-like Fianna Fáil manifesto. Now he surprised questioners by gleefully welcoming the advent of the party's flood of new backbenchers: 'They're all mine!'

Chapter 8

1977: SECOND COMING

The terms of the Irish Times Trust, drawn up in 1974, gave it the status of a charitable trust, empowered to donate money to worthy causes including North–South reconciliation. From time to time subsequently, critics like the *Phoenix* satirical magazine mocked the fact that it made no such donations. The provision was only a cover for the reality, that the trust was a tax dodge and a means for the directors to enrich themselves. That was obvious to the journalists, who were dismayed and sought ways of exerting their influence on what came to be called the 'corporate governance' of the company. They set up a committee, on which I served, to examine the terms of the deal, but only a couple of us understood anything about corporate finance or governance, or about the extraordinary, not to say unique, authority conferred on McDowell as chairman of the trust and the company.

McDowell, under the terms of the deal, could not be removed from office even by a unanimous vote of his fellow-directors (all of them, in any case, appointed by himself). The rationale for provisions of this kind—and for the transaction itself—was that the status of the trust would protect the paper from a takeover bid by predators. In the real world, no company is safe unless it can trade competently and profitably. The disasters of the period 1974–77 put the independence of the company, and the survival of the newspaper, in doubt.

Trouble made itself felt from the beginning. The country's economic difficulties continued, with dire effects on advertising revenue especially in the two most important areas, property and recruitment. Editorially, the paper deteriorated. This was only partially a consequence of a shift in policy from Gageby's excessive nationalist enthusiasm and from the grasp of the *Zeitgeist* under the Gageby–Foley axis—although the shift disturbed many readers. More important was that under Pyle's erratic guidance the publication became dull, an unforgivable thing for any newspaper. The circulation fell sharply, and with the fall came a loss of revenue similar to that felt in advertising. Projections for profits were wholly unrealistic, and by early 1977, at the latest, the company was close to, if not actually in, a position of 'reckless trading'.

Few of the journalists could guess the critical nature of the financial position or the extent to which executives on the other side of the house shared their anxieties. Their main concern was the diminution of editorial standards and the paper's appeal to readers. They set up another committee under the aegis of the National Union of Journalists chapel (office branch) and produced a document for submission to the board. McDowell held several meetings in the 'bunker' with the father (chairman) of the chapel, Paul Gillespie. Gillespie did not enjoy these encounters, and I can well understand his discomfort. In later years I endured many such conversations myself. I found no meeting of minds, but instead had to listen to long, impenetrable speeches from McDowell. Gillespie for his part found that they increased his suspicions of the chairman.

It seems to me very likely that the meetings formed part of a process designed by McDowell to shore up his own position. He wanted to ascertain the feelings of the staff, including their views of Pyle's editorship—though he did not discuss this question openly with Gillespie—and to maintain his relations with the chapel. Had he by then begun to ponder the return of Gageby, or did he have in mind the appointment of someone else? At what stage did he make contact with Gageby? I fear that I do not know the answers to any of these questions, but I certainly do not accept the theory that the two had maintained constant contact ever since 1974. All the evidence suggests that McDowell acted belatedly and reluctantly.

In *Bright, Brilliant Days*, Andrew Whittaker reveals that in March 1977 he met the chief executive of the Bank of Ireland, Ian Morrison, and urged him to use the power held by the bank in view of the indebtedness of the *Irish Times* to remove both McDowell and Pyle. Whittaker acted on his own initiative. I believe that similar moves had been in train for several months by then, and the dates, in so far as I know them, bear me out.

Another important figure in the *Irish Times*, Peter O'Hara, the managing director, was also acquainted with Morrison and informed him, without McDowell's knowledge, of the company's desperate financial position. I consider it certain that Morrison began to act before he was approached by Whittaker. Although he gave Whittaker no hint, the developments I am about to relate must have had their origins earlier than March 1977.

With or without the knowledge of the bank, McDowell and Gageby made contact and arranged the series of moves that followed. Gageby invited Pyle to lunch and discussed the fall in circulation with him. He told me much later that he was dismayed by Pyle's complacency, but Pyle told me later still that he had guessed at once what was in train and saw no point in trying to defend his untenable position. Gageby asked him if he had any objection to his meeting the chapel officers. Pyle had of course no option but to agree. He sent for Gillespie and met him, not in his own private office but in the adjacent room occupied by myself, Bruce Williamson and Dennis Kennedy. This happened, to the best of Gillespie's recollection, in March. A critical point, therefore, had been reached at the time of Whittaker's approach to Morrison, and the moves that culminated in the Second Coming must have started at some earlier date.

Pyle told Gillespie, in my hearing and that of Williamson and Kennedy, that Gageby would like to meet the chapel officers. I was astonished that he should discuss such matters in front of us, but there was no need for secrecy. All the chapel officers would know almost at once, and then everybody would know.

About the same time, Donal Foley initiated a memorable conversation with me. It happened on a sad occasion, a memorial Mass in the University Church on St Stephen's Green for a young mutual friend, Helen Gavigan. She had served on the Northern Ireland desk in the Department of Foreign Affairs and had thus become known on the Dublin social scene beloved, most of all, by the SDLP. In July 1976 she had been one of the guests at the reception for Christopher Ewart-Biggs, where I found her in a state of exaltation. She had just been told of her first foreign posting— as first secretary in the Irish embassy in Paris, an appointment to dream of. But when she went for the mandatory medical checkup the doctors found that she had cancer. Treatments failed. The cancer spread, and she died within a few months.

After the service, Foley took me to a nearby pub. As soon as we had seated ourselves and ordered our drinks, he came straight to the point: 'Fergus is on the skids.'

I replied laughingly: 'Donal, the dogs in the street know that.'

'Who is it to be?'

'Donal, it has to be you.'

He shook his head. 'They'll never give it to me. It has to be you.'

For some time, I had avoided any serious conversation with him on the subject. I now said he must know the position I had adopted for the previous six months or more. I had been approached by various persons of standing among the staff—desk editors, chapel officers and so forth—who had identified me as the front-runner for the succession to Pyle on the assumption that Foley was out of the running. I had told all of them that I did not consider myself a candidate and would continue to support Foley. He now repeated that he did not have a chance, and urged me to go and see Gageby.

For some reason which I cannot recall, my encounter with Gageby did not take place for another six weeks or so. By then, Gageby had entertained the chapel officers to a prolonged, lively, alcohol-fuelled lunch at which everybody spoke with unusual candour.

There was no more need for discretion than for secrecy. A meeting of the chapel had already passed what amounted to a motion of no confidence in Pyle. Kennedy voted against it. I abstained. I lament very few incidents in my life, even instances of foolish or dangerously impulsive behaviour, but I have always regretted this one. I felt that I could not vote confidence in an editor in whom I had no confidence, and that if I did so I would lose credit with the staff. I was eager to maintain that credit, and not from any unworthy motives. I did not see it as a marker for my own ambitions but as necessary to retain my influence in coming events which I hoped would restore stability. Nevertheless, in recounting this event I do not think I am being excessively scrupulous. I was wrong to act as I did, and I very much doubt that I would have lost anything by voting differently.

At last I met Gageby in his house in Rathgar and wasted a beautiful late-spring afternoon drinking great quantities of rotgut wine (which he drank as copiously as the excellent burgundy he supplied for his dinner guests). We talked round and round the one subject that mattered. Much of the conversation centred on his lunch with the chapel officers. He said he had been taken aback to find that Pyle, formerly held in affection by the staff, had now become thoroughly disliked. I said Pyle had brought this on himself by his impossible combination of appalling inconsistency and a dictatorial manner. As the conversation went on, it seemed to me more and more clear that Gageby was hinting at his own return. Daringly, I said: 'Douglas, I don't believe in Stuart restorations.' He reacted with a look of surprise, not with the glare of intimidation that one might have expected. Then he said: 'Who is to be, so?'

'It has to be Foley.'

'That would never do. It would kill him.'

'Then it has to be me.'

This was bravado. Clearly something had already been cooked up, and neither Foley nor myself was part of it. The arrangements for Gageby's return were by then well advanced, with an undertaking from McDowell that he would have a totally free hand in respect of editorial policy, which chiefly meant the 'national question'. Andrew Whittaker had advised Ian Morrison to oust McDowell, but the Bank of Ireland considered overturning the terms of the trust too difficult and complex an operation. Three months later, I was not surprised when Gageby came back, restored confidence and reconstructed the operation—with the help of a brief upturn in the economy in the late 1970s, and a gift from the bank, which wrote off a million pounds of the debt. It also sent a team into D'Olier Street to investigate the company's finances and to repair them in tandem with the financial director, Derek McCullagh, and with Louis O'Neill, the former general manager who had left to run a subsidiary company but returned as managing director.

Journalists assumed that the bank had insisted on the return of both Gageby and O'Neill. In recent times two incidents have cast some doubt on that assumption. A very well-informed member of the establishment has told me that the bank was concerned about the running of the company, not the identity of the editor; and Andrew Whittaker relates that for some unknown reason, Ian Morrison did not like O'Neill. But presumably Morrison could have had no objection to the placing of responsibility in the hands of men of proven ability. In the event, O'Neill and McCullagh worked arduously and played an important part in restoring the company's fortunes.

I often think of the unintended irony of Gageby's remark about Foley, who did not regain any of the influence he had enjoyed in Gageby's first reign. He died only four years later, aged fifty-seven. I often think, too, with compassion, about Fergus Pyle, who also died before his time. For all his incompetence and bad behaviour, he did not deserve the treatment he got. He had known, for perhaps as long as a year before his downfall, that he was doomed, but he had to carry on somehow until the thread broke. After his downfall he served for a while as press officer for Trinity College, a capacity for which he was no better suited than for the editorship of the *Irish Times*. Then he came back to the paper as a sort of roving correspondent, as amiable as he had been before his ill-judged promotion.

One might admire his Christian humility (he was a dedicated member of the Church of Ireland, with High Church tendencies) but I am made of different stuff. When he returned to the paper, Gageby, much to my surprise, asked me if I had any objection. I said that of course I had none.

In the meantime the idea got about that I had met Gageby to urge him to return—almost the exact opposite of the truth. But I welcomed the Second Coming, and I cannot doubt that it was the right decision at the time. Such was the condition of the company's finances and the editorial decline of the *Irish Times* that only he could have saved us. He had the confidence of the board, the staff and, crucially, the bank. He was lucky in that the newspaper's finances improved quite rapidly, largely on account of the general economic stimulus provided by the government's bizarre decision to implement all its promises to the electorate on taxation regardless of the prevailing world economic circumstances, but I do not believe that Foley, myself or anyone else could have equalled his success in the following years. Indeed, in all probability, without Gageby the paper would not have survived.

———

It has been speculated that Gageby's Second Coming was in some way connected with the Fianna Fáil general election victory. The two events may not have been entirely coincidental.

During the election campaign Pyle was not alone in believing that the Tullymander would deliver a majority for the coalition. On the day after the election, before a single vote was counted, a lead story appeared in the paper, written by Dick Walsh. It proclaimed that the coalition had won. Never count chickens before they hatch out.

When Fianna Fáil won, Pyle was devastated. He wrote an editorial suggesting that the loss of Garret FitzGerald and Conor Cruise O'Brien (who lost not only his cabinet post but his Dáil seat) had made the world, not just Ireland, the poorer. He only reluctantly accepted that the Irish voters had made a firm democratic decision, never mind the reasons, when they gave Lynch more than half of their first-preference votes. By now he was totally out of touch with the feelings of the electors including the middle-class electors, of such overwhelming importance for the *Irish Times*. But I must share some of the blame. I too had thought the Tullymander would work.

Lynch during his four years in opposition had tried to fortify himself against the Haughey faction by drawing a coterie of bright young men closely around him. One of the most notable was his press secretary, Frank Dunlop, who decades later would testify to the Flood Tribunal (renamed the Mahon Tribunal in the course of its sittings) that he had bribed councillors on behalf of property developers to vote for planning changes.

I had grown friendly with Dunlop. Journalists liked him, partly for one of the reasons why they liked a much more considerable person, Muiris Mac Conghail, the man who had made a sparkling name for himself as a television producer and who served as the coalition's press secretary between 1973 and 1977. Some of us thought, in our innocent way, that we could see a new openness in government and opposition media relations.

Long afterwards Dunlop published his memoirs under the title *Yes, Taoiseach*. In that book he disclosed that while working for Lynch he had also worked for his rival, Haughey, driving him to dinners on the 'rubber chicken' circuit. Considering the multiplicity of the dinners, and the large attendances, I cannot understand why we did not know this. More remarkably, how could Lynch not have known? A person who was close to him during his years in office is quite certain that he did know, but forgave Dunlop. Possibly he was motivated by something other than Christian charity. He may have felt that if he took any action it would be interpreted as a sign of weakness.

Dunlop has told the Mahon Tribunal that he did not keep comprehensive notes but relied on his memory. His memory evidently is not comprehensive, since in *Yes, Taoiseach* he omits an extraordinary event which involved myself.

That event, which permanently changed my relationship with him, concerns the dismissal of the Garda Commissioner, Edmund Garvey, in 1978.

I was flabbergasted when he approached me one day and told me that the Lynch government wanted to force Garvey's resignation because they believed he was a British spy. They thought, he said, that it would be a good idea if the *Irish Times* carried an editorial calling for the Commissioner's resignation.

I told him that this was one of the worst ideas I had heard in my life. What grounds for suspicion did the government have? One of Garvey's most important duties—arguably the most important of all—was combating terrorism. In the course of this essential work he held regular meetings (with government sanction) with his Northern counterparts at which the two sides exchanged information and discussed how they could prevent IRA attacks with mortars and other weapons across the leaky border and intercept persons fleeing from the North to the Republic. What information they exchanged (which would be of little use to either side unless it was fairly comprehensive) and how they managed activities on the ground, were matters for the judgment of the Commissioner and his senior officers in border areas. This emphatically did not make him a British spy. If the government did not have confidence in him, for reasons which only the cabinet could judge, they should sack him. Besides, the editor of the *Irish Times* was a former Military Intelligence officer who had never forgiven Lynch for the treatment meted out to Michael Hefferon in the Arms Crisis. Any approach to him would blow up in their faces.

But Dunlop persisted. He came back to me a day or two later, saying that he wanted to bring the Minister for Justice, Gerard Collins, to meet Gageby in the *Irish Times* office. I spoke to Gageby. His eyebrows twitched, but he told me to arrange the meeting and it duly took place—but with one absentee. Dunlop came alone and did all the talking. Gageby to my recollection said nothing at all, but merely let Dunlop make his unconvincing case. As soon as he left, Gageby sat at his typewriter and wrote an editorial, but not the editorial Dunlop wanted. It said what I expected, that the government should do its own dirty work. He wrote the headline himself, 'Weaseling', insisting on spelling it the American way. Spelling aside, the word summed it up.

When preparing these memoirs, I found that Collins formed no part of my mental picture. That is no surprise. Not only did he not attend the meeting, he knew nothing about it.

Although Dunlop in his book makes no mention of the incident, he says that he had a blazing row with Collins and that the government, without reference to himself, then issued a statement announcing Garvey's dismissal. Collins would have had good reason for annoyance had he known about Dunlop's demarche to the *Irish Times*, but he has informed me that he had absolutely no recollection of any such row and that it came as a total surprise to him when I contacted him thirty years later and asked him to set the record straight. He has also told me that he is quite certain that Lynch had nothing whatever to do with Dunlop's initiative. In addition, he regards it as simply ridiculous that anyone could have believed the Commissioner to be a British spy.

It has been speculated that Lynch wanted Garvey out of the way for a reason far removed from the one given to me by Dunlop. Garvey was a disciplinarian—surely a point in his favour, not to his detriment—and

Fianna Fáil backbenchers heard, and passed on, innumerable tiresome complaints from members of the force who disliked his strict enforcement of the rules that governed them. His successors had to live with a perception that once he went the regime would become easier and that gardaí could contest any action of their superiors that caused them discomfort, like a transfer to another station. I do not attribute scandals like the outrageous activities of some officers in Donegal, investigated by the Morris Tribunal, to the events of the 1970s, but at a less serious level standards of discipline in the force deteriorated and morale declined. It is sad to see fine young people joining the force with the best of motivations, only to be disillusioned by bad management or political interference.

In fairness to the Lynch government, however, it has to be said that Collins was not a man to be influenced by deputies' complaints. On the contrary, he was known for his contemptuous attitude to 'Blaneyite' backbenchers whom he suspected of taking too tolerant a view of subversive activities. And the government, in his opinion and that of Lynch, had genuine cause for loss of confidence in the Commissioner. The associations representing the lower and middle ranks of the force had earlier expressed their own lack of confidence in him—though whether they should have had the right to do that must be debatable.

——

The improvement in the economy did not last long. The second oil crisis of the 1970s struck with similar force to the first one, and it hit Ireland particularly hard because of the new government's daft fiscal policies. The public finances went into a tailspin. It was meat and drink to Haughey, who had been an outstanding finance minister and whose contempt for the policies of the Lynch coterie was well known. The backbenchers were restive, and Haughey's people exploited their discontents. Their private mutterings grew into public challenges.

When they came to a crisis it was not on economic questions but on issues arising from the continuing troubles in the North. The government had consented to reconnaissance overflights of the border by the British army. When this became known to the dissident backbenchers, a revolt occurred at a meeting of the Fianna Fáil parliamentary party. Claims were made that Lynch had misled them. Colley, in charge of affairs during Lynch's absence in the United States, mishandled the response.

Worse still for Lynch was that at the same time he lost two by-elections in his own Cork back yard. What now of Honest Jack, the man with the pipe and the nice manners, whose popularity within the party rested on his electoral successes? Fianna Fáil are in business to gain and hold office, and electoral failure is the most grievous sin a leader can commit.

Unknown to Haughey, Lynch had planned to retire in 1980 and hand over to Colley. Haughey's supporters calculated that they could win a leadership election (confined to Fianna Fáil deputies) without any great difficulty. They were fortified by their hero's escape from a trap set for him by the now-fading Taoiseach.

Lynch had appointed Haughey Minister for Health in the hope of wrong-footing him on the issue of contraception. The sale of contraceptives was banned, but huge numbers of people (possibly including a majority of young married couples) evaded the ban by illegally importing condoms and other contraceptives from Britain and Northern Ireland and pharmacies in Belfast and border towns did a thriving business. Years earlier, the women's liberation movement had shown up the absurdity of the law by bringing quantities of condoms from Belfast and ostentatiously displaying them at the railway station when they arrived in Dublin. Clearly the time to change was more than ripe, but what to do in the face of powerful opposition from the bishops and from conservative Catholic organisations? Haughey, having consulted the bishops, came up with a proposition so laughable that words cannot adequately describe it. He brought in legislation which permitted the sale of condoms to married couples on a doctor's prescription. This he called, shamefully, 'an Irish solution to an Irish problem'. He was ridiculed, but he was also praised for his ingenuity.

Still some of his supporters were uncertain, not to say panicky: nobody panics more often or more conspicuously than politicians who see the glittering prize near their grasp but cannot be sure they will close on it. They believed he could win against Colley, but not necessarily against a more competent man and one with solid support among the wider public. Des O'Malley was loyal to Colley and did not think that he himself had yet attained the stature of a leadership challenger. But what if a third candidate emerged? What if P.J. Hillery resigned the presidency, found himself a Dáil seat and stood for the Fianna Fáil leadership?

Regardless of its source, the idea was intriguing. If anybody could have united the party (a most doubtful proposition) it was Hillery. But the obstacles were insuperable. In the first place, the operation would be immensely tricky. Lynch would have had to persuade Hillery to resign the presidency and would have had to induce some backbencher to give up his Dáil seat so that Hillery could return to the Dáil at a by-election. Secondly and crucially, Hillery did not want to become Taoiseach in any circumstances, least of all in a situation in which he knew he would face endless trouble from the Haughey camp. Nevertheless, some of Haughey's people saw his resignation as within the bounds of possibility and wished to ensure that if he did resign he would do so in disgraceful circumstances. He had to endure a spate of lurid rumours, to the effect that he had a mistress in Dublin or Brussels or one in each location and that his marriage was breaking up. He tried to counter them by inviting the editors of the national newspapers to meet him at Áras an Úachtaráin. There he told them little else than that he had no intention of resigning. They suggested that he should meet the political correspondents. He did so, and repeated what he had told the editors. The meetings must have been hideously embarrassing, since everybody present had heard the inspired rumours.

Had somebody else heard them—specifically Pope John Paul II, who visited Ireland in September 1979? Of course he had. The Vatican is very well informed, and John Paul II would have been briefed on all the main personalities he would meet on his trip, as well as the political background.

Had he also heard stories about two clerics, Father Michael Cleary and Bishop Eamonn Casey, who took a prominent, hugely overplayed and clownish part in the proceedings? Cleary lived as 'man and wife' with his housekeeper. Casey fathered a son during an affair with an American divorcee, Annie Murphy. Perhaps not. Their sins were a pale shade of pink by comparison with the unspeakable behaviour of hundreds, perhaps thousands, of clergy who engaged in gross child sex abuse. Though all the scandals would not erupt for several years, undoubtedly some bishops knew. They covered up, and very likely they concealed what they knew even from the Vatican.

Conservative Catholics, meanwhile, were ecstatic. They saw the appearance of this glamorous Pope, one of the outstanding men of the age, as an encouragement for their campaign to 'restore traditional values' and specifically their opposition to divorce and abortion. The first was banned by the constitution and it would take a referendum to remove the ban. The second was a matter for legislation. Demands for the legalisation of abortion were feeble at best, but the 'pro-life' movement would call for a referendum to enshrine it in the constitution. It would take nearly two decades, and bitter controversies with spectacular political consequences, for an increasingly secularised country to defeat them and implement all the main points of the 'Liberal Agenda', and even after a preposterous five referendums on the subject of abortion the issue has not been fully settled.

Most of the country saw the visit as an occasion for joyous celebration. A few dissented. They foresaw the triumph of the conservatives, with marginalisation of Protestants and liberal Catholics. Bruce Williamson plunged into gloom. I told him that any triumph would be temporary and that a rapidly modernising country would not tolerate church domination. I failed to console this natural-born pessimist.

His view was a world removed from that of Gageby, who loved John Paul II as he loved other larger-than-life personalities. He called a meeting of the *Irish Times* editorial staff and told us that this was the biggest story we would cover in our lives. My colleagues must have observed my look of disdain at this ridiculous statement. Along with a million other people, he attended the Pope's Mass in the Phoenix Park and wrote a piece which began with a Biblical quotation. Subsequently he devoted lavish coverage to John Paul II's visits to Scotland and Mexico, in which the Irish public had little interest.

At home, I had been involved beyond the call of duty in the coverage. On the climactic Sunday, I rewrote much of the lead story, and I wrote the main headline: OUTPOURINGS OF JOY AND FERVOUR. My colleagues, knowing my sceptical cast of mind, gave me funny looks. But that was what the story was about.

And the Demon King, who had been mostly out of sight during this festival?

Three months later, Haughey contested the Fianna Fáil leadership election with Colley. He won, but not by the margin he had expected. He then declared that the defeated candidate had pledged his loyalty, but Colley disputed that. He was deeply disappointed and worried about the party and how the country would fare. How far would he go in expressing his discontent? For a man of principle who had publicly denounced 'low standards in high places', the choice was stark: to accept the reign of a man whom he deeply distrusted, or to vote with his faction in the Dáil against Haughey's nomination as Taoiseach, split the party and put it out of office.

Garret FitzGerald in his memoirs writes of contacts with Colley and his own ephemeral belief that Colley would vote against Haughey. I have never been satisfied on the point, but I can bear FitzGerald out to this extent, that his trusted adviser Alexis FitzGerald told me that he expected that sensational outcome. I could not believe that Colley, born into the Fianna Fáil Old Guard who so valued loyalty and discipline, would go to such an extreme. In the event, he voted for Haughey's nomination. But bitter divisions would continue until long after his early death.

I never doubted that Haughey would win out. Indeed, I never doubted that even if another candidate—Hillery or O'Malley—had attained the leadership he would persist in his efforts to reach the top by any means. Back in 1966 the former Fine Gael leader James Dillon had warned the Old Guard that 'he will break your hearts.' He did.

During the long run-up to December 1979, I was on friendly but guarded terms with him. We lunched more than once in a favourite haunt of his, the Royal Hibernian Hotel. He repeated his criticism of the 1977 manifesto, deplored the state of the public finances, and assured me that once he became Taoiseach he would bring them under control. Many other journalists, and figures in the establishment, especially the business establishment, heard the same message and believed it.

At one of our lunches he hinted delicately at an invitation to Innisvicillane, his private island off the Kerry coast. With I hope equal delicacy, I declined. I would probably have accepted an invitation to lunch or dinner at his Kinsealy mansion, though that would have been a close call. I certainly could not see a holiday as his guest on Innisvicillane as in accordance with journalistic ethics. It would have ranked me with his cronies. We were bound to fall out sooner or later, and he lived by such maxims as 'those who are not with me are against me' and 'the enemy of my enemy is my friend'. To him, the very idea of journalistic ethics was absurd. I did not attempt to explain it.

Shortly after he became Taoiseach he made a television address in which he told us all that we had been living beyond our means and must now tighten our belts. This pleased me, much as it pleased the stock market and politicians like Des O'Malley. But almost immediately he shirked the decisions, like control of public spending, necessary to rectify the country's finances.

When it later emerged that he had accepted enormous sums of money from businessmen, people were outraged that he had lived a lavish lifestyle while telling the rest of us that we should pinch and scrape. We may never know the full extent of the operation. One of the many tribunals of inquiry tracked down sums of more than IR£8 million, but I have it on good authority that the true figure exceeded IR£30 million.

I was more annoyed by his cowardice and opportunism. Had he kept his word, he would have had to engage in something close to all-out war with the public sector unions. He would have risked strikes in services like transport, a potentially lethal threat to his popularity and future electoral prospects. But had he succeeded, he would have done his country great good and he might have been forgiven for his greed.

Fianna Fáil's hypocrisy and their uncanny knack of rewriting or obliterating uncomfortable bits of history made themselves manifest then and since in their ability to lay their blame for our fiscal troubles on others. For years, they denounced the Cosgrave government for doubling the national debt and made their point felt, but the Lynch and Haughey governments doubled it again. At the time, however, I was more disturbed by the sights that accompanied Haughey's accession to power. A large gang of drunken louts gained access to Leinster House, cheering and jostling. We would see worse in the coming years during the failed 'heaves' by his internal enemies, when his supporters' numbers grew and their activities became more outrageous. In the most disgraceful incident of all, James Gibbons was knocked down and kicked within the precincts of the House.

There had been somewhat similar scenes in earlier times, but usually at election meetings, not in Leinster House. In the 1960s, Neil Blaney and Kevin Boland had run by-election campaigns for Lynch. David Thornley said that their menacing air, and the open intimidation of voters by their followers, frightened him. Also in the 1960s, John M. Kelly wrote a thriller, *The Polling of The Dead*, which portrayed associates of the Fianna Fáil Party who would stop at nothing, even murder. The first was overstated and the second close to caricature, but I would remember Thornley's remark during one of the heaves, when wavering backbenchers received telephoned death threats and one of them said that he was 'frightened beyond being frightened'.

———

On his return to the *Irish Times* in 1977, Gageby gathered the editorial staff for what he called a 'shout-in' instead of then fashionable 'talk-in'. There was very little talking, and no shouting. He gave us a vague outline of his plans to revitalise the paper and said that he meant to stay for only eighteen months or two years, by which time his successor would have emerged. I was standing at the back, and was a little embarrassed when people at that point turned round and looked at me. He watched without changing expression, but I think he was taken aback, and I am sure he was displeased, to discover how high I stood in the staff's respect and affection.

Not long after, I was summoned to the bunker for a meeting with him and McDowell. I did not enjoy it, but evidently neither did they. It was their turn for embarrassment, because they could not avoid the question of sectarian prejudice. After some beating about the bush, McDowell said he understood that I had been uneasy about Pyle's appointment and Foley's treatment. I did not deny it. Then McDowell said: 'Other things being equal—of course they never are—the next editor of the *Irish Times* will be a Roman Catholic.' Gageby turned to me and growled: 'You'd better start going to Mass again.'

He held another but smaller staff meeting (these pseudo-democratic events soon dwindled to nothing) when he appointed me night editor with chief responsibility for the production of the paper. He told my colleagues, in a light enough but meaningful way, that I was very popular but my popularity would not last when I asserted my authority and tolerated no excuses. In the event my popularity increased because the staff responded to firm direction from someone they trusted, as they did both me and Gageby.

I had just enough time to organise a 'back desk' with close communication with the newsdesk before we entered a mini-crisis. For countrywide distribution, we relied on CIÉ, who now discontinued their late-night trains and substituted trucks which left their depots much earlier. For the first time, the *Irish Times* had to take deadlines seriously, and I had to bear down hard on the newsdesk and the chief sub-editor to enforce them. These deadlines were far easier to meet than the appallingly restrictive regime, dictated by commercial and printing requirements, that prevails universally at present, but it was fairly tough going for at least a year.

Gageby meanwhile set about what his critics unfairly called taking the paper downmarket. Similar and stronger criticism has been levelled at other newspapers in recent times, with mixed justification: for example, *The Times* and the *Daily Telegraph*. But upmarket and middle-market newspapers everywhere have maintained their serious and well-informed editorial core, and no law requires readers to plough through sheaves of colour supplements and pieces detailing the writers' dietary habits or their emotional problems consequent on having sexual relations with their dumped former partners. As to Gageby, he caused a stir when he despatched Maeve Binchy to write a series on French seaside resorts, accompanied by pictures of luscious young women, most of them almost naked. Nobody would blink now, and even then the sight quickly palled; I dubbed the series A Beach Too Far. But the text was worth reading to admire the writer's incomparable gift of observation.

His interest in the North was as intense as ever. In *Bright, Brilliant Days*, Fionnuala O Connor has described the dinners at which Gageby entertained the members of the *Irish Times* Belfast staff and encouraged them to report instances of 'normal life' and to take drives up the Antrim coast road, which he considered the most beautiful place in Ireland. He also conveyed a more relevant message, his overwhelming enthusiasm for John Hume's work, his subtlety of mind and his dedication to non-violence. The idolatry of Hume was not entirely to the taste of many journalists working for our own newspaper and other media, since Hume's relations with the media were, to say the least, prickly. In time, however, as she observes, they came to share Gageby's admiration for him.

In their never-ending search for heroes, Gageby and Healy identified Haughey and FitzGerald, with Haughey very much in front, as the two 'charismatic' figures who would lead the country in the next decade, placing us on the correct economic path and bringing about a peaceful Northern settlement. Dennis Kennedy summed up Gageby as 'a political animal'. Kennedy argued fiercely with him about the Northern question, on which their views were poles apart, but he told me that that did not matter: the editor of the *Irish Times* should be 'some kind of political animal'. This did not involve any great interest in the minutiae of politics; on the contrary, he preferred the broad brush-strokes and issues of personality and was too greatly influenced by his own likes and dislikes.

Paul Tansey in his contribution to the Whittaker book recounted a revealing incident. During one of the failed coups against Haughey, after the emergence of O'Malley as his chief opponent, Gageby tried to persuade Tansey that Haughey was more worthy of support than his challenger. He had a similar conversation with myself, in which he dwelt on the less laudable aspects of O'Malley's prickly personality. When Gageby consulted key members of the staff, Tansey saw it as an example of collegiality. In my own essay in the same book, I complain, to the contrary, about the absence of collegiality. It strikes me as a curious example of intelligent and truthful persons coming to opposite conclusions from virtually the same experience.

Another striking example of the misunderstanding that surrounds

Gageby's methods and his relationship with Healy appears in Dermot James's history *The Irish Times: From The Margins to The Centre*. He quotes an editorial published in 1982: 'How Mr Haughey can live with colleagues who spread not only dissatisfaction with his management of the party and the state, but disparagement of his personal qualities, is hard for those outside politics to understand.' He goes on to remark that several journalists, myself included, had commented on Gageby's friendship with John Healy, 'leading to a feeling that Gageby was unduly influenced by him, and a number of them felt that this extended to his opinion of both Charles Haughey and Fianna Fáil.' Whatever about the conclusions of other critics, I do not subscribe to the idea that his eccentric views of these matters should be attributed solely or chiefly to Healy's influence. His own prejudices counted for more. He summed them up in a private conversation with me in which he said: 'If the Fianna Fáil Party can't get rid of Haughey, so much the worse for them.'

Fergus Pyle had revelled in the details of Brussels negotiations and the complexity of the compromises hammered out by representatives of the member-states. Nothing could have been better calculated to switch readers off. At one point the paper ran a self-publicising advertising campaign, no less, illustrated by a picture of a story across the top of a front page. The headline contained the three dreadful words 'EEC fish limits'. I complained that it might as well have said 'don't bother to read this.'

Gageby and Healy did not concern themselves greatly with fishing limits, but continued to bang on about the glory of European unity and Franco–German reconciliation. Yet Gageby refused to recognise the reality that European unity must have a military dimension. His views had been shaped by his wartime experiences; he considered Irish neutrality a fundamental principle; he deplored what he saw as its erosion by the various treaties in which the member-states ceded more centralised power to the European Commission and the Council of Ministers, and until the very end he supported the hollow formula whereby Irish governments, especially Fianna Fáil governments, redefined 'neutrality' merely as a refusal to join military alliances. This he described as honourable, a view which I did not share and which I thought weird in a man who knew so much about how wartime neutrality had come about and how it operated.

In the early 1960s, Seán Lemass had wanted to join the European Economic Community, precursor of the European Union, along with Britain, and he wanted to find out if Nato membership was a prerequisite for Irish entry. His sources of authoritative information were few, since the diplomatic service was seriously under-staffed, but he had excellent reason to believe that it was indeed a prerequisite. To sound out public opinion, he 'flew a kite'. Micheál Ó Móráin (the same man who would later, as Justice Minister, be mangled in the Arms Crisis) made a speech in his Mayo constituency advocating Nato membership. Everybody assumed, rightly as I am certain, that he did so at Lemass's instigation. The criticisms that followed centred less on the issue itself than on allegations that Ó Móráin was drunk or that members of his audience were drunk (evidently the critics were unsure whether either was true or which allegations would carry more weight). The debate died down when the EEC negotiations failed, and by the time the next round of talks succeeded and we entered the Community on 1 January 1973 we had discovered that we did not in fact have to join Nato.

When the North erupted in 1969, Haughey invited the British ambassador, Sir Andrew Gilchrist, to Kinsealy, where he put forward a daring proposition. Britain should cede sovereignty over Northern Ireland to Dublin. Thus the nationalist aspiration for unity would be achieved. But in return, Dublin would hand the unionist government even greater powers than Stormont had previously enjoyed—in effect, independence apart from powers reserved to the British government over, for example, foreign affairs. British defence interests would be safeguarded. Guarantees of rights for the Catholic minority, one may safely assume, would have had no greater meaning than those dreamed up by Harold Wilson in the following decade.

Such proposals got an eerie echo in the 'Boal plan', drawn up, perhaps coincidentally, perhaps not, about the time that Haughey became Taoiseach in 1979. The author was Desmond Boal, a leading Belfast lawyer and a friend of Ian Paisley. Haughey was then trying to use Boal as a conduit to Paisley and was, as always, certain that Paisley would eventually rule Northern Ireland. He believed he saw the Big Man's hand in the Boal plan. He pondered the defence question, and skirted the issue of Nato membership by suggesting a bilateral defence pact to Prime Minister Margaret Thatcher. She was interested, but her advisers told her that there was no advantage for Britain in the proposal. In the event of a crisis, the Irish, who relied entirely on the Western allies for their security, would do whatever was required of them.

Haughey's methods of cultivating Thatcher were highly characteristic. Shortly before he met her at 10 Downing Street, I had a chance encounter with Michael Mullen, a Haughey admirer and a hard-liner on the Northern question. He told me that Haughey had acquired a Georgian silver teapot as a gift for her. Haughey found out, presumably from Mullen, that the *Irish Times* intended to publish this story. He tried to have it suppressed, but I wrote it and it appeared in the paper, giving rise to much public amusement and many jokes about 'teapot diplomacy'.

Whether there was much substance in their first meeting is questionable. However, their second meeting, in Dublin Castle, seemed to hold out promise of concrete progress in Anglo-Irish affairs. Thatcher brought with her to Dublin a large and impressive team of ministers, including not only the obvious names like the Foreign Secretary, Lord Carrington, but the Chancellor of the Exchequer, Sir Geoffrey Howe (who found his inclusion in the expedition hard to understand). The communiqué issued at the end of the meeting announced the establishment of a team to conduct 'joint studies' of Anglo-Irish issues, including institutional questions. The government hailed this as an enormously important development which would raise discussion of the Northern issue to what Haughey called 'a new plane', meaning in essence that the two governments could devise and impose a Northern solution over the heads of the local parties. But the Foreign Minister, Brian Lenihan, slipped up badly when he said that the studies would concern themselves with constitutional questions when he should have used the term 'institutional'. Soon afterwards, on the fringes of a meeting of European heads of government, Thatcher furiously berated Haughey, who passed on the reprimand, with interest, to Lenihan. Her own anger was not directed chiefly at Lenihan but at Haughey himself for exaggerating the import of their discussions. The incident undermined any trust that may have existed between them, and relations were further, and gravely, damaged on the issue of the Falklands War.

When the Argentines invaded the Falkland Islands, which they called the Malvinas, the European Union countries imposed economic sanctions on the Buenos Aires regime. Ireland's participation was far from universally popular at home, where Fianna Fáil supporters in particular thought the islands should belong to Argentina anyway. The sacred word neutrality was invoked, and the small matters of international law and our credit in Europe and the United States disregarded. The militant Fianna Fáil view was expressed by my old friend Niall Andrews, now a member of the European Parliament, when I met him at a party at which he kept shouting the slogan 'Viva Malvinas!' It was expressed to greater effect by

Haughey's Defence Minister, Paddy Power.

When the British sank an Argentine capital ship, the *Belgrano*, Power declared that the British were 'now the aggressors' and called for a policy revision. Whether this statement was inspired from above is not known but can be guessed. Haughey followed it up promptly. He not only cancelled Ireland's participation in the European sanctions but called for 'a ceasefire in place', which would have permitted the Argentines to retain the territory they had seized. The embarrassment was enormous, not least because Ireland at the time held a seat on the United Nations Security Council. The issue was finessed by the Irish ambassador, Noel Dorr, but we were rescued mainly by the rapid and conclusive British victory. At the time, however, and for many years to come, Haughey's recklessness was bitterly resented in the British establishment and dismayed our friends in the government and the administration. It would be left to Garret FizGerald to pick up the pieces.

————

During my conversations with Haughey between 1977 and 1979, I had raised the question where he would find the talent to fill the ministries. He replied dismissively that he had plenty of suitable talent available to him. I remained doubtful.

At first he tried to unify the warring wings of his party by retaining Colley in the cabinet notwithstanding the latter's openly stated lack of confidence in him, and appointing like-minded persons such as Des O'Malley and Martin O'Donoghue to important ministries. But as the dissidents continued their efforts to overthrow him, he switched his ground and drew loyalists about him. His most spectacular, and ultimately fatal, appointment was that of Seán Doherty as Minister for Justice.

Doherty, a former member of the Special Branch, was a man of considerable intelligence and charm, but utterly unfitted for the job. He had no understanding of his constitutional responsibilities, but spent his time pursuing vendettas in his Roscommon constituency and getting himself mired in several scandalous events. These have been so frequently and so thoroughly detailed that it would be pointless to rehearse them here and I will mention only two.

The first would become more important for its repercussions than for its gross impropriety. Doherty ordered the telephone tapping of two journalists, Bruce Arnold and Geraldine Kennedy, future editor of the *Irish Times*. For me, the queerest aspect of the tapping was that it happened legally, on a warrant, instead of in the customary secretive and illegal manner.

The second was the arrest of a murderer, Malcolm MacArthur, in the Dalkey apartment of the attorney general, Patrick Connolly. The two were personal friends, and Connolly had no idea that MacArthur had committed any crimes before visiting him. He took the event so lightly that he tried to continue with his holiday plans and flew to New York. At the airport he received a message ordering his instant recall to Dublin, where Haughey sacked him. Haughey had already described the incident as 'grotesque, unbelievable, bizarre and unprecedented'. Conor Cruise O'Brien seized on the words to create the acronym GUBU, which immediately entered the language and remained there. It marked the culmination of 1982, the Year of the GUBU. Haughey's second government, formed in March of that year, lasted only nine months. It also marked the culmination of a period of extraordinary political instability, with three general elections in less than eighteen months.

When Haughey fell, Fine Gael and Labour formed a coalition under Garret FitzGerald, and the new Minister for Justice, Michael Noonan, disclosed the facts of the telephone tapping. Noonan thought this would provoke a final, and successful, Fianna Fáil backbench 'heave' against Haughey. He was almost right. Haughey might well have lost a confidence vote at a parliamentary party meeting had not the chairman, Jim Tunney (dubbed 'the Yellow Rose of Finglas' from his habit of wearing a yellow rosebud in his buttonhole) adjourned the meeting on spurious grounds. That bought Haughey a little time, during which an operation was mounted to change the minds, or at any rate the votes, of the dissident backbenchers. Where persuasion failed, threats and blackmail worked. When the parliamentary party met again, it voted confidence in him by a whopping majority.

Fianna Fáil deputies and party activists, never comfortable in opposition, settled down to a period in which their attitudes to their leader varied from enthusiasm to grudging acceptance. On the surface, he seemed to have achieved unity of a sort. But underneath, the signs of future trouble were unmistakable. Haughey was now determined to rout his enemies and in particular O'Malley, who had replaced Colley as the dissident leader. He also hoped to neuter Doherty, who was deprived of the Fianna Fáil parliamentary whip but was soon taken back into the

Fianna Fáil fold. Doherty, however, was not for neutering. He deeply resented being made the scapegoat for an action, the telephone tapping, which as the whole country believed had Haughey's full knowledge and approval. He told anyone who would listen—journalists as well as politicians—that he was carrying about with him 'two buckets of shit'. One day, he implied, the buckets would be emptied over Haughey's head.

The *Irish Times* meanwhile continued to occupy its normal position, the high moral ground, but Gageby was not happy. If Haughey went, O'Malley was now viewed by most observers the favourite to succeed him, and Gageby viewed an O'Malley leadership with the utmost distaste, partly for personal reasons and partly because he considered O'Malley 'weak on the national question'. On the other side of the House, he liked FitzGerald—though he hated FitzGerald's Labour coalition partners—and he would soon grow to like him more.

I don't know if he ever intended to fulfil his 1977 promise to retire within two years, but I very much doubt it. If he did at first, he changed his mind quickly, and let the chapel know. Mary Maher, a stalwart of the chapel and one of my closest friends and allies, asked me for my opinion. I replied: 'Mary, I'm fucked.' I could see at once that Gageby meant to buy time to find challengers to me.

Having previously promised the succession to myself and Donal Foley, he now went on to make similar offers, some more firm than others, to several people, of whom the most significant were Conor O'Clery and Conor Brady.

One afternoon I chanced upon Benedict Kiely and Seán J. White in Buswell's Hotel. They had looked forward eagerly to my success and had been dismayed to discover that I had challengers. 'And they're all called Conor!' At Donal Foley's funeral in 1981, Mickser Hand offered me odds of six to four that O'Clery would be the next editor. I said I would take the bet in thousands. He refused to go as far as that, but he made it clear that he thought I had lately made a false move.

Having got the back desk and the sub-editing operation into shape, with invaluable help from a sound man, Pat O'Hara, a model for all chief subs and night editors, I took what amounted to a sabbatical, writing political 'thinkpieces' and making frequent visits to Belfast and London. On one of the latter, I attended the Labour Party's notorious Wembley conference of January 1981 in the company of Dáithí Ó Ceallaigh, then a junior diplomat in the Irish embassy, later ambassador. At that conference Michael Foot visibly lost all control over his party, which voted for a crazy system of electing the leader and deputy leader and ensured the defection of the 'Gang of Four' led by Roy Jenkins and the foundation of the rival Social Democratic Party (SDP). Ó Ceallaigh was close to Neil Kinnock, and that evening we dined with the future leader and half a dozen other people. I have seldom seen a man so deeply plunged in gloom as Kinnock on that occasion. Perhaps he foresaw how dreadful a task awaited him if and when he succeeded Foot. In the event, he would do a magnificent job of initiating the reforms completed (not to say overdone) by Tony Blair. For both of them, the role of Peter Mandelson would be immensely important. I already knew Mandelson as a television director. Both in that capacity and later as Northern Ireland Secretary in Blair's New Labour government I thought him unlovable, but I admire his staying power as a politician.

A trip to Washington yielded more entertainment. I was there on St Patrick's Day 1981 when the new American President, Ronald Reagan, attended his first lunch at the Irish embassy. He was still in the process of forming his first administration, and the ambassador, my friend Seán Donlon, who observed the fall of every sparrow in Washington, was at pains to ease the difficulties inherent in the (to us) strange American system, in which a Republican President had to work with a Democrat-dominated Congress. Among the guests was Lawrence Eagleburger, whom Reagan had nominated for one of the top foreign affairs jobs and who was a hate-figure for right-wing Republicans because of his association with Henry Kissinger. He would have to face congressional hearings on his appointment. While the guests assembled in the embassy and waited for the President to arrive, he was on tenterhooks. In an attempt to make light conversation, I asked him how long he had served in the State Department. He replied: 'Too fucking long.' End of conversation.

Donlon saw to it that Eagleburger was seated with Reagan, Senator Edward Kennedy, and 'Tip' O'Neill, Speaker of the House of Representatives. Whatever impression he made on Kennedy and O'Neill, he evidently failed to make the President understand that he was his nominee for an appointment of world significance. After lunch, Reagan asked Donlon's wife: 'Who is this guy Eagleburger? Is he the German ambassador?'

Donlon presented Reagan with a parchment purporting to show his descent from King Brian Boru, victor of the Battle of Clontarf in 1014. I have no idea how the heraldic experts expected to prove such an impossible proposition. I never saw the parchment and I am pretty sure that I was not meant to see it. But Reagan was enchanted. His eyes misted over as he made his speech of thanks. People who deride him as a B-movie actor are mistaken. He played the role of President of the United States with confidence and aplomb every day for eight years. And at least one of his habits could be commended to other world leaders. During one of the many crises of his reign, a White House spokesman described his anxiety: 'The President is having sleepless afternoons.' Other leaders allow themselves to be inundated with paper and fatigued by ceaseless travel. They give themselves no time to think. Not that Reagan did much thinking.

Chapter 9 ∾

| 1983: AT THE COALFACE

M y easy life as a correspondent did not last long. I was drawn back on to the night desk, this time with the title of deputy editor and with an even more arduous job than enforcing deadlines.

The *Irish Times* board had decided that we must have colour printing and new presses, and that we must change from hot metal to computerised print technology. In my opinion, they planned the operation atrociously.

We needed all these things, but we needed them all together. Logically that meant a new plant (eventually built, at a reputed cost of ir£60 million, at Citywest) and not the almost impossible arrangements made in all three areas in D'Olier Street. My readers will not wish to know all the details of these moves, so I will describe them as briefly as is consistent with clarity.

The board thought colour advertising essential for revenue, and perhaps it was. But since our single aged press had no colour facility, we could manage only with a clumsy system which may have cost us more than we gained. Pages were printed, or part-printed, in the *Irish Independent* in Abbey Street and fed into our press. This awkward arrangement led to delays and breakdowns.

Infinitely worse were the problems surrounding the next stage, the arrangements for photo-setting and make-up. It was decided that we should run both the old and new systems in tandem for a period of several months. This meant that in addition to the usual setbacks associated with such a change the press had to carry both metal plates and much shallower plastic plates. The plastic plates were fixed to 'saddles' to give them the correct depth. For the printers, getting the register right was a nightmare.

In addition, insufficient thought had been given to the proper organisation of the new, or half-new, technology. In the composing room where former hot-metal compositors cut up the material with scalpels and glued it on to pages, and in the subsequent operations prior to printing, each of the old hot-metal functions was replicated. Constant arguments about productivity took place between the management on the one side and the printers and their unions on the other. They would never be resolved until, as inevitably happened, the role of Linotype operators was abolished and journalists input the copy directly and made up the pages on screens, the present system.

My own function was to supervise the production from the editorial viewpoint and, while doing everything in my power to maintain standards, to agree the compromises necessary to produce the paper on time, or at all. I am proud that, partly owing to my efforts, we did not lose a single edition during the changeover. But I still shudder when I look back over those terrible months, when we did not know from minute to minute what crisis would overtake us.

I could not have succeeded without what must have been a unique degree of co-operation from the printers. From London, where wages were paid to hundreds of non-existent workers and receipts were signed by 'Mickey Mouse', to Washington, where presses were sabotaged and copies of the *Washington Post* flown by helicopter from the roof of a blockaded building, the sins of printers were scarlet. Nothing of the kind happened in Dublin. On the contrary, the *Irish Times* printers 'pulled out' and worked without stint in every emergency, and every night brought an emergency.

By contrast, I got very little help from Gageby. He did not attend any of the weekly production meetings at which I agonised over technical details with representatives of the management and resisted their demands that we should make fewer requirements of the production side and 'cut our cloth according to our measure'. He had no interest in the tremendous possibilities offered by the new system. On one particularly bad night— when, unusually, he came in to observe the production himself—he panicked and said in the presence of several compositors and overseers that we should abandon the project and go back to hot metal.

I was impatient with the inadequacy of our plans and the inordinate length of time the changeover was taking. Plainly direct input and page make-up by journalists were the future, and in the early and middle 1980s we were not part of the future. Gageby was not enthusiastic about my trips to Britain and the United States to observe the introduction of the new technology there, and somebody—no one would tell me who—vetoed another trip, to Florida, where the production manager, Jim Cooke, had learned that matters were more advanced than in the major American cities.

The supposed rationale for this nonsense was that we must not alienate the print unions and that we must move in tandem with the other Dublin newspaper managements. I remain convinced that the *Irish Times* could have made a separate deal with the unions, who knew perfectly well that their craft would not last for ever and took the sensible view that they must forfeit their jobs sooner or later at the right price.

Finally our antiquated press was dismantled. The Linotype machines were donated to the Coptic church in Egypt, where it appeared nobody had the money to invest in new technology. A team arrived from Germany to build the new *Irish Times* press. While this work went on, the paper was printed by the *Irish Independent*, who had spare capacity.

Gageby told me that the board wished to congratulate me on my work during the upheaval. I reminded him of an old saying about the three most useless things in the world: 'a man's tits, the Pope's balls, and congratulations from the board'. I don't know if he passed it on.

——

Conor Brady had left the *Irish Times* briefly to edit the *Sunday Tribune*. Here I must correct an error in the first edition of the memoirs (2008) of my friend Seamus Martin, who writes that I was turned down for the job and that Geraldine Kennedy thought I would have been a better choice than Brady. I was not turned down; I never applied. Geraldine Kennedy and Mary Holland, both of whom worked for the *Tribune* at the time, asked me to talk to the proprietor, Hugh McLaughlin, and I visited him at his house in Foxrock. I found that he favoured Jim Farrelly of the *Irish Independent*. We parted amicably. McLaughlin then proceeded to launch a daily newspaper with Farrelly as editor. The rationale for the move is difficult to understand. It was speculated, then and since, that McLaughlin hoped for an instant success and handsome revenue, part of which could be employed to prop up the *Tribune*. If that was his pipedream, it evaporated quickly. The new publication survived for only one week, and the ownership of the *Tribune* changed hands. Brady became editor in the middle of the turbulence. If the paper failed to prosper under his editorship, he was not to blame.

Brady came back to D'Olier Street in 1983 to take up an undefined job in the office of the managing director, Louis O'Neill. During his spell in the *Tribune*, he and Gageby had kept in close touch. One night Pat O'Hara went into the *Irish Times* editor's office with some query. He found Bruce Williamson there, in a state of alcoholic gloom. Williamson was not interested in the query but in conveying a message. 'It's Friday night, dear boy,' he said. 'On Friday nights the editor always dines with Mr Brady.'

Those close to me among the chapel officers and the editorial executives were greatly agitated by Brady's return, as also were the many outsiders who took an interest in journalism (as witness my encounter with Benedict Kiely and Seán J. White). They suggested that I should 'do something.' But what?

He did not remain long in O'Neill's office but came back to the editorial department as an assistant editor with responsibility for features. This further, clearly pre-planned move engendered more agitation among the staff. Again, I saw no way to assert my position. Brady approached me and told me that he had no plans to challenge me for the succession, but I did not pass on the contents of our conversation to my friends. Gageby was aware of the apprehension and concern among the senior staff. He buttonholed me, not in the office we shared but in the newsroom, for just long enough to say: 'You don't have to worry. You're still the front-runner.' I was far from reassured. To call me the front-runner was if anything a diminution of my supposed status, that of the anointed successor. I took it as a very bad omen.

I might have been even more unhappy if I had known something I did not learn for many years: that Gageby made a practice of asking close friends outside the paper their opinion as to who should succeed him. More precisely, he invited them to name Brady, and when my name was mentioned he fell silent. I seem to detect an analogy here with his attempts to get Paul Tansey and others to share his preference for Haughey over O'Malley as leader of Fianna Fáil.

Perhaps it is as well that I did not know. It was bad enough to know something that even I could not fail to spot: that Brady soon came to be regarded by some of the more astute staff members as Gageby's representative on Earth. (My former mentor Ken Gray was seen, in a somewhat similar way, as McDowell's representative on Earth.) Whether or not Brady felt himself in some sense Gageby's spokesman, he played the part firmly when a group chaired by myself met to conduct interviews and make a recommendation on the appointment of the next news editor.

The editorial committee, who hailed every specious favour they received from the management as a giant step towards influence and 'transparency', were represented on the panel. This was merely cosmetic.

In reality they had no power whatever and in any case the final decision would rest with the editor, but everybody likes the feeling of holding power and influence. Everybody, that is, but me. If there is one thing I hate more than conducting job interviews, it is being interviewed myself. The procedure in the case of appointing a news editor was especially irksome, since the outstanding candidate was Pat Smyllie, son of Donald and nephew of Bertie, and I knew that Gageby had no intention of promoting a member of that family.

When the interviews concluded, the five members of the panel mulled over the merits of the candidates. All but one of us spoke about Smyllie's abilities as a sharp news man and his impressive performance at his interview. Then Brady said that we all knew Gageby wanted to give the job to Conor O'Clery and we had better recommend him. Since this was the obvious truth, there was no more to be said. I went off and told Gageby how much Smyllie had impressed us. He made no comment, but proceeded with O'Clery's appointment.

O'Clery had been, and would be again, a first-class correspondent, showered with well-deserved prizes, but the job of news editor requires qualities of a different kind. Although he and I had long been firm friends and would soon resume our friendship, we had serious disagreements over the handling of stories and I was displeased when he appointed Kevin Myers to write the daily column An Irishman's Diary.

He made the appointment against the expressed wishes of the editor, who wanted a different kind of Irishman's Diary. I too favoured a different model: an upmarket gossip column, somewhat on the lines of those in the London 'heavies'—probably with more than one contributor—and not an opinion column. When Myers used it as a vehicle to express his own opinions, Gageby could have reacted in either of two obvious ways. He could have put up with it, and perhaps he should have because it was beautifully written, albeit in a style much too reliant on hyperbole for my own taste, or he could have moved Myers to other duties. Instead, he constantly bullied and harassed him and when he did not wish to do his own bullying he used Ken Gray to act as a persuader. The most intense conflict occurred on the subject of Myers's obsession with the first world war. He wanted the Irish dead commemorated. So they should be, and so they have been since, but Myers wanted more: he insisted that they were entitled to commemoration by the Irish state. I see no reason, and evidently Gageby saw no reason, why the state should officially honour men who fell in a conflict which occurred before the state was founded.

But Myers stood his ground and in effect Gageby tolerated it, perhaps because he knew that the writer had a large and enthusiastic following. Whatever the reason, I don't think Gageby comes well out of the affair. Myers for his part continued to fight his own war through a second editorship and a part of the third. He finally left the *Irish Times* during the reign of Geraldine Kennedy and carried his column with him to the *Irish Independent*. Such was his cult status that one friend of mine told me he had ceased to buy the *Irish Times* after fifty years and switched overnight to the *Independent*.

O'Clery had difficulties in his personal life which I thought might be eased by a change of scene. I therefore decided to send him, with his consent, to London and to appoint another Northerner, Eugene McEldowney, in his place. McEldowney proved to be an excellent news editor, but it was O'Clery who benefited most. He shared my intense interest in Anglo-Irish affairs and developed exceptionally well-informed contacts in London. One of them gave him a series of exclusive stories. He would ring me to say: 'It's the same source. He's never let me down.' This had the opposite effect from the one he intended. It made me nervous, because contacts often let you down, but the man in question (of course O'Clery did not reveal his identity, but I guessed it) never let him down.

I sought and got Brady's support for my plan to move O'Clery to London and appoint McEldowney. Was that a tacit admission of my own diminishing influence? If so, I was not conscious of it at the time, but by then I deeply distrusted both Gageby and McDowell. I could also see that executives on the commercial side resented Gageby's lack of care for their concerns, sometimes expressed in a dismissive and even insulting manner. They wanted him out, but they did not want me in: they wanted Brady.

Numerous meetings with McDowell did nothing to quell my fears. He would meet me in the bunker or give me lunch in a private room in the Kildare Street and University Club. On those occasions he did all the talking. Each time that he piled more work and responsibility on me, he said that my acquiescence neither brought me closer, nor took me any distance from, realising my 'aspirations'. I wanted to reply, and perhaps I should have replied: Hang on! I had every right to object to a formulation which suggested an ambitious young (by then not so young) man pushing himself forward. In 1977 I had refused even to consider the question until Foley insisted. On Gageby's return, he and McDowell had raised it themselves. Since then, as McDowell must have known, I had received promises from Gageby and unmistakable hints from himself—until he felt certain that no matter what happened, he would retain my services.

As time passed, Brady began to express a different line on his own plans on the succession. In several private conversations, he was dismissive of Gageby's passions for Wolfe Tone, Newgrange, the army and the SDLP, and made it clear that he thought the editor had outlived his usefulness. He did not conceal his own ambitions, but he said that McDowell hated having to make his mind up and it suited him to have both of us in place. 'If it's you, they lose me. If it's me, they lose you.' I did not bother to remind him of his earlier assurance. Rather, I was surprised at his impatience. I was now over fifty years old, and Brady was fifteen years younger. The longer Gageby stayed, the worse for me. I could wither on the vine.

By then my situation was almost as nightmarish as it had been during Fergus Pyle's reign. I tried to handle it in the only way I knew, by remaining totally loyal to Gageby and refusing to encourage any dissent. But three events had the extraordinary effect of undermining Gageby's position and mine at the same time.

When Brady was offered the editorship of the *Sunday Independent*, he declined, apparently because the terms did not include membership of the *Independent* board. When Louis O'Neill heard about the offer, he was greatly alarmed. He sought means of persuading Brady to stay in D'Olier Street. Brady was promoted to deputy editor and given a seat on the *Irish Times* board. As a sop, I got the ridiculous title of senior deputy editor. McDowell had a genius for inventing titles.

I was already a member of the board, a powerless and dubious honour. The system was that the members of the trust first met separately; then they had a discussion with the editor or acting editor; then the full board, including the executive directors, met; then everybody mingled for lunch—eaten standing up, so that discomfort was added to insufferable boredom. I found the governors of the trust, as McDowell pompously called them, ill-informed about journalism and, surprisingly, for the most part lacking political shrewdness or insight. I did not know by what criteria they were appointed, and all I can say for certain is that McDowell privately did not forbear to boast of his (imaginary) good judgment and how he had excluded at least one eminent Northern Ireland citizen. My *bête noire* was Professor James Meenan, who treated me with bland contempt. His attitude may have derived from his membership of a notable Fine Gael family. Notwithstanding my friendship with Garret FitzGerald, it seemed that some in that party had never forgiven me for my opposition to coalition all those years ago.

Even less did I enjoy the couple of occasions on which I appeared before the trust as acting editor during Gageby's holidays. The proceedings were so tightly controlled that I was not given an opportunity to answer, for example, questions about the paper's Northern policy. At one meeting I could hear people asking one another, 'what did he say?' As I opened my mouth to explain matters more loudly and at greater length, McDowell called a halt.

My periods in the editor's chair were spoiled, the first time by Gageby and the second by powerful signs—to me but not many others, for most of the staff continued both to idolise Gageby and to expect me to occupy his place permanently very soon—of intrigue and disloyalty to myself. On the first occasion, Gageby telephoned me from France at least once a day, questioning me closely about what I was doing and getting in the way of my work. Ken Gray, to his visible discomfort, had taken a temporary desk in the editor's office to watch me on McDowell's behalf. Evidently he told the chairman about the calls, for McDowell vetoed them the second time round. But it was disgraceful and humiliating for me to be treated in this fashion.

I suspect that matters came to a head when Gageby fell and broke his leg while walking on a river bank close to his country house in Meath. Opposing factions saw opportunities in the accident. Bruce Williamson took me up the back stairs to a tiny office usually reserved by Gageby for exceptionally private business. He told me that this gave me my chance and I must seize it. But how? How, in practical terms? And how, consistently with remaining loyal to Gageby? He had no idea, and neither did I.

Gageby came back to work, leg in plaster, in short order. He may have feared the consequences of a long absence. McDowell fussed about arrangements to help his mobility. Williamson's explanation for the agitation was that 'the chairman knows Douglas is a lucky man.' But his luck was running out.

On his first day back, he sat across the room from me. I happened to look up from my work and catch him watching me with a stare of deep-seated malice which unnerved me. That, I fancy, summed things up. He must have known my ill-directed loyalty to him, which had prevented me from giving the slightest hint that I was eager to take over soon and begin to reconstruct the paper into something better suited to the age we lived in. He must also have known that McDowell was under pressure from the commercial side to let him retire and put Brady in his place.

New departures were certainly urgent. Gageby's eccentricities had begun to verge on the intolerable. He had always had a very queer writing style, full of bald statements and non-sequiturs. When some issue presented itself in which I knew he had a particular interest, I would say 'Douglas, you'll want to write the editorial on this yourself' and he would reply 'no, no, you can do it more elegantly.' I would write the leader, only for him to repeat much the same sentiments in his own erratic style the following day. Sometimes he would write the headlines as well. One example that sticks in my mind is GOTTERDAMMERUNG FOR FIANNA FÁIL. But this example of daft exaggeration was small compared with the rambling and inconsequential leaders, with Wolfe Tone and Newgrange mixed up in the same paragraph, which he now wrote more frequently, and even less intelligibly.

On day-to-day matters, he gave less and less guidance. His contributions to editorial conferences became less frequent and less relevant, usually consisting only of unhelpful grumps about trivial things. On one occasion, though, he made a justified complaint about the general appearance of that day's paper. The back desk had had a bad night of it, and no matter how hard we tried, we had found it impossible to force even the late edition into the shape we wanted. Exhausted and irritable, I said: 'You can't win them all, Douglas.' He shut up, and so did everybody else.

His political eccentricities culminated in his reaction to the Anglo-Irish Agreement in November 1985. To outward appearance he was still sprightly for his age, sixty-six, but his behaviour exemplified his failing grasp.

—

In 1983 FitzGerald had set up the Forum for a New Ireland, which sat for a year and produced a report. All the 'constitutional' parties on the island were invited to participate, but the unionist parties predictably declined and the membership reflected what FitzGerald hoped would be a consensus in moderate nationalism.

As so often, enthusiasts exaggerated the import and prospects of the enterprise. John Healy, presumably with Gageby's approval, said that the forum should properly be called the Council for a New Ireland; in effect, a sort of embryo all-island parliament. That was entirely absurd, and people of a more practical and sceptical cast of mind saw it as a device to prop up the SDLP against the growing power of Sinn Féin.

This power derived in large part from two epochal developments, the H-Blocks hunger strike and the new Sinn Féin–IRA 'Armalite and ballot paper' strategy. The first was a tragedy. The second initiated the moves whereby the so-called 'republican movement' would eventually forswear the Armalite rifle and its other weapons and bring it into government in the North, though not, as its begetters claimed and hoped, in both parts of Ireland. Both illustrated the strategic intelligence of the leadership under Gerry Adams and Martin McGuinness and the ruthlessness and cynicism of its methods. They also demonstrated the failure of the 'Ulsterisation and criminalisation' policy introduced by Merlyn Rees in the 1970s.

Rees had abolished the practice of internment without trial and imprisoned only persons convicted by the courts of terrorist offences. These were subjected to the ordinary rules, obliged to wear prison clothes and perform whatever work was required of them, and denied free association. The prisoners' leaders revolted, and a series of escalating protests culminated in the hunger strike in which ten men died in the H-Blocks in the Long Kesh internment camp, renamed the Maze prison.

At first the IRA leaders opposed the prisoners' action, but they quickly came to realise its potential political advantages. Bobby Sands, the first man to die, was elected to the House of Commons in a by-election while on hunger strike. The nationalist population did not blame his death, or those of the nine who followed, on the IRA. They blamed the British government and Margaret Thatcher personally. They did not regard the hunger strikers as criminals but as political prisoners who should be permitted to wear their own clothes and express their status through their own organisation. They saw Thatcher's obduracy as cruel and unjustified. They despaired of moderate politics and swung towards supporting Sinn Féin at the polls and giving aid and comfort to the IRA, whether by reason of conviction or intimidation. Such was the atmosphere in which the New Ireland Forum met.

The initiative cannot be dismissed as a total failure, because FitzGerald and his Foreign Minister, Peter Barry, afterwards built on its work to considerable effect. But the forum undoubtedly failed in two crucial objectives, achieving nationalist consensus and protecting the SDLP from the inroads of Sinn Féin. And its proceedings were discouraging. The Catholic bishops were as smooth as silk but said nothing to please unionists—or liberal Catholics—and Haughey took an atavistic and unrealistic stand which made the report all but worthless as a basis for

Anglo-Irish or North–South negotiations.

It described 'a unitary state' as the favoured outcome. This was done at the insistence of Haughey, who privately did not believe in such a fantasy for one moment. The other options named were federation or confederation, and British–Irish 'joint authority' over Northern Ireland. Haughey could argue that nationalists could and should begin negotiations, if any, from their hardest position and soften the line if talks made progress, but a unitary state was neither a practical proposition nor the one he privately favoured, which had a strong flavour of federation about it. As to joint authority, it echoed a proposal for a condominium made by the SDLP many years earlier. Since then, the destruction of the power-sharing executive and the triumphalism of Rees's constitutional convention had demonstrated the unwillingness of unionists to agree to an acceptable form of devolved government in the North, John Hume certainly had despaired of that, and Gerry Fitt, whom he had replaced as leader of the SDLP, saw no alternative to the indefinite continuation of British direct rule. But none of the options was likely to be at all attractive to British pragmatists. Privately, and sometimes publicly, those most sympathetic to Ireland expressed their disappointment and what they saw as a most unhelpful report. Margaret Thatcher stated her views more robustly.

She expressed herself in characteristic terms at a press conference following a meeting with FitzGerald and Barry, outlining each of the proposals and declaring: 'That is OUT.' Her statement became known as her 'out, out, out speech', and her arrogant manner caused enormous offence in Ireland. This was communicated to Ireland's friends in Britain, notably in the Conservative Party, who urged her to adopt a more placatory attitude. She was swayed, too, by the skilful diplomacy of FitzGerald and Barry, who swallowed their annoyance and set about repairing relations. Talks were entrusted to two teams, each composed of four brilliant officials. Both governments acted on their advice. The result was the Anglo-Irish Agreement, which gave the Irish government a recognised role in Northern affairs, exemplified by the creation of a secretariat based in Belfast.

The agreement, reached over the heads of the Northern parties, infuriated unionists. Hundreds of thousands attended mass meetings at which they listened to inflammatory speeches. Ian Paisley shouted: 'Never, never, never, never!' The Secretary of State, Tom King, was physically attacked. He observed caustically that unionists said no to everything, but sooner or later they would have to say yes to something.

Haughey's reaction, meanwhile, was disgraceful. Had he negotiated the agreement himself, he would have presented it as a nationalist triumph. Now he was petty enough to resent FitzGerald's success. He rejected the accord as a humiliating sell-out, and sent Brian Lenihan to the United States in the hope of undermining the consensus by persuading the Irish-American leaders to reject it. Lenihan, who knew that his mission was as hopeless as it was ill-advised, got a cold reception, in part because those leaders entertained deep and well-justified suspicions of Haughey dating from an incident that had occurred during his first period in office.

Irish-American opinion had long been divided between the moderates led by the 'Four Horsemen'—Senator Kennedy, Speaker O'Neill, Senator Daniel Patrick Moynihan and Governor Hugh Carey of New York—and the intransigents who varied from outright IRA supporters to people who simply disliked everything British and Irish co-operation with Britain. The latter, though less influential than the Four Horsemen, were well organised and well funded and had strong contacts with Fianna Fáil as well as Sinn Féin. Probably acting under Blaney's influence, Haughey decided to move Seán Donlon from the Washington embassy and send him to New York as ambassador to the United Nations. Donlon enlisted the aid of the Four Horsemen, who insisted that he must remain in Washington and that there must be no change, real or apparent, in Irish government policy.

At home, in 1985–86, it was made clear to Haughey that he was badly out of touch with public opinion, and at odds with much of his own party. Mary Harney, one of the most prominent younger figures in Fianna Fáil, quarrelled with him on the issue. Des O'Malley defied him on a separate question, contraception. Haughey imposed a three-line whip on Fianna Fáil deputies to vote against a family planning bill brought in by the coalition Health Minister, Barry Desmond of Labour. O'Malley abstained, withstanding ferocious threats, and made a famous speech in which he declared that 'I stand by the Republic.' He had already lost the Fianna Fáil whip, but that did not satisfy Haughey, who proceeded to have him expelled from the party. A meeting of the national executive duly obliged. Among the brave handful who opposed the expulsion was a young woman called Mary Hanafin, a future cabinet minister. Arguably this open vote, and the open votes on which Haughey insisted when Fianna Fáil parliamentary party meetings discussed his leadership, contravened the party's constitution, but once again Haughey got away with it.

However, his treatment of O'Malley had repercussions which would soon bring him grief. O'Malley, Harney and others disillusioned with both Fianna Fáil and Fine Gael founded the Progressive Democrats, who at the general elections of 1987 and 1989 would eat into the Fine Gael vote but, more significantly, would make it impossible for Fianna Fáil to achieve the Dáil majority which Haughey had confidently expected in both elections.

———

Gageby was delighted with an agreement which, as he saw it, gave the unionists the kicking they deserved. Although I did not share his almost irrational hatred of unionists, I largely agreed with him. Again and again, they had rejected every attempt to bring about equality for Catholics. The two governments had every right to impose a framework within which the Northern parties, if they so chose, could work together for a settlement based on power-sharing, much like Sunningdale. We did not know then that the settlement of 2007 would take a form very different from that of 1973–74, a *mariage de convenance* between the instigators of the Troubles.

Apart from his own prejudices, I think he was influenced, as usual, by John Hume, and also by a clever initiative from the foreign affairs department, in which I thought I detected the hands of Garret FitzGerald and Seán Donlon, by now secretary of Foreign Affairs. Gageby was invited to Iveagh House for a briefing and an advance sight of the document. His support was assured. However, he took it to excessive lengths.

Naturally he gave the event extensive coverage and published the text of the agreement in full. Fair enough, but he did not stop there. From time to time, he devoted a full page of the paper to a reprint of the text. Not only was this exceedingly odd when unaccompanied by any relevant report, it provoked resentment on my part for an unrelated reason. Gageby, as I have already said, took little interest in the requirements of the coalface workers in matters of production, including pagination. The number of pages in the paper was determined on the basis of the proportion of editorial matter to advertising, and the management disliked demands by the chief sub-editor and myself for extra pages when the news flow was exceptionally heavy. Gageby did not forbear to berate us, even when he himself had agreed to the change in pagination. Yet he now whimsically wasted space on republishing a document already in the public domain.

I incline to think that, somewhat as with his floating Brady's name in conversations with his private friends, he was trying to persuade himself, more than his readers, of the merits of the Anglo-Irish Agreement: specifically, that it constituted a stage on the road to a united Ireland. It did not, and neither have any of the subsequent political developments. Now and again some part of the truth—acknowledged, however unwillingly, by the people of the Republic—seemed to be making itself felt even by him. Once he mused, in print, that 'France was France without Alsace–Lorraine and Ireland is Ireland without the North.'

John Martin in *The Irish Times: Past and Present* says that during the last year of Gageby's reign I was regarded as the de facto editor. That overstates the case. I did what Gageby wanted, or—increasingly—what I thought he wanted. It was difficult for me to take any initiatives of my own apart from the scores of day-to-day decisions which the job entailed. Gageby scarcely listened to my demands for an improved design, and my pleas for a rapid and complete move to the new print technology were ignored or vetoed.

I did have the support, usually the enthusiastic support, of the staff. Most of them obeyed my instructions as faithfully as they had ever obeyed Gageby's. But in other ways, touch with reality was growing more feeble outside as well as inside the editor's office. A majority on the editorial committee engaged in self-delusion. Ideally they would have liked the next editor to be elected by the journalists, a system adopted by some enlightened newspapers. Had that been agreed, I would have had the support of at least 70 per cent—some of the more enthusiastic put it at 80–90 per cent, but that was unrealistic. I was also the choice, as Gageby and McDowell must have known, of the part of the intelligentsia who took an interest in the affairs of the *Irish Times*. One went so far as to seek supernatural aid. Breandán Ó hEithir, then living in Paris, sent me a postcard to tell me that he had lit a candle at the shrine of his 'favourite Virgin' in Notre Dame Cathedral. But I doubted that she would perform the same feat for me as she had done for King Pelayo at Covadonga.

There never was the remotest chance of an election. Instead, McDowell offered what he called 'a negative sieve', and the editorial committee accepted it. I was deeply unhappy. What did a negative sieve mean? Either it meant a veto or it meant nothing. And plainly it did not mean a veto.

Gageby announced his retirement on 30 August 1986. As a final (but not yet parting) gift, he ordered a late-night revamp of the paper to feature sensational coverage of a summer flash flood on the Dodder, which he had witnessed from his house. Nobody was even slightly injured, but hundreds of houses were flooded including, as it happened, that of the editor of the

Irish Independent, Vinny Doyle. Gageby's own house, on an eminence above the river, was untouched. Alarmist forecasts that bridges would be washed away were shown by morning to be ridiculous.

I suspect that those in charge of the print operation printed at most a few hundred copies for sale on the streets of Dublin and, much more to the point, for the editor to see. This was not the first example of nonsensical waste of money and labour, and I don't suppose it was the last.

My own not-quite-parting gift to the *Irish Times* followed the batty divorce referendum dreamed up by Garret FitzGerald. He had somehow persuaded himself that the electorate were ready to remove the constitutional ban. The opinion polls in the early part of the campaign seemed to bear out his optimism: they showed a large majority in his favour. But as the campaign went on, opinion swung against him. It was swayed by the activities of the conservative Catholic organisations, supported by the bishops and much of the minor clergy, who delivered inflammatory sermons reminiscent of an earlier age. But it may have been more greatly influenced by the fears of the rural population, especially the farmers and their wives. Campaigners told the wives that if we voted for divorce their husbands would leave them and take up with younger women, and they would lose their property rights. On polling day, the proposition was rejected by a whopping majority. The ban would not be removed for another two decades.

On the afternoon the result became clear I went into work to find most of the staff in the depths of depression. They had fervently supported the Liberal Agenda and hoped, notwithstanding the opinion poll evidence, for a successful outcome. I spent much of that evening rallying them, telling them that we would recover from the setback and live to fight another day. Gageby—unusually for him on an important occasion—was nowhere to be seen.

I was already out of sympathy with his attitude to the question. As an argument in favour of Irish unity, he had advanced the thesis that we needed to incorporate the large Northern Protestant population to help us to liberalise our constitution and laws. That always struck me as a patronising approach. We would embrace the Liberal Agenda when a Catholic majority came to defy the church, as had happened on contraception and would happen in the course of time on divorce and abortion too. The Northern Protestants, and the subject of a united Ireland, were not relevant.

The divorce referendum may be called the last nail in the coffin of

FitzGerald's coalition, but the coffin itself was constructed on more quotidian lines. By the summer of 1986 the government was in a state of decay, caused by disagreements between Fine Gael and Labour which made it impossible to bring the economy and the public finances under control. Unemployment and emigration—ominously, middle-class emigration—had soared. Plainly the coalition had lost any ability to govern. The mood of the country was dismal. Unprompted, I wrote an editorial which argued that there was no way in which the coalition could revive its own or the country's fortunes and that it might as well call a general election in the autumn instead of waiting until its term expired the following year. I submitted it to Gageby, who approved its sentiments but instructed me to add a line to the effect that, all this notwithstanding, FitzGerald should remain in office to nurture the Anglo-Irish Agreement. Readers had no difficulty spotting that this was a blatant contradiction of what had gone before. What were we trying to say?

Chapter 10 ✍

| 1986: DARK DAYS

Conor Brady in his memoirs says that he and I learned of Gageby's intention to retire at a meeting on 28 August at which arrangements were begun for the next steps. He is mistaken. If a meeting took place on that date, I was not present, and neither was another person he names as being present, the former assistant editor Dennis Kennedy. Kennedy was not there, and he could not have been there. He had left the paper and was living in Belfast. He pointed this out in a review of Brady's book which he wrote for a Dublin magazine.

Brady says that had the appointment of the new editor been made at once, there would have been no doubt about the outcome. True. But the appointment was not announced until 15 December. There was plenty of time for intrigue and treachery, which now reached their height.

Orderly arrangements were not made on 28 August or, to my knowledge, any other date. The interval of three and a half months was filled by confusion and demeaning antics, not all deliberately designed to undermine me but all, in one way or another, to my disfavour.

At the outset, McDowell told me that he wanted the members of the trust, who had got little out of their membership except IR£4,000 a year (since massively increased) to have a share of the limelight. This did not mean that he would allow them to have any real influence on the decision. Formally, the appointment would be made by a meeting of the full board, comprising the trust members and the executive directors. In reality, only four people would count: McDowell, Gageby, Louis O'Neill and Ken Gray. It could be assumed that O'Neill would support Brady and that Gray would take the same line as McDowell. Meanwhile, the trust members got lollipops in the form of the establishment of three-member sub-committees to interview several candidates.

That was farcical in itself and in the way it operated. Any foreign candidates enticed by a glowing advertisement inviting applications may have thought the operation was entirely above-board, but everybody in Dublin knew the choice rested between only two people. That must have been obvious to any members of the trust who still had their wits about them, but some were silly enough to grasp the opportunity for pointless posturing. One of the local applicants was Maurice Hearne, an editorial writer on the *Irish Independent*. He told me that he was interviewed in the private room in the Kildare Street and University Club where I had met McDowell so often. He described one of the three trust members who conducted the interview, Thekla Beere, a former government department secretary, as gesticulating and expostulating when he criticised the *Irish Times'* lack of professionalism: 'Oh! Mr Hearne, how could you say such a thing?'

I caught a glimpse of Thekla Beere shortly after it was all over. I was lunching with someone in the United Arts Club. She was at another table. As she rose to leave, she spotted me and dodged behind another person to avoid having to speak to me. I suspect that someone had told her what had really been in train.

I mention this degrading nonsense only because the trust's role may have had some minor significance, which I will discuss in a moment. To return to the events which immediately followed the announcement of 30 August: McDowell told me that in view of my standing in the race I need not submit an application, but he soon changed his mind and instructed me to do so. In addition, he required written presentations from Brady and myself setting out our views on the paper's character, ethos and so forth and our plans for the future; and he subjected me to no fewer than three formal interviews.

It seems that Brady submitted a lengthy document in which he discussed advertising and circulation in addition to editorial matters, and made proposals for expansion in such areas as consumer affairs. I confined myself to discussing the newspaper's ethos and modus operandi, and my plans to build on its existing strengths and reputation, in a document of about 2,000 words. McDowell read it before circulating it to the board. He was dissatisfied and told me to rewrite it. I did so, but the message remained the same. The *Irish Times* had a unique standing in Irish society. It was almost a great newspaper and could become a truly great newspaper. But in many ways it did not serve its readers well. Fundamentally, it lacked the consistency that should accompany its authority. This fault was reflected not only in editorial policy but in the writing quality, which varied from the excellent to the plodding and uninformed and at worst to gross errors in grammar, spelling and punctuation. Our supposed traditional standards in these matters must be upheld while we modernised and sharpened our focus.

I did not go into detail on news coverage, features, layout or pagination. I had firm ideas on all of these, which I wanted to implement urgently, but I saw no point in including them in my submission. The executive directors were supposed to understand these questions without being told, and the trust members would certainly not understand them. Neither would they understand it if I said that I meant to rid the paper of one of its besetting sins, self-indulgence, and insist on greater professionalism. No point in baffling them.

Yet I was even more dissatisfied than McDowell with what I had written and with the revised version. At the core of my discontent was my position, moral and practical, in relation to Gageby. The mugwumps on the trust had little interest in such things as design, but even the dimmest of them had some grasp of editorial policy and its defects. They wanted editorials that addressed the issues of the day in a pragmatic and comprehensible manner, not rambling thoughts. Most of them would have been gratified to hear me say that I would banish Wolfe Tone and Newgrange. No doubt McDowell would have been equally pleased if I had said so at one of our many meetings. But I had to remain loyal to Gageby, Wolfe Tone and Newgrange notwithstanding, even though I entertained a well-founded suspicion that he would not be loyal to me.

My suspicion deepened as the long-drawn-out process went on. Gageby's absences became more frequent, and more and more decision-making rested with me. I bore myself confidently: too confidently. The staff looked to me for leadership, and most of them felt it was only a matter of time, and not much time, until my position was confirmed. Among the majority, this mood prevailed throughout, but from about the middle of October those who looked into matters more deeply could see a change. For myself, I told those in whom I confided that I was determined to regard my chances as 50–50, but privately I could see the prize slipping out of my grasp.

About that time, it worried me to detect, as I thought, an increased aloofness in the attitude of both Gageby and McDowell towards me. The open favour for Brady's candidature on the part of the commercial executives was nothing new. McDowell had led me to believe that the role of the trust was insignificant. However, from time to time since then rumours have reached me of outside influence, possibly exerted through trust members. I have wondered whether someone had a word with James

Meenan—although, in view of his existing hostility to me, a word might not have been needed. At any rate, I was interviewed by one of the three-man trust panels at which nobody asked me a single question except Meenan, who chaired it. It was a profoundly unsatisfying encounter.

A more satisfactory interview, or so I thought at the time, was conducted by a panel composed of more knowledgable people, led by Gageby and McDowell. Gageby asked me whom I would appoint as deputy editor. (He seemed to be asking me what I would do when, not 'if', I got the job. If, as I believe, he had made up his mind years earlier to ensure that I never got it, this was a remarkable piece of deception.) I said I had one or two names in mind but did not wish to disclose them at that point. Nevertheless, he began to mention a name. McDowell stopped him. He then wrote something on a piece of paper and handed it to me. It was the right name: 'Joe Carroll'. That was perceptive of him, because I had never given him any hint that I had Carroll in mind. I may have expressed admiration for his work as a reporter.

McDowell asked me whether, as editor, I would retain Conor Brady's services. I replied: 'Certainly, so long as he does what I tell him.' Nobody made any comment.

Years later, I was angered to read a passage in Brady's memoirs in which he said that certain journalists expected promotion from me. He said in addition that I was popular among the left-wingers and had once stood as a Labour candidate. My candidature had occurred seventeen years earlier. On the more substantial point, I had never promised promotion to anyone. On the contrary, I had told one person, Mary Maher, that I would like to demote her, not promote her, because I wanted her to leave her executive job and go back to writing. I did not speak, then or later, to Joe Carroll. I had discussed my plans for the paper with just one person, who already held a very senior position. I have some reason to believe that Brady did not know how close I was to that man.

As decision time came near, I continued to behave as if all were well. I knew no other way to behave. Deep down, however, I knew that I was done for.

There were a few others who in their hearts knew, or at least feared, the same thing. With weeks to go, the editorial committee met—without my knowledge—and discussed whether they should make a demarche to McDowell. Two of the five members, Mary Maher and Noel McFarlane, voted to take some action. They were outvoted.

Could they have done me any good? In a word, no. McDowell might have wanted me to have the job, but by now the procedures he had set in train were unstoppable. They included (was this legal under the company's articles of association?) forbidding myself, Brady and two other members to attend the board meeting which ratified the decision already made in his discussions with Gageby, O'Neill and Gray. Everything depended on Gageby. Had he supported me, that would have been the end of it. It is hardly worth speculating whether the editorial committee might more profitably have approached him instead of McDowell, but the thought occurs to me that had they done so, both Gageby and McDowell would have supposed that they had acted at my instigation.

——

On the afternoon of Monday 15 December 1986 Thomas Bleakley McDowell handed me a most unwanted Christmas present.

The day had begun with a telephone call from my old and cherished colleague Peter Tynan O'Mahony, by then in retirement. He wanted to congratulate me on the elevation he expected for me, and to give me some sound advice, which he delivered at great length and in a ponderous manner.

At midday I went to see the dentist. He congratulated me on the dazzling appointment of which he had heard in a pub the previous night.

I knew better. Although I kept up appearances until the very last moment—and kept up my spirits, even in my unhappy private musings—I had every reason to expect bad news, not good.

The previous Thursday, McDowell had invited me to his Whitechurch mansion, where I listened to him, as I had listened on so many earlier occasions, rambling round the subject at issue. As always, he did almost all the talking. At a late stage, he began to hint at alternative appointments for me, for example London or Washington. I said, sharply enough, that I would prefer to be editor.

Nothing further of any consequence was said, and I told nobody about the conversation. But I could not misread the message, which confirmed not so much a doubt or a fear as a certainty. Had he intended to appoint me, he would surely have discussed with me my contract and my remuneration—and insisted on my disclosing Joe Carroll's name to him, along with the names of others whom I would wish to promote. Not even Gageby would have appointed anyone to a position of such consequence as deputy editor without McDowell's knowledge and consent. It was all over, or so I thought. There were more kicks to come.

On Monday, McDowell met me in the offices of a firm of accountants in Harcourt Street. The large building appeared to be deserted. We went upstairs, past empty rooms, into a corridor in which he had some difficulty finding the right office. He fumbled with keys. At last we got ourselves inside and seated. He muttered something about the necessary procedures having been observed, then he came, uncharacteristically, quickly to the point: 'We're giving the job to the younger man.'

Much as I had prepared myself, firmly as I had believed that I could come to the denouement with fortitude and without emotion, the words hit me like a physical blow. For a couple of seconds I was unable to make any reply.

He filled the silence by asking me if I would like a shoulder to cry on. He said that he had Bruce Williamson standing by, knowing how close I was to him. Or perhaps I would just like to be left alone in the room for a little while? For a mad moment I thought of asking him whether he meant to leave me with a revolver and a bottle of whiskey. Then I pulled myself together and told him that I would say only two things. One, I would do and say nothing undignified. Two, he must tell Gageby that when he made the announcement to the editorial staff, as he shortly would, on no account must he mention my name. He replied that this would be difficult. I said that, difficult or not, I insisted on it.

There was nothing more to be said, but he had not finished talking. He said that 'you're still Jim Downey.' Oh yes! I thought, the great Jim Downey with his career all behind him at the age of fifty-three. He also said that I must not give any radio or television interviews. I thought that pointless and bordering on the offensive.

Outside the building (still no sign of human life) he shook my hand and congratulated me on my dignity. This I considered much more offensive. What had he expected? Angry words? Violence? A tearful breakdown? What was his own notion of standards of behaviour? I made no reply, but climbed into my car and went home.

The house was empty. I was too agitated to sit down, read a book, watch television or listen to music. I paced about until Moira came home and calmed me. In the next couple of hours, she was followed by Rachel and Vanessa. Rachel, poor thing, was unable to contain her tears. She had lately graduated from journalism school and had been in the company of some of her former classmates when the news, which none of them expected, came through. To cheer us all up, I opened a bottle of champagne. By some chance, we had three in the house. One, an excellent vintage (1978), had been given to me weeks earlier, for unstated reasons, by T.B. McDowell.

Our conversation, devoted entirely to a discussion of what had happened in the *Irish Times* in the preceding months and years, was interrupted every few minutes by phone calls. At first I persuaded Moira to take the calls, but this was too burdensome for her. The callers ranged from close friends inside and outside the paper to people she hardly knew, or did not know at all. At last I agreed that I must answer the calls myself. I did not relish the task. Taking calls of commiseration is not an agreeable activity at best, and no amount of gratitude or courtesy could make me bear with one senior commercial executive who had the brass neck to tell me that he felt for me but had supported my rival. In other words, he claimed an influence denied to the journalists.

It was late at night, and the girls had gone to bed, before one of the callers informed me of something that angered me much more. That afternoon, Gageby had climbed on to a chair or a desk (subsequent accounts differed) in the newsroom and announced Brady's appointment. His words fell into an astonished silence. Then he said: 'Jim is being well looked after.'

Did he mean that as a deliberate insult, or did he just blurt it out when he saw the reaction to his statement? I think it was deliberate. I had tried to guard against patronising remarks by telling him, via McDowell, that he must not mention my name. I had feared something like this, but nothing quite so bad. He had spoken of me as if I were some old retainer, pensioned off after a lifetime of humble service, who should be grateful for any crumbs (they turned out to be small enough) his patrons chose to give him.

Furious and not entirely sober, I phoned McDowell and berated him for failing to keep Gageby quiet. He made a half-hearted attempt to conciliate me and said we would speak soon. Moira and I finished the last bottle and went to bed. I suppose I slept.

McDowell and I spoke again sooner than I had expected.

With wonderful timing, the *Irish Times* management had fixed 15 December as the date for the office Christmas party. While I was holding my own champagne-fuelled wake at home, the journalists and the commercial executives came together to celebrate a birth. The former were in no mood for celebration, but the latter were. A couple were so carried away by the success of 'our man' that they made provocative remarks. Now, they said, the hacks would know who was in charge. Scuffles broke out. Nobody was hurt.

This was not the last occasion on which my adversaries boasted of their success. Months later, one of them taunted Breandán Ó hEithir, who had to be restrained from hitting him.

McDowell used the incident at the office Christmas party to turn the tables on me. When he next phoned me, he said that the 'generosity' with which I would be treated depended on my kicking the staff into line. That stoked up my anger further. I was entirely innocent, and I had no intention of inciting any trouble. It would have run contrary to my obsession with behaving well and maintaining my dignity.

Worse was in store. On Christmas Eve I had lunch with one of the most senior journalists, a staunch supporter. We ate without appetite and drank hardly anything. When we mulled over the debacle, he gave his opinion that the events of the preceding months had made no difference: 'This decision was made years ago.' I went on to a party in the house of a like-minded person. When I came home, Moira told me that Gageby had telephoned twice. Impeccable timing again. While he was ringing, I had been telling the people I met—and I told others shortly afterwards—that they must do their best out of professional pride and that they must accept the promotions they would soon be offered.

———

McDowell now met me several times, mostly in a tolerably amiable atmosphere. He took me to lunch in his club and gave me some fine claret. When I remarked on the quality, he said that he had given Gageby a bottle (or bottles) of even better wine. Why on earth did he bother to tell me that? Possibly as a means of informing me, in his indirect way, that Gageby had not gone entirely willingly. If so, the wine was a sort of compensation for him. It was no compensation for me.

He chided me for not returning Gageby's phone calls. Douglas, he said, was most upset. I made no reply. I was not going to tell him what I was doing at the time of the calls. I saw no need to defend myself.

When we met in the bunker, the atmosphere was more businesslike. He sacked me from my job as senior deputy editor and forced me to resign from the board. He showed me the clause in the articles of association which provided that if I refused to resign he could sack me. I signed the piece of paper he put before me. All this was done in a light-hearted way. Only later did I discover that friends in the business community were angered when they heard of it, because a forced resignation suggests that someone has done something wrong, and I had done nothing wrong.

My friends inside the *Irish Times* were upset also. The medical correspondent, Dr David Nowlan, protested to Ken Gray, who told McDowell. I was summoned to another meeting, at which I felt obliged to say that I had made no complaint but had merely informed my friend of the true situation. McDowell seemed satisfied—not that I had anything to confess. Then Ken Gray popped out from behind a screen, like a character in a farce.

Earlier, McDowell had outlined three options to me: London, Washington, or early retirement. The terms for early retirement would have given me a pitifully small income. Had I been a little younger, I would have grabbed the Washington job with both hands, but at this stage it would have been too inconvenient for family reasons. McDowell bounced me into making an early decision, and I agreed to return to London.

A more delicate operation remained to be performed. McDowell invited me to meet himself and Brady in the bunker. I shook Brady's hand and wished him well—or perhaps I should say, wished the paper well. Then I went upstairs to an editorial conference chaired by him. It was an uncomfortable experience. People kept casting sly or puzzled looks at me. I said nothing. They could take my presence as an endorsement, or in any other way they wished.

I regarded all these proceedings as contemptible and humiliating. I would have felt even more disdain and helpless anger had I known the lies spread about me in the months before, of which I would hear sooner rather than later: excessive drinking and lacking the Protestant work ethic. The first was ironic if it came from Gageby, whose consumption of brandy had been awesome not long before. The second, which found its way into the senior common room in Trinity, was laughable. But there was a third, which gave a cold insight into the minds of the trust members. They had been told (by whom, I don't know, but clearly the intention was to delude them) that Brady was the choice of the staff. Presumably none of them checked.

Some little consolation came from a flood of cards and letters. Pat Foley, Donal's widow, wrote: 'I feel the same way I did in 1974—hopping mad.' Kevin Myers sent a note full of sympathy and insight. I valued his generosity greatly, because he and I had had strong differences over his political opinions and his writing style.

Breandán Ó hEithir, now back in Dublin, advised me never to forgive but to seek revenge. I said that people had destroyed their lives in the pursuit of revenge and in any case I had no means of achieving it. Forgiveness was another matter.

———

I went back to London to settle into a new office, this time in the PA–Reuters building in Fleet Street, and to look about for a place to live. In my hotel I found a message from Maeve Binchy, wisest and kindest of women. It consisted of a bottle of champagne, a guide to the best entertainments available, and a greetings card inscribed with an instruction that I was there to enjoy myself. All through the following year I would rejoice in the love of other friends, Mike Burns, Aidan Hennigan, Bernard Purcell, London editor of the *Irish Independent*—and the inimitable Gery Lawless.

I found Conor O'Clery in a state of suspended animation. The *Irish Times* has had praise lavished on it for the decision to make him the first Irish permanent correspondent in Moscow. But the decision was not the dashing new departure frequently claimed; it was a matter of expediency. Its real purpose was to make room for myself in London. O'Clery's appointment was announced at the same time as mine, but he had still to go through all the bureaucratic procedures required under the cumbersome communist system. Week after week dragged by while he waited for the Soviet embassy and Iveagh House to wring answers out of Moscow. It was tedious for him, because he was a social animal with innumerable contacts and he must have grown weary of hearing people asking him when he would leave. At last the procedures were completed and he began his spectacular new career as a foreign correspondent, serving in Asia and, most notably, in the United States.

For myself and my family, the inconvenience was less than a move to Washington would have entailed, but it was quite bad enough. Vanessa was still in University College Dublin. Moira divided her time between Dublin and London. Rachel came over to take up a job, for which she had been head-hunted, on a weekly paper aimed at the Irish community. We lived in a flat in Beckenham, greatly inferior to the pleasant little house we had occupied nearby in the early seventies.

But the flat was a trifle, and I could easily have found a better one. Now that my dealings with McDowell had ended, now that I could relax and need not maintain an outward appearance contrary to my inner feelings, my gloom increased. What gave me the most anguish was to contemplate the people who had shafted me. I had believed that they and I were engaged in a great enterprise and that I could go on to make it greater. Instead, my career was in ruins and I was left to contemplate what a bloody fool I had been.

There is a scene in that marvellous movie *Some Like It Hot*, in which a friend tries to console Marilyn Monroe when she thinks she has been dumped by Tony Curtis, masquerading as the heir to Shell Oil. She says that wherever she goes in the world during the rest of her life, she will always see the Shell sign and be reminded. No matter where I went or what I did or how long I lived, I would never escape far more numerous reminders of the *Irish Times*.

I renewed my acquaintance with the Palace of Westminster, almost though not quite as jolly as ever, but with a noticeably lower rate of alcohol consumption. I did not bestir myself to seek out exclusive stories, and indeed the political scene in early 1987 was not such as to demand great exertion. Margaret Thatcher would shortly call an election. She would assuredly win it. The prospect did not please me. The need for some of her reforms was undeniable, ever since Labour fumbled their opportunities. But even if I could ignore (and I could not) the devastation of communities that followed her victory in the miners' strike, I could not abide her philistinism, which reached its lowest point with her breathtaking statement that 'there is no such thing as society.'

My opinion of her fell further during and after the extraordinary general election campaign. Nothing could have prevented her from winning, but she behaved as if she were fighting a close contest. She quarrelled with her closest associates, like Norman Tebbit. She disliked her party's advertising campaign, and brought one lot of advisers into 10 Downing Street through the back door while the rival lot left by the front door. I attended her daily press conference on 'Wobbly Thursday', a week before the election, when her campaign stuttered. That may have owed something to a minor health problem, but the assembled media felt that, as we say in Ireland, 'she was losing the run of herself.' This was close to the truth. Shortly afterwards she lost the services of the invaluable Willie Whitelaw, who resigned as leader of the House of Lords, pleading ill-health, and of her superb cabinet secretary, Robert Armstrong. Over time, it came to be accepted that from then on she was out of control. Her insistence, against all sage advice, on bringing in an unfair and unpopular poll tax, and falling out with an excellent Foreign Secretary, Sir Geoffrey Howe, on the issue of Europe, would lead to her defenestration by her own cabinet.

Labour, meanwhile, had recovered to some extent from the divisions of the early eighties and the disastrous leadership of Michael Foot. The party owed a great deal of the improvement in its fortunes to Neil Kinnock, who had regained most of his optimism and high good humour and who initiated a successful reform programme with important help from Peter Mandelson. It profited from the failures of the Liberal–Social Democrat alliance. Soon I would witness the long-drawn-out suicide of the Liberal Party at two conferences, the first at Harrogate, the second at Blackpool. But if Labour was no longer 'unelectable', it was still a long way from being elected, and Kinnock would never be prime minister.

The Tories, as the party in power, were inevitably more interesting. I liked the 'wets', much as I had liked the very similar pro-Europeans in an earlier age. Some of them were the very same people, like Kenneth Clarke, who might have made a great Conservative leader if the party had not been so hopelessly divided on the European question.

Among the liveliest of my new acquaintances was another 'wet', Richard Needham, Earl of Kilmorey. Later, as a Northern Ireland junior minister, he gained brief notoriety when he expressed his scathing view of Margaret Thatcher on his car phone. The IRA had tapped his phone, and the tape got into the public domain and reached the ears of the Prime Minister. To her credit, she ignored it.

Needham was a splendid mimic. He could have made a fortune on television. He had worked in South Africa for an Afrikaner tobacco baron and had a perfect command of the Afrikaner accent. In Belfast, he found time to get instruction in the various Northern accents, not just the regional variations but the differences between, for example, east and west Belfast.

We lunched together one day in London, after which we returned to the Palace of Westminster through the St Stephen's entrance. One of the first statues one sees there is of Henry Grattan, who contrary to the usual Irish assumption did not disappear from the scene after the dissolution of the Irish House of Commons but sat for twenty years at Westminster. Needham remarked: 'Our lot got made earls for supporting him.' I said: 'I think, Richard, your lot probably got made earls for opposing him' (meaning, on the Act of Union in 1800, which Grattan famously denounced). At a very high-powered conference which we both attended at one of the Oxford colleges, the wine was, most unusually, very bad, and sparse to boot. At last, dinner guests began to club together to buy wine for themselves and those nearby at a laughable £2 per bottle. Needham saved himself and his neighbour, Tim Pat Coogan, £2 by calling the waiter and saying that 'Mr Coogan has got a bad bottle. You had better bring us another.' The waiter could see that they had finished the first bottle. While he went off with bad grace to fetch the wine, Coogan expostulated, whereupon Needham said: 'Yes, and that's how we got the land off the Catholics, too, and held on to it.' He was amused that anyone should care about his little manoeuvre, or whatever deals his ancestors had cut in 1800 or how they had grown rich in a previous age.

I went to the theatre. I took pleasure in the company of artists and theatre people in the Chelsea Arts Club, to which I had access by virtue of my membership of the United Arts Club in Dublin. I attended many lively parties, some in the Irish embassy. At one of these, Mike Burns noticed a familiar face among the waiters.

He had lately settled in as the RTÉ London correspondent. Before living in London full-time, he had been back and forth, setting up a new studio. On these trips, he customarily stayed in the Irish Club, but on one occasion there were no vacant rooms and the club sent him to a bed-and-breakfast establishment in Kensal Rise, since partly gentrified but then very much a 'low-rent' area. He didn't mind. The sheets were clean, the Irish breakfast was good, and there were no formalities like signing registers.

When he paid the bill on leaving, the proprietor said: 'Do you mind me asking … isn't your name Mike Burns?'

'Yes.'

'Do you mind me asking … didn't you use to be on the radio at home?'

'Yes.'

'And on television?'

'Yes.'

'Do you mind me asking … didn't you use to be a … star?'

'Well …'

'Do you mind me asking … haven't you come down in the world?'

When the proprietor, in his second capacity as a waiter, saw Burns at the embassy, he may have concluded that his former guest had not fallen too far in the world.

The Kensal Rise bill, by the way, must have been tiny by comparison with the one presented to Burns, Hennigan and myself for a magnificent dinner, in a private room in the very grand Boodle's Club. It was in honour of retiring officials from Dublin and Stormont, and was organised by Ted Smyth, at this time press counsellor at the London embassy and a member of Boodle's. Burns and I would of course get our shares repaid when we submitted our next expenses claims to our employers. How would Hennigan fare with the infamously parsimonious *Irish Press*? Try as I might, I could never afterwards make him tell me if he had to pay out of his own pocket.

But the social life did not prevent me from having nightmares every night for a year. Attempts to comfort me were unavailing. One was made by Fergus Pyle, of all people. When he visited London I took him to dinner, and he ate and drank heartily: his own travails had not affected his appetite. He called me 'the journalist's journalist', the ultimate professional (he could have added, by comparison with Gageby, the brilliant amateur). Poor fellow! He was quite well aware of his own failings.

My work was pleasant, my position privileged, but as time went by, I felt more and more out of place. At one time, I could have happily forsaken the ambition to edit the *Irish Times* in favour of writing political commentary for the paper, and I would not have been worried about 'coming down in the world'. But that was no longer an option. In the Westminster lobby, I looked around at men in a somewhat similar situation to mine, men who had once been thought front-runners for the editorship of Fleet Street newspapers. They were writing political colums—but for other papers. I began to realise that I had made a bad mistake by not severing my connection with the *Irish Times* decisively, in December 1986; and I began to ask myself what I could and should do now.

Throughout, I was still obsessed with good behaviour. I wrote to Bruce Williamson, knowing that he would pass the letter on to McDowell, to tell him that if I chanced to meet Douglas Gageby I would be civil to him. McDowell thereupon invited me to one of the ghastly lunches that followed board meetings. Gageby greeted me warmly, I responded with (I hope) cool civility. They insisted that I should cross the room to speak to James Meenan, who dismissed me with his customary cold contempt. Another typical reward for my silly attempts to behave well.

At that point I had not yet decided on my next move, but as the months passed my ideas took firm shape. One answer had always been obvious.

For many journalists of my generation, the dream had always been to run their own paper, even if only a provincial weekly: not just to edit but to own it, free of a proprietor's whims. I decided to launch a national weekly devoted to politics and the arts. Apart from my own desires, I believed (as I still believe) that Ireland needed such a journal.

The next time I went to Dublin, I sought a meeting with McDowell and told him that I wanted to leave the paper, but I would have to get far better compensation than he had offered earlier. He made a much-improved offer, which I accepted. It comprised a tax-free lump sum, a pension and a widow's pension. I calculated that I could launch the new publication with my lump sum and the money I raised among my friends. My pension was far too small to live on. The *New Nation*—not a weekly but a monthly publication, as those I consulted wisely insisted—would have to prosper.

It did not. It survived for only ten issues. Regrettably, those who had invested lost their money; less regrettably, since the responsibility was all mine, I lost a lot more. Yet it deserved better, not so much because of the political writings by myself and the few people I managed to recruit as because of the splendid book reviews commissioned by my literary editor, Professor Terence Brown, who got a miserly reward for his work.

In retrospect, I reckon that in order to succeed, the *New Nation* would have needed at least five times, more likely ten times, the amount of capital available to me. Many similar enterprises have failed for the same reason. The exceptions, alas, tend to be the journals that preach the current modish, and grotesquely ill-named, 'neo-conservatism'.

———

In the first issue of the *New Nation*, published in November 1988, I wrote a piece entitled 'Our Weird Consensus'. It criticised the political and economic consensus which had developed since Charles J. Haughey's return to office at the beginning of the previous year.

They say that oppositions do not win elections, governments lose them. The FitzGerald coalition was already dead on its feet when it lost the 1987 general election. The newly-founded Progressive Democrats cut heavily into the Fine Gael vote. They did much less damage to Fianna Fáil, but they prevented Haughey from achieving an overall Dáil majority and his new government could be brought down at any time by defections or by deputies' absence through illness.

He and his outstandingly competent and tough Finance Minister, Ray MacSharry, set immediately about repairing the shaky economy. For this, he has had all the credit due to him and more besides. Such was the calamitous state of the public finances that he had no choice but to cut and cut again. Frank Cluskey commented that 'Mao Tse-tung couldn't have done anything different.' Nevertheless, MacSharry deserves generous praise for his courage.

The Fine Gael leader, Alan Dukes, made a speech in which he outlined what became known as the Tallaght Strategy, from the location in which he delivered it. He said that his party would support the new government's restrictive measures in the national interest. He was motivated both by patriotism and by expediency. He had lately won the party leadership as FitzGerald's hand-picked candidate in a vote of the parliamentary party— by a margin which was not publicly disclosed. Many in Fine Gael would have preferred Peter Barry. Dukes wanted to buy time in which to copperfasten his leadership.

The Tallaght speech shocked the party. Deputies and grassroots thought that Fine Gael should have mounted the kind of opportunistic opposition characteristic of Fianna Fáil and brought down the minority government at the first opportunity, on some issue on which Labour and the PDS would have supported them. Longer-headed people thought that while Dukes was right to endorse the necessary cuts in services, he had undermined, instead of strengthening, his position in his own party. Ruairi Quinn, afterwards leader of the Labour Party, told me: 'He should have done it but he shouldn't have said it.'

The consensus extended much more widely than its parliamentary manifestation. In particular, the business community, the media and a majority in the trade union movement formed part of it. Unions with all or most of their members in the public sector had a great deal to gain from 'national partnership agreements' which would trade tax cuts for pay restraint and which gave the unions a share in a large range of public policy formation. For two decades, the system would be nurtured by a great negotiator, Bertie Ahern, first as Labour Minister, then as Taoiseach.

But where did that leave parliament? And where did it leave public discourse? In years to come Stephen Collins, of the *Sunday Tribune* and later of the *Irish Times*, was probably the first political journalist to attack the system as undemocratic and as contributing to the irrelevance of the Dáil. My own criticism in 1988 was founded more on my fears for the level of public discourse.

Seán Mac Reamoinn was a close friend of mine and had been even closer to Donal Foley, whom he encouraged in his commitments to liberal Catholicism and the Irish language. He edited a delightful book, *The Pleasures of Gaelic Poetry*, and contributed to upmarket journals like the *Tablet*. He was better known as a wit. He made a gloss on the maxim that 'inside every fat man is a thin man trying to get out' with the quip (wrongly attributed to Seamus Kelly) that 'outside every thin woman is a fat man trying to get in.' On his more serious side, he was one of the founders of a left-wing Catholic journal, *Alpha*, whose birth coincided with that of the *New Nation*. The editor, Peadar Kirby, constantly denounced the 'corrosive cynicism' which he saw as rampant in our society. I could not have known how feeble Irish public discourse would become over the next twenty years, and Kirby can hardly have known how much that would swell, and be swollen by, the cynicism he deplored.

Haughey for all his posturing as a democrat, a patriot and a lover of the arts and the company of intellectuals made the biggest contribution of the generation to cynicism and corruption. He did not introduce corruption into Irish political and business life—no society is free of it—but he brought it to unimagined new heights and his very presence at the head of affairs gave a nod-and-wink sanction to the practitioners.

The calamitous consequences, which would contribute heavily to the eruption of the economic and financial crisis in 2008, included apathy and undue scepticism on the part of the electorate, expressed in the common phrase 'they're all the same.' This is unfair to the decent majority in Fianna Fáil and most other parties, and makes it harder to identify and punish the numerous real culprits.

But corruption in any case is inevitable in the context of a sudden and enormous increase in wealth and a gigantic property bubble. It can be controlled only by endless vigilance, stringent regulation and strict accountability. From 1987 onwards, and especially during the Celtic Tiger boom which lasted, roughly speaking, from 1993 to 2007, all of these went out of the window. Bribes to councillors brought appalling planning decisions, leading to social and environmental disasters. Parts of our hitherto incorruptible public service came on board.

Corruption, however, was only one element in the endless undermining of the administration and the parliamentary system. The crucial damage was inflicted by the ever-increasing denial of accountability. By 2008 the Dáil, sitting for fewer than a hundred days a year and dominated by a government without a legislative programme, would become powerless and almost irrelevant. Over the years, hundreds of quangoes had been established, accountable to nobody and giving ministers a shield behind which they can hide. The most notorious example is the Health Service Executive. Meanwhile, mandarins resist the politicisation of the civil service itself, but they have fought a losing battle, and no wonder: since 1987 Fianna Fáil have been in office, in one coalition or another, for all but two and a half years.

The beneficiaries have been the rich, especially developers—and the public service, who have profited in a remarkable degree from a myth which grew up in the 1990s. According to the myth, private sector employees had gained the greatest benefits from the boom. This applied with special force to the new high-technology entrepreneurs and to exceptionally highly-skilled people working for multinational companies, thousands of whom were thought to earn over a million a year. In point of fact only a handful earned anything like that, and those few who did got the market rate for their work. They also ran the risks associated with markets, and many lost their jobs in the 'dotcom meltdown' of the year 2000. But the government set up a committee to 'benchmark' public service and public sector workers, to bring them up to the supposed earnings in the private sector. Evidently the benchmarking committee, like the government, subscribed to the myth. It made a series of recommendations, the criteria for which were never published. In the outcome, average public service earnings rose to an average far higher than the private sector average, at the expense of the taxpayers.

Then and since, there has been too little public protest at the atrocious way the country is run. And there are obvious reasons. Living standards rose. Until 2007, we had virtually full employment, by contrast with the earlier high unemployment and emigration which we had almost taken for granted. Universal free higher education (university tuition fees were abolished by a Labour Party minister) encouraged parents' confidence in their children's opportunities in life. Happy with such comforts, people by and large were too willing to put up with the glaring inadequacies in health, transport and other services and to ignore the corruption and the imminent crisis in education. They had their discontents, above all the drugs crisis, the rate of serious crime and the growing public disorder, but they heard few calls for radical reform of the system and if they did hear them they did not believe that their own participation in democracy would bring it about.

| 1990: A NEW START

R eform of one particular kind was urgent, and even if I did not have a publication of my own in which I could thunder for it, I was happy to campaign for it in a different role.

While I was still editing the *New Nation*, the *Irish Independent* invited me to contribute occasional articles. The first approach came from Gerry O'Regan, then deputy editor, but I thought I detected the hand of the editor, my old *Irish Press* comrade and *Irish Times* Club drinking buddy Vinny Doyle, who in his own unique way was as much a marvel of Dublin journalism as Douglas Gageby.

The *Irish Independent* was founded by William Martin Murphy in 1905. Under the ownership of Murphy, one of the most successful Irish businessmen of the age and a Home Rule member of the House of Commons at Westminster, it rapidly became the highest-selling newspaper in the country. Among his other enterprises was the Dublin United Tramways Company. He abhorred trade unions, and his confrontation with the union led by 'Big Jim' Larkin and James Connolly brought about the 'great lock-out' of 1913, when thousands of workers' families came close to starvation. The Catholic church arrayed itself in all its might on Murphy's side. When the union chartered a ship to take children to Liverpool, where working-class families could at least afford to give them something to eat, clerics mounted a protest on the quayside in an attempt to prevent them from boarding. It was only one incident in what the church, and the paper, saw as a war against communism and revolution.

Murphy has never been forgiven for the events of 1913, nor has he been forgiven for an editorial published by his newspaper in the aftermath of the Easter Rising in 1916.

The leaders of the insurrection, and large numbers of their followers, were sentenced to death under martial law. Most of them were reprieved;

fifteen were shot. The executions were not carried out all at once but piecemeal, over a period of weeks. To add to the horror, their families and sympathisers did not know who would live and who would die, or when. One likened it to watching 'blood seeping under the door'.

In the midst of this, the *Independent* called for leniency for the rank and file among the captured insurgents but harsh treatment for the remaining leaders under sentence of death. Not only could the demand for strong measures have only one meaning, the targets were equally clear. The two leaders still alive were Seán Mac Diarmada and Murphy's old enemy, the socialist revolutionary James Connolly. Both were shot. Connolly met his death propped up in a chair. He was unable to stand, having been gravely wounded in the fighting.

The *Irish Times* took an almost identical editorial line, but the *Irish Times* was a unionist paper and the *Irish Independent* a nationalist publication, owned by a former nationalist MP. The blame fell on Murphy personally, and that has remained largely the case to this day—unjustly, as it would appear. Murphy said privately that he did not approve of the sentiments expressed in the editorial, but felt that he had to maintain public silence because he did not wish to let down the editor, T.R. Harrington. When he visited London, where he had many political and business contacts, it incensed him to hear people speaking with approval of the executions. That, he said, 'got my Irish blood up.'

John Dillon, deputy leader of the Home Rule party, protested (to an unsympathetic House of Commons audience) both on moral and expedient grounds. He foresaw that the executions would swing Irish opinion away from moderate nationalism towards support for another insurrection. Indeed they did, along with other British mistakes such as the ill-judged and failed attempt to introduce conscription to Ireland in 1917–18.

None of this, however, prevented the *Irish Independent* from achieving the highest circulation of any paper in the country and establishing itself as the organ of Catholic Middle Ireland. Its opinions, cogently and often elegantly expressed, were those of the Catholic middle class, urban and rural; in other words, extremely conservative. After independence, it fervently supported the provisional government in the civil war, and it continued to support Cumann na nGaedheal and their Fine Gael successors through numerous political upheavals. Its dedication to the church, expressed both in its reverential treatment of papal and episcopal utterances and in publishing clerical minutiae, was total. Meanwhile, its news coverage was unrivalled and remained so despite the best efforts of the *Irish Press* from 1931 onwards. And no rival came near it in its appeal to advertisers.

Under the ownership of the Murphy family, but more so after the advent of Tony O'Reilly, it continually expanded its operations, launching or acquiring new titles and eventually becoming the core of a global media empire. Throughout, the market-leading morning paper sailed on.

But by the 1980s old formulae needed revision. The revision carried out by a new editor, the then still youthful Doyle, made the old guard among the journalists and some in the management shudder.

It was signalled by his decision to support the proposal to legalise divorce in 1986. At the time, the 'Catholic' newspaper's favour for divorce legislation alienated the more conservative readers and caused a temporary loss of advertising, but over the years that followed his judgment would be vindicated. Two decades on, Doyle's achievement can be summed up simply. He accommodated the *Irish Independent* to the revolutionary social changes then occurring or about to occur, while maintaining its standing as the newspaper of Middle Ireland—which itself has changed beyond the recognition of his predecessors.

Something else was about to change: my relationship with him. We would remain drinking companions, enjoying regular Wednesday-night sessions in a pub near the Indo office along with Michael Wolsey, then deputy editor of the *Independent*. At work we became firm comrades, and I developed an admiration for Doyle that none of his eccentricities could diminish. Long after, on the night he retired, he said to me: 'Never a cross word.' It was true.

My first impressions of Abbey Street were far more positive than I had expected. I might regard D'Olier Street as my real home, but I found the *Independent* infinitely more professional and more news-conscious. If I sighed over having been denied the chance to reform the lackadaisical and self-indulgent culture of the *Irish Times*, working for Doyle was exciting for an old-time news man like myself.

To be sure, he and his editorial executives might sometimes take their enthusiasm too far. As they said themselves, he would 'do anything for a story'. Having got hold of a good one, he and they would exert themselves to see how much they could 'firm it up'. Can we say this? Will the facts we know for sure support such-and-such a conclusion? Finally, will we go for it? Occasionally that ended in going too far, and perhaps falling foul of the libel laws or the NUJ code of practice. But old-timers who cling to the time-honoured belief that boundaries are there to be tested have the right attitude. Heaven help journalism if the new generation loses it.

I will write in due course about an epochal decision to breach boundaries deliberately, that of Geraldine Kennedy in 2006. Would Doyle have published the story which sparked off Bertiegate and would bring about, eighteen months later, Bertie Ahern's premature resignation as Taoiseach? Would I? Of course. But an editor has to make many fine judgments, especially about legal advice. The country has become so litigious that quite innocuous material has to be referred to lawyers, and the difficulties of carrying out worthwhile investigative journalism are enormous. We shall see whether the advent of a Press Ombudsman and a Press Council will improve our lives. That will not happen unless the government delivers on its side of the bargain, reform of the defamation law, and by the end of 2008 the reform still had not made its appearance.

Doyle's working methods were extraordinary. I firmly believe in 'hands-on' editing, but I found it amazing when I first saw him, as was his custom on Friday nights, sitting at the back desk with his sleeves rolled up, performing the function of a night editor or chief sub-editor. That sometimes included drawing page designs on paper, the system that preceded computerised screen layout. It amused me to see that his proficiency as a layout artist was at about the same level as my own, in other words barely average. You can't have everything.

He had often been accused of 'lifting' stories: having reports from the first editions of other newspapers rewritten and published without sufficient checking and without attribution. By my time, he had abandoned the practice, whether because of pressure from his own staff and from the NUJ, or because of the mellowness of increasing age, or because of the danger that the other paper's story might be totally wrong. One night, we were chatting about instances of reporters allowing themselves to be carried away and writing stories unsupported by the facts. I instanced a striking example from the *Irish Times*, published shortly before I joined the *Independent*, and said: 'I can't understand why nobody spotted that it simply couldn't be correct. At least,' I added cheekily, 'you didn't lift that one, Vinny.' He confessed that he had thought quite seriously of lifting it before his better judgment prevailed.

Here I may as well make a confession of my own. I pride myself on a life-long adherence to the highest standards of journalism, but I take a more tolerant view of lifting than some of my colleagues. Not many editors, deputy editors or night editors of considerable newspapers could say with their hands on their hearts that they have never been tempted to take a chance on lifting a story whose importance and plausibility could not be ignored.

I have never known anyone more steeped in the craft than Doyle or better informed about the newspaper business in general. He took a passionate interest in the ups and downs of newspapers, the rises and falls in circulation, the takeover bids and commercial decisions, not just in the Independent group but far more widely. He greatly admired the *Daily Mail* and in particular its long-serving and immensely successful editor David English. The *Mail*'s politics chimed with his own. It did not chime with mine, and I viewed with a mixture of amusement and horror the way it mixed, and still mixes, its political prejudices with its news coverage. But I admired its attention to every little detail, and its unerring aim for the 'G-spot' of its readers, almost as much as Doyle did.

He tried consciously to suppress, but occasionally gave in to, his own sensationalist instincts in the interest of keeping the paper in the middle of the market, in both commercial and journalistic terms. That meant performing a fine balancing act which he carried out in the normal style, by giving prominence to sensational stories (especially about crime, an obsession which has come to be shared by almost everyone) while at the same time publishing well-informed and well-written analytical pieces about domestic and foreign events. He recognised the talents of David McKittrick and of Robert Fisk, possibly the best reporter in the world and without compare in his writings on the Middle East. He was lucky in that at the time of the Iraq war he had Fisk's reports available to him because he took a news service from the *Indo*'s sister paper, the *Independent* of London.

He was lucky, too, in that he had in Wolsey a deputy whom he could trust completely. Wolsey was an honest man, a total professional, and a thinker. He was invaluable to Doyle; and in time, he would become invaluable to myself in a different way. We constantly discussed, often at considerable length, the handling of editorials and 'thinkpieces'. We did not always agree, but I always profited from our conversations.

Although Doyle never quarrelled with Wolsey or myself, he often quarrelled with others. For one thing, he was combative by nature; for another, he seldom bothered to explain how some course of action he required of a person (usually an editorial executive) was necessary. Those who questioned his decisions got brusque answers, and those passing by his office heard loud voices. It was fairly clear that confrontations also occurred with senior management over such questions as budgets, but he never spoke about them to me. He was immensely discreet, and as to myself, the less I knew about the internal politics of the Independent group the better I liked it: I had been more than sufficiently bruised by the *Irish Times* office politics.

When I began to attend editorial conferences, I witnessed no confrontations to speak of. Doyle did not believe in wasting time conducting 'inquests' into the blunders of the previous night. Reprimands were rare, and surprisingly mild. It tickled me to observe once or twice that the culprits did not seem to realise that they had been told off.

Yet he had strong opinions, not to say prejudices, about almost everything from politics to art. His favourite novelist was not one of the classical writers, but Norman Mailer, whose readers can be sure of sensation. He underestimated his own grasp of politics and political personalities, subjects on which he was very shrewd. I shared one of his particular likings, for Albert Reynolds. Reynolds was a most unpopular Taoiseach, and he made some colossal errors of judgment. Under his leadership, Fianna Fáil attained a record low 39 per cent of the vote. (It has been forgotten that the second, third and fourth record lows at general elections were scored by the man with the supposed magic touch, Bertie Ahern.) But Reynolds played a shrewd and skilful part in Northern affairs. Lately it has been all but written out of history, but Doyle and I recognised it. When he was forced to resign, he told Doyle: 'No regrets, Vinny, apart from one thing. I had something going in the North.' It would remain for Ahern to complete the 'something'.

Doyle had a particular dislike of RTÉ, which he regarded as cutting into the advertising revenue of the print media: he had an exaggerated view of the damage thus caused. He somehow convinced himself that RTÉ's dual revenue stream, from the licence fee and from advertising, was unique in Europe: it was not. His complaints about the station may or may not have influenced readers and they probably did no harm one way or the other, but they coincided with another, unrelated campaign, this one waged by the *Sunday Independent* against an imaginary RTÉ–*Irish Times* 'liberal' axis. People who are prejudiced against the Independent group tend to assume that the papers owned by it take an identical line. It is impossible to persuade them that they have their own, sometimes conflicting, editorial policies. I cannot count the number of times I heard it alleged that 'Independent Newspapers' opposed the Northern peace process. In point of fact, the *Irish Independent* consistently supported the process notwithstanding its deep reservations about the rise of Sinn Féin. It stood by Reynolds at one bleak moment when it appeared that hope of turning the IRA to non-violence had evaporated. An editorial adopted a gloomy tone but went on to say that Reynolds still stood by his belief in ultimate success, and that his optimism must be taken seriously. Reynolds assumed that the chief editorial writer, Seán Cantwell, had written the leader. He instructed Seán Duignan: 'Tell Cantwell that he's got it right.' Actually I had written it, but Cantwell would have said the same things.

A little story against myself: After Reynolds reached agreement with John Major on what amounted to a joint Anglo-Irish Northern policy and scored a temporary triumph when the IRA declared a ceasefire, I said to him: 'Albert, I never doubted you.' He gave me a funny look. Like everybody else, I had had my doubts, and he knew it.

He knew equally well where stories, and memorable phrases, came from. He got a bad press, but he might have got a worse one had it not been for Duignan's enormous popularity. Duignan wrote a hilarious book, *One Spin on the Merry-Go-Round*, based on the diaries he had kept during his time as press secretary to Reynolds. In it he tells of a lunch with me at which, when into our second bottle of wine, we discussed the nervousness of Reynolds and his ministers, who feared that they might lose the referendum on the Maastricht Treaty in 1993. I asked what they were going to do to win the electorate over.

'We'll have to strike terror into their hearts.'

I wrote a piece for the *Irish Independent* in which I quoted this comment. As always, I tried to conceal my source, hoping Reynolds might think that it came from some minister. But he knew at once, and chided Duignan.

Doyle showed himself at his most combative, not on policy questions but when it came to the endless war over the annual circulation figures. Newspaper editors and managements find ways to present their figures, good or bad, in the most favourable light. In the case of the *Indo*, Doyle presented them in his own incomparable way. Late in his reign the *Examiner*, edited by Brian Looney, announced its intention to achieve a genuine national circulation and overtake the sales of the *Irish Independent*. The *Examiner* is a very good newspaper, but the notion of a Cork-based paper beating the giant *Indo* was far-fetched. When the circulation figures showed that the *Examiner* had not only failed in this aim but that its sales in Dublin were too small to measure, Doyle wrote a few triumphant paragraphs which appeared on the front page of the *Irish Independent*. Our production editor, Michael Hilliard, chuckled with me over the way the piece was written. I said: 'The words sledgehammer and nut come to mind.' Afterwards, we teased Doyle. He was not in the least embarrassed. The following day, a longer piece appeared 'by Garret O'Connor', a byline he sometimes used. It repeated not only the sentiments of the previous day, but whole paragraphs word for word. Doyle was not a man to be put off by little jokes about sledgehammers and nuts.

On the night he retired, he was surrounded in a local pub by staff members weeping into their pints. Brian Looney came in. Instead of ordering a drink, he stood in front of Doyle and delivered a prolonged impromptu eulogy. Sam Smyth interrupted the flow to say: 'You're not auditioning, Brian.' Looney was not auditioning but speaking from the heart. Well done.

———

As time went by, my contributions to the *Independent* grew more frequent. I wrote comment and analysis on both domestic and foreign affairs, and editorials in the absence of Seán Cantwell. Then and later, there was no interference with my byline pieces: I could write what I liked, subject to the usual constraints in relation to libel, contempt of court and good taste. Editorials are a horse of a different colour. A leader writer is not employed to express his or her own opinions but those of the editor. I had done that in the *Irish Times* and had no compunction about doing the same in the *Irish Independent*.

That does not have to reduce an editorial writer to a mere hack. Doyle, Wolsey and other senior people consulted me and took my opinions on board. I exerted some influence on the paper's policy on several issues, notably the abortion referendum of 2002. I was the first person in Abbey Street—possibly the first in the Irish media world—to spot that the referendum proposal was not 'liberal', as the Fianna Fáil–Progressive Democrat government claimed, but yet another attempt to overturn the Supreme Court judgment in the 'x' case. This judgment had legalised abortion if a danger existed to the life of the mother, and held that a threat of suicide constituted such a danger. The *Irish Times* somehow failed to see the core point of the government's proposal and carried an editorial supporting it. In the face of its readers' outrage, it quickly reversed its line. When chided for inconsistency, it weakly pleaded that it had misunderstood the issue. The *Irish Independent* made no recommendation one way or the other. The proposal to overturn the Supreme Court judgment was narrowly defeated, not because of anything the newspapers said but because the conservative camp was split. Abortion legislation will come eventually, thereby completing the main points of the Liberal Agenda.

As was obvious to all with an interest in these matters, Doyle employed me as part of his liberalising policy, as well as for authoritative comment on politics and style of writing. He and Cantwell had had many sharp differences of opinion. Cantwell was a sweet man, well informed, widely read, interested in the sensational current events in Russia and one of the few Russian speakers in the country, but deeply conservative and imbued with the old *Irish Independent* values, like a fondness for Fine Gael. During the general election campaign of 1992 I asked him jestingly: 'What line are you going to take, Seán? Anyone but Fianna Fáil?'

By then, however, old allegiances had been shaken by the enormous changes in social attitudes, in the political system and in the massive economic improvement which would soon earn Ireland the tag of the Celtic Tiger.

In 1989 Haughey, after only two years in office, called a general election. He made the wrong judgment and listened to the wrong advisers. He and they thought that Fianna Fáil had seized the right moment to win the overall Dáil majority which had eluded them in 1987. Instead, although they took 45 per cent of the vote, the same as in 1987, they lost four Dáil seats and could not form a single-party government, even a minority government. They had to turn to the Pogressive Democrats, so recently their bitter enemies.

On the night of the count, when the results were becoming clear, I was in an RTÉ television studio, helping to analyse the returns for the viewers. Those in the studio could watch two monitors in addition to the set transmitting the programme. Haughey appeared on one of the monitors, O'Malley on another. The look of distaste on Haughey's face was marvellous. He may not have known at that stage how much more he would have to swallow in the near future. In the event, he swallowed almost everything.

The PDS had won only a handful of seats, but that was enough: they made up for the seats Fianna Fáil had lost. Mary Harney saw at once that the party had a unique chance. At her urging, they decided to reject any proposition for giving outside support to a Fianna Fáil minority government and to insist on membership of a coalition. For Fianna Fáil, this meant abandoning a 'core value', and many at all levels of the party baulked at it. Not so Haughey, who was willing to throw core values overboard in order to retain the captaincy of the ship. He appointed Albert Reynolds and Bertie Ahern to conduct negotiations with the PDs while he himself carried on parallel talks with O'Malley. When agreement was announced, Fianna Fáil cabinet ministers could scarcely conceal their disbelief. The Progressive Democrats got two seats in the cabinet, a junior ministry and large dollops out of the deep trough of patronage.

But if the unreconstructed elements in Fianna Fáil hated the deal, the business community loved it. It gave them something they always want, stable government. And they would soon learn that Fianna Fáil have little difficulty in accommodating themselves to their partners, of any colour. Three years later, they would take on board virtually the entire policy platform of their next junior partners, Labour—before the negotiations to form a coalition even began. In 2007, by contrast, they would give their new friends, the Greens, little or nothing by way of stated policy, but would hand them the two ministries of the greatest importance to them, Environment and Energy. Between 1989 and 1992 the captains of industry and finance were more than happy with a government that continued to maintain control of the public finances and had O'Malley as Minister for Industry and Commerce. At business dinners, I met life-long members of the establishment willing to state, with little or no prompting, their new-found political preference: 'Fianna Fáil–PDs'.

Large sections of the urban middle class did not go so far as to vote Fianna Fáil in the 1990 presidential election. They had an attractive alternative, which seemed to epitomise the spirit of the age. The Labour Party, led by Dick Spring, was enjoying a resurgence. Spring had an imposing team of advisers, among them Fergus Finlay, John Rogers and the future leader Ruairi Quinn. To oust Fianna Fáil from the presidency for the first time ever, they found a candidate in the celebrated civil liberties lawyer Mary Robinson. Nobody could have any doubt as to where she stood on the Liberal Agenda. She ran nominally as an independent, but she was heavily backed by Labour and Quinn was her election director.

She was greatly helped by the dire state of Fine Gael. Alan Dukes, still bruised by the adverse internal reaction to the Tallaght Strategy, promised a party conference 'a candidate of substance'. His audience raised the rafters with a chant of 'we want Garret!' But Garret FitzGerald had no desire to stand. He rejected the invitation, and so did Peter Barry. At last

Dukes found a candidate in Austin Currie, in former times one of the leaders of the Northern civil rights movement, now trying with very limited success to make a career in Dublin politics. Most voters in the Republic were unaware of his considerable talents, and unlike Robinson he had no special appeal to women voters. Indeed, prominent Fine Gael feminists openly deserted their party for the duration of the campaign and worked for Robinson. It was a calamity.

A worse calamity was to befall the Fianna Fáil candidate, Brian Lenihan. He was chosen with the grudging endorsement of his old friend Haughey. He had lately undergone a liver transplant in the United States, and although his doctors declared him fit for the stress of a campaign there were continuing doubts about his health. He was on strong medication which affected his memory.

The events that followed have been described in Emily O'Reilly's book *Candidate* and in my biography of Lenihan, but I think it worth elaborating on my own recollections and conclusions. During the campaign it emerged that a tape existed of an interview he had given to a research student called Jim Duffy. Under pressure from Fine Gael and from the *Irish Times*, Duffy released the tape to the newspaper. Ken Gray and another *Irish Times* executive, Eoin McVey, played it at a press conference in the Westbury Hotel in Dublin.

The subject was a sensational incident in 1982, when FitzGerald had lost office following what amounted to a vote of confidence in the Dáil. That night, several telephone calls were made to President Hillery with the object of persuading him to refuse FitzGerald a dissolution of the Dáil and allow Haughey to try to form a government and thus avoid the inconvenience of a general election.

It so happened that Hillery had lately met King Juan Carlos of Spain. The story goes that the king had told him about an infamous incident that had occurred in the Cortes in Madrid. A demented Civil Guard officer who wanted to overturn the democratic reforms had invaded the parliament chamber, fired shots and caused deputies to duck for cover. He then demanded a telephone on which to ring the king's private number. As Juan Carlos reached for the phone at the other end, an aide put his hand across and prevented him. Had he taken the call, the officer would have been able to claim (truthfully) that he had spoken to the king and (untruthfully) that he had found him sympathetic. It would hardly have provoked a constitutional crisis, but it could have done great damage to the king's important role in nurturing Spanish democracy.

Whatever the truth of this yarn, wherever Hillery learned that kings and presidents wait for someone else to pick up the phone, those who tried to speak to him that night in 1982 failed. The phone was answered by an aide de camp, Captain Oliver Barbour, who told the callers that the President was unavailable. He stood firm when Haughey threatened him, saying that he would ruin his career. Later, in an emotional passage in the Dáil, Haughey said that he would never insult an army officer. He had been accused of threats, not insults. More lurid stories soon circulated, such as that Haughey had himself driven to Áras an Uachtaráin but was turned back at the gates. Hillery reportedly was furious, both at the threats to Barbour and the impropriety of pressurising him to refuse the dissolution of the Dáil.

Who else tried to phone him that night, on Haughey's instructions? Certainly a front-bencher, Sylvester Barrett, who made two attempts, first alone, the second time accompanied by Lenihan. In an interview for my Lenihan biography, he denied that Lenihan had also telephoned Áras an Uachtaráin. Although I have described Barrett as a man of known veracity, I now think it more likely that he handed the phone to Lenihan and that Lenihan did speak to Barbour, though not of course to Hillery.

Lenihan in the Duffy interview said that he had indeed spoken to Hillery, who dismissed him angrily. That may have arisen from a tendency to embroider the facts, but it is at least equally probable that his recollection failed him. By the time the tape came into the public domain, he had forgotten that he ever met a student called Jim Duffy. He wanted to approach Hillery and ask him to state the facts. His campaign director, Bertie Ahern, vetoed this ridiculous idea. Lenihan then rushed to a TV studio and told the nation that according to his 'mature recollection' he had not made a phone call to President Hillery that night in 1982. His statement was laughed at, and his campaign was in tatters.

The PDS saw their chance to seize the high moral ground. They demanded that Haughey should force Lenihan to resign as Tánaiste and Defence Minister, and threatened to bring down the government if he did not comply. Haughey decided to abandon his old friend. But the resignation did not come as quickly and easily as he hoped, or at all. Frantic efforts were made by Haughey's people to contact Lenihan, while the Lenihan family closed ranks against the pressure. In Athlone Brian's sister Mary O'Rourke told an emissary, Pádraig Flynn, in colourful terms, to get back across the Shannon and into his Mayo homeland post haste. Other emissaries redoubled their efforts. Also in Athlone, a helicopter 'buzzed' the house in which Lenihan was staying, hovering outside the window of the bedroom he occupied with his wife Ann. Finally Lenihan returned to Dublin, accompanied by family members, and went to see Haughey at Kinsealy. There he was presented with a resignation statement which included a sentence to the effect that no pressure had been put on him. He refused to sign. Haughey went into Leinster House and obtained the sanction of the Fianna Fáil parliamentary party to act freely. He did not state his proposed action in so many words, but its nature was obvious. He then informed the Dáil that he had sacked Lenihan. Immediately afterwards Lenihan came into Leinster House. He was surrounded at once by sympathisers, many in tears.

Lenihan's was not the first head chopped off at the behest of the Progressive Democrats, and it would not be the last. A young deputy, Seán Power, asked Haughey what he would do when the PDS came looking for his own head. We would not have long to wait before we found out. When the next crisis came, Haughey would find his standing in his party undermined by this act of betrayal.

At least one of his closest associates, a man who worked with him for many years, thought that he could face down the Progressive Democrats' demand. 'He should have told the PDS to fuck off.' So he should.

Throughout the convulsions, the opinion polls went wild. After Duffygate, Lenihan's support dived. After his dismissal from the cabinet, it soared. When the votes were counted, Lenihan had Fianna Fáil's customary 45 per cent, Robinson 39 per cent. She was elected on Currie's transfers.

Long after, while discussing Duffygate with me, Sylvester Barrett said that 'the whole thing was a Fine Gael set-up.' Lenihan himself held the same opinion. He also believed that the *Irish Times* had given the Duffy tape to the nation's and the world's media in the Westbury Hotel in order to give the story the widest possible circulation. I challenged this view in an article in the *Irish Independent* in which I said that the *Irish Times* should have held on to its 'magnificent scoop', published it as an exclusive story, and the world-wide coverage would have followed; I attributed the Westbury incident to cold feet; and I asked for an explanation and an apology. In 2008 my criticisms were reprinted at some length in Dermot James's history of the *Irish Times*. By then, Conor Brady in *Up With The Times* had more or less accepted the version of events given by myself and Emily O'Reilly. He did not explain why the decision was made to hold the Westbury press conference.

Fine Gael's tactics in the affair have attracted surprisingly little comment over the years. To me, they remain mysterious. If, to quote Sylvester Barrett again, 'the whole thing was a Fine Gael set-up', what did they hope to gain? They knew that their candidate stood no chance. If they succeeded in damaging Lenihan, they would simply throw the election to Robinson.

Lenihan gave his own lively account in *For The Record*, written at speed and launched, to the applause of a huge throng of the great and not-too-good, in the Berkeley Court Hotel. Late in the evening I was drinking with a knot of people who included Derek Dunne, a fine freelance journalist whose talents were sadly lost to us when he died very young. I told a story about an eminent colleague preparing to go out and vote on the day of the presidential election. As he was putting his coat on, his wife asked: 'Who are you going to vote for?'

'Brian Lenihan.'

'You mean to say you're going to vote for Brian Lenihan although he lied to the Irish people!'

Dunne said: 'I voted for Brian Lenihan BECAUSE he lied to the Irish people.'

Only joking. Maybe.

———

Haughey's crisis came to a head at the turn of the year 1991–92, when he sacked Albert Reynolds and Pádraig Flynn from his cabinet for withholding their support from him and when Seán Doherty decided that the time had come for him to deploy his 'two buckets'.

Doherty appeared on a television programme called *Nighthawks*, a mixture of satire and entertainment, and dropped strong hints. He cannot have intended to let the matter rest there. The public reacted mostly with hilarity, the government with alarm. He then called a press conference at which he said that Haughey had known all along about the telephone tapping. Haughey called his own press conference and gave an impressive performance at which he said that Doherty was a self-confessed liar: he had given conflicting versions of events. This was not enough for the PDS. Nothing short of Haughey's resignation would satisfy them. Seán Power's question about chopping off heads had been answered.

From time to time, rumours have surfaced, abated, and surfaced again to the effect that Doherty or other persons had documentary evidence of Haughey's involvement in even more scandalous dealings. No evidence to support the specific allegations has ever become public, although Haughey's finances have been closely investigated by two judicial tribunals.

Haughey resigned with great aplomb, quoting Shakespeare and Yeats and claiming, like Othello, that he had 'done the state some service'. Privately, he still had an item of the first importance on his agenda. He wanted to deny the premiership to the hated Reynolds and hand it to Bertie Ahern, who came under ferocious pressure from Kinsealy to declare himself a candidate. But Ahern was doubly preoccupied. He had lately succeeded Reynolds as Finance Minister and was preparing his first budget. Besides, his marriage had broken down and he was living in a flat above his constituency office in Drumcondra. One of Reynolds's chief supporters said that people liked to know where the Taoiseach slept at night. This was a gross intrusion into his private life, but Ahern himself would raise the issue again during the Bertiegate affair of 2006–08. Reynolds for his part believed at first that Ahern would support him, and privately called him his 'lieutenant'. When it became clear that the Finance Minister was wavering, one of Reynolds's supporters derided him as 'the rat in the anorak', a reference to his unusual sartorial style. The bitterness of these months, on top of the turmoil of the Haughey era, inflicted deep wounds which would not be healed until Ahern became Taoiseach in 1997 and united the party. Meanwhile, Reynolds enjoyed something close to a walkover in the leadership contest when Ahern decided against standing. The two candidates who opposed Reynolds got only a handful of votes between them.

But his victory was illusory. So far from setting about healing the divisions in Fianna Fáil, he worsened them by sacking eight cabinet ministers in the 'St Valentine's Week Massacre'. And his relations with the Progressive Democrats went from terrible to impossible. His own opinion of his government partners was expressed publicly, not by himself but by someone very close to him, a young deputy called Brian Cowen: 'If in doubt, leave them out.' Cowen, like Reynolds and like Haughey before he ditched the 'core value' of single-party government, still hoped for the overall Dáil majority which would never come.

One of the many judicial tribunals was sitting. This one, under Mr Justice Liam Hamilton, inquired into malpractice in the beef industry. Reynolds and O'Malley both gave evidence. Reynolds accused O'Malley of recklessness and of mendacity: a strange allegation against a man of O'Malley's known integrity. The PDS walked out of the coalition and a general election was held. The campaign has been described by Seán Duignan in *One Spin on the Merry-Go-Round*. It was a shambles from beginning to end, and towards the close Reynolds began to muse: 'Labour will drive a hard bargain.' Even then, he could not bring himself to envisage the scale of the defeat. Whereas Fianna Fáil fell to a record low, Labour, buoyed up by Mary Robinson's victory in the presidential election and the 'Spring Tide' on which their leader coasted, took a record 19 per cent and thirty-three Dáil seats.

Spring entered negotiations with John Bruton, who had replaced Alan Dukes as leader of Fine Gael. Their personal relations were poor, Spring's attitude to Bruton arrogant, and his demands excessive: he sought a rotating premiership. Nevertheless, they might have agreed to form a 'rainbow coalition' with Democratic Left although the three parties, and any bits and pieces they might find to support them, would have fallen just short of a Dáil majority—and although a strong objection prevailed within Fine Gael to an alliance with Democratic Left, a party which had descended from the 'Official' Sinn Féin and IRA. It has always been widely believed that Bruton shared this objection. Not so. He was willing to take Democratic Left into government, but his front bench vetoed it. It was a reasonable decision, not necessarily because they doubted the small party's newly acquired democratic credentials but because of the fear of instability consequent on the formation of a three-party coalition which would not have commanded a Dáil majority. (As chance would have it, two by-election victories would change the parliamentary landscape sufficiently to make a rainbow coalition an option for stable government in 1994.)

As Christmas 1992 approached, Reynolds watched keenly and waited for his chance. Fortune and timing favoured him. His adviser Dr Martin Mansergh prepared a document for negotiation with Labour: it was crammed with Labour policies. At this crucial time, Reynolds attended a European summit meeting in Edinburgh, at which he came away with a gift in EU funding for Ireland of a supposed IR£8 billion. Who could resist such temptations? Answer: quite a lot of people in the Labour Party, who harboured a deep distaste for Fianna Fáil. When decision time came, Spring called a meeting of his advisers. They split down the middle, and he cast the deciding vote himself, in favour of entering a coalition with Fianna Fáil.

Reynolds gave Labour baskets full of plums. He and Spring appointed several excellent ministers. They went to work with enthusiasm, helped by a system of 'programme managers'. Tellingly, all but one of the Fianna Fáil appointees were civil servants, whereas Labour chose advisers who came from different backgrounds. The Labour programme managers made it their business to ensure that their party's policies were implemented. This had the potential to be a very good government.

None of them knew just how lucky they were. During the interregnum at the turn of the year 1992–93 a currency crisis had shaken the Exchange Rate Mechanism (ERM), the precursor of the European single currency. We needed to devalue the Irish pound within the European Monetary System, but we could not act until we had a government. As soon as the Fianna Fáil–Labour coalition was formed, Bertie Ahern as Finance Minister devalued the currency. Along with the European funding, already granted or in train, it was one of the chief spurs that brought about the Celtic Tiger. Given a normal term of office, the Fianna Fáil–Labour coalition could campaign in the next election in the midst of unprecedented prosperity.

But there was a fatal flaw at the heart of the government. Just as no trust had existed between Reynolds and O'Malley, no trust existed between Reynolds and Spring. The cloud of the Beef Tribunal hung over this government as it had hung over the last. The tribunal's report was expected in the summer of 1994. Before its publication, a report appeared in a Sunday newspaper to the effect that Labour would judge the Taoiseach on the basis of the tribunal's findings. The source was obviously Fergus Finlay. Reynolds was furious. When the report arrived in his hands, he and a group of advisers searched for a passage that would appear to vindicate his actions years earlier as Minister for Industry and Commerce. When they found one, he instructed Duignan to release it to the media. Duignan pleaded with him to do nothing until he consulted Spring, but he insisted. The coalition did not split for several months more, on the proximate issue of a delay in acting on a warrant for the arrest of a paedophile priest, Brendan Smyth: an affair, as it turned out, of panic and confusion, not scandal or conspiracy. But the row over the Beef Tribunal report had already left the government dead in the water.

Ahern took over from Reynolds and began another set of negotiations, with the object of renewing the Fianna Fáil–Labour coalition. The talks had reached their final, tidying-up stages, and Ahern expected to become Taoiseach within twenty-four hours, when a story by Geraldine Kennedy appeared in the *Irish Times* which gave further damaging details of the Brendan Smyth affair. Spring broke off the negotiations and entered talks with Bruton. This time, the prospect of office worked wonders for the Bruton–Spring relationship and brought their negotiations to a rapid and successful conclusion.

Once again, we had a pretty good government. But if there had been a fatal flaw in the last coalition, there were two in this one.

When the electorate in general, and especially the business community, saw the endlessly increasing prosperity and the record growth rates, they wanted a bigger share. Specifically, they wanted cuts in taxation, above all cuts in income tax. Afterwards, the Finance Minister, Ruairi Quinn—the first Labour minister to hold the job—said that he might have been 'too conservative'. To my way of thinking, conservatism is a virtue, not a fault, in a finance minister in the middle of a boom. But Fianna Fáil would not have hesitated to distribute all the goodies available, and more besides.

Secondly, and crucially, the middle-class electors who had voted for Mary Robinson in 1990 and Dick Spring in 1992 had always deplored Spring's decision to ally himself with Albert Reynolds, and they did not forgive him when he changed sides. As the popular expression had it, 'they waited for him in the long grass.' When the rainbow coalition went to the country in the 1997 general election, the voters took their revenge. Labour's vote, and share of Dáil seats, nearly halved. Spring resigned the party leadership and was replaced by Ruairi Quinn. Bertie Ahern barely improved on the dismal Reynolds performance of 1992, but he was able to form a Fianna Fáil–PD minority government with the support of a few independent deputies.

| 1997: PAYBACK TIME

On the day before the 1997 general election, the *Irish Independent* carried a front-page editorial calling on its readers to vote for Fianna Fáil and the Progressive Democrats and declaring that 'it's payback time': time for the electorate to enjoy, by way of tax cuts, the fruits of the boom. I wrote most of it. The phrase 'payback time' and the statement that Irish taxpayers had been 'bled white' over the years were Vinny Doyle's. A reference to restraint in public spending was urged by Brendan Keenan, but I would have needed no encouragement to make the argument on public spending.

Normally I would not discuss facts like these in print, but most of them have long been in the public domain and the phrase 'payback time' has been notorious ever since. There is nothing odd about my own role. As I have remarked above, the job of an editorial writer is not to express his or her own opinions but the opinions of the newspaper as instructed by the editor, as stylishly and convincingly as possible, and in the 'payback time' case there was a special reason why I should labour to make the editor's point. I had lately taken over as chief leader writer on the retirement of Seán Cantwell, and had made just one condition in my discussions with Doyle. I told him that I would take whatever line he pleased on any issue but one: he would have to find somebody else to express the paper's support for the broadcasting ban on Sinn Féin spokesmen because I thought it wrong that the paper should take that view while thundering for press freedom. I might as well not have bothered, because hardly were the words out of my mouth than the minister with responsibility for broadcasting, Michael D. Higgins, removed the ban. But I felt honour-bound as well as duty-bound to make the case as well as I could.

What prompted the *Irish Independent* to abandon its traditional loyalty to Fine Gael and come out so strongly in favour of Fianna Fáil? After his retirement, Doyle told me that Brendan Keenan had sent him a memorandum pointing out that we could afford tax cuts if the government restrained public spending. There was no very striking difference between the taxation policies on offer, but it seemed reasonable to suppose that we had a better chance of cuts in income tax rates from a Fianna Fáil–PD alliance than from a rainbow coalition composed of Fine Gael, Labour and Democratic Left (who would shortly amalgamate with Labour). In point of fact, Ruairi Quinn had been an outstanding finance minister. We did not know that under the Fianna Fáil–PD government spending would go out of control.

Other explanations have been mooted. The parent company had been angered by the failure of the Bruton government to assert the legal rights of a subsidiary company in respect of a television distribution system, undermined by campaigners who had set up their own illegal 'deflector' system. Talks between officials and the company's representatives were said to have been difficult and confrontational. A simpler theory was that Tony O'Reilly had made up his mind to commit his flagship newspaper to Fianna Fáil. Of course newspaper editors know what proprietors want, usually without being told, but I have no personal knowledge of any instance of proprietorial interference in the *Irish Independent*. My own contacts with O'Reilly were exclusively social, and chiefly as his guest at dinner parties.

Theories like these ignore the simplest explanation of all. One of the outstanding elements in Doyle's success—and one of the reasons why he kept the newspaper's traditional firm grip on a rapidly changing Middle Ireland—was his instinct for the readers' desires. It supported the abolition of university tuition fees. It campaigned for low mortgage interest rates. And it always liked cuts in income tax rates.

For three reasons, I doubt if the editorial changed voters' minds. First, people commonly make their decisions five days or so before an election. Secondly, newspapers influence their readers in many other ways besides leading articles, and the 1997 election was a good example. On the surface, Bertie Ahern fought a far better and livelier campaign than the outgoing Fine Gael Taoiseach, John Bruton. He appeared to enjoy unique popularity. His lightning tours of shopping centres, his evident amiability, the hugs and kisses from female admirers, were reflected in the television clips and the colour pieces in the newspapers. Thirdly, he profited from the collapse in the Labour vote prompted by the anger of middle-class voters who had supported Robinson in 1990 and Spring in 1992 and who had been shocked by Spring's decision to enter government with Fianna Fáil.

Nevertheless, many people persist in believing that Payback Time was a major factor, indeed the biggest factor, in Ahern's victory. One Fine Gael deputy told me he had no doubt whatever that it changed everything.

The *Irish Independent* went on to advocate the Fianna Fáil–PD option again in 2002 and 2007—much less enthusiastically on the final occasion, when the PDS tore themselves apart on the issue of Bertiegate during the election campaign. At the polls they were all but wiped out, falling to their lowest Dáil representation ever, two seats. Although Mary Harney continued to sit in the Dáil as an independent deputy, and retained her Health portfolio in the new Fianna Fáil–Green coalition, they voted themselves out of existence as a party.

———

For several years, while working for the *Independent*, I also wrote political columns for Andrew Whittaker in *Irish Business* and for Dan White, John McGee and Vincent Wall in *Business and Finance* magazine. White and Wall had both been classmates of Rachel at her journalism school. I enjoyed the work enormously because it gave me the freedom to make experiments in style denied to editorial writers. One piece for Whittaker was in the style of a Molly Bloom soliloquy, one for White a parody of a Shakespeare play. They did not always please the businessmen who read those magazines (one of my friends took great exception to my criticisms of the Dublin Chamber of Commerce) but I discovered that I had a surprising fan in Bertie Ahern, who had my columns sent up to him every week along with his official papers. They also impressed the panel of judges for the European journalism awards, who gave me three prizes for my work for *Business and Finance* and the *Irish Independent*.

I was unable to take part in the competition for the national media awards, since I was one of the judges myself. The chairman was my dear friend Michael Mills, former Ombudsman and onetime *Irish Press* political correspondent. I had the honour of speaking at his funeral in April 2008. He died one day after P.J. Hillery, whom he admired fervently for the way he upheld the constitution and the stability of the political system in times of turbulence.

The members of both panels liked fine writing, campaigning journalism, and articles bearing the marks of much thought and research. Quite right, but nothing beats a good old-fashioned scoop. One such was a story by Sam Smyth in the *Sunday Independent*. It concerned a house extension for the Communications Minister in the rainbow coalition, Michael Lowry, paid for by Ben Dunne, then the head of the giant Dunnes stores retail chain. It was the first in a series of astounding disclosures which culminated in the revelation that Charles J. Haughey had received regular donations, amounting to many millions, from a group of businessmen. We gave Smyth the top prize that year.

Ever since, most of the investigative journalism carried out in Ireland has been crime-related or tribunal-related. Much of it is first-class, but I worry about it. The tribunals inquire into scandals of the past, often the relatively distant past. We learn too little about the scandals that occur in our own time—and continue every day, and have grown worse, to the point where they have come to threaten the country's economic independence and political stability. The media, like the law, are slow to catch up with the culprits—if they ever catch up—and in Ireland and everywhere else they seldom dig far below the surface.

Ireland is the second most litigious country in the world after the United States. And unlike the Americans, we labour under special handicaps in the laws relating to libel and contempt of court. Ludicrous sums are awarded in damages to plaintiffs in libel actions. Media organisations are obliged to retain expensive lawyers 'on call' to advise them. If they dare to go to court, they have to face the prejudices of jurors. I have attended the High Court in Dublin only twice in my life, once as a witness for the *Irish Times*, once for the *Irish Independent*. I was not called to give evidence on either occasion. I recall vividly the first case, in which a destitute plaintiff sued the *Irish Times*. The facts were not at issue. The paper had made an innocent mistake (for which it apologised, but under our batty laws the apology did not count) and would have to pay damages. It intrigued me to observe the way the jury hung on the words of the plaintiff's counsel and so obviously contrasted his client's poverty with the supposed vast wealth of the *Irish Times* executives sitting in the court. In a case involving the Independent group, jurors may reflect that Tony O'Reilly is a very rich man and can afford to pay any damages they may choose to award, and may forget that they are there to decide the merits of the case regardless of the litigants' means.

But there is a bigger obstacle in the way of deep investigative journalism, especially any attempt to expose the practices which have shaken the banking and construction sectors. It costs a lot of money to employ teams of reporters to dig into a story, perhaps for months on end, with no guarantee of results, and few newspapers can afford it. I have seen news editors, in desperation to cover the news of the day, pulling reporters off investigations and reassigning them to current markings.

To do them justice, Irish daily newspapers carry lengthy and informative articles on serious current issues, often deploying experts and/or campaigners to state both sides of an argument. And to do RTÉ justice, in recent times it has done excellent investigative work on both radio and television. None of this, nor the universal practice of employing specialist correspondents, nor yet the splendid tribunal-related work of some *Irish Times* reporters, compensates for the absence of special investigative teams.

The Independent and Examiner groups have to think of their shareholders. The Irish Times has no shareholders to worry about. And it has plenty of money—or did have until the domestic and global financial crisis struck in 2008.

But no Irish newspaper has, or could ever have, the resources required to give the full context of the news it reports or the opinions it expresses. We often hear that Irish decisions are made in Brussels, not Dublin. That understates the case. Decisions are made in Washington, New York, Beijing, Frankfurt, which may affect us more than any decision made within our own administration. With globalisation, the influence of small countries and even second-rank countries is inevitably limited, and so is the ability of their media to catch up with the deeper meaning of world events.

While I was struggling in vain to keep the *New Nation* afloat, the revolution of 1989–91 was under way in central and eastern Europe. Terence Brown urged me to find some way to report the events that began with the demolition of the Berlin Wall and culminated in the collapse of the Soviet Union. I had no means of complying.

The fall of communism was greeted by enthusiasts with proclamations of a 'new world order'. If what has happened since could be called a world order of any kind, it is worse than the old one. For a while it seemed that we would have to come to terms with a system based on one superpower, the United States, instead of two. The enthusiasts forgot that power politics, like nature, abhors a vacuum. A new superpower, China, struggled to be born. Beijing began to exert a colonial-type influence, mostly malign, in Africa. India joined the race to become an industrial giant, but India, like Japan, is effectively an ally of the United States. Two countries of immense geopolitical importance, Pakistan and Afghanistan, fell into a condition close to anarchy. The troubles of the Middle East grew more and more intractable, and were massively worsened by the declaration of war on the West by al-Q'aida in 2001 and the Iraq war which followed.

The Soviet collapse unleashed a crime plague of unexampled proportions in Europe. Trafficking in illegal drugs is one of the biggest industries in the world. Along with it go other criminal activities on a vast scale, often run by the same people, like trafficking in women and children for the purpose of prostitution. The profits made from growing opium poppies in Afghanistan are a trifle by comparison with the world-wide earnings from money laundering.

We are all far behind this deadly game—and even farther behind the semi-legitimate games played by intelligence services and by the military-industrial complex. Meanwhile, climate change threatens the very existence of the human race. Some in the West look on it with complacency, even view it as something potentially advantageous to a country like the United States, blessed by geography as in so many other ways. A race is under way to exploit the resources hidden under the melting polar icecap. It could lead to war, and so could the friction that will be inevitable once American and Chinese geopolitical interests collide.

In fairness to the leading Irish newspapers, they try to communicate to their readers that, as A.J. Liebling put it in the middle of the twentieth century, 'the world is one, and could be one less any minute.' Crucially, they understand the importance of our membership of the European Union and the urgency of preventing us from becoming second-class citizens in a 'two-speed Europe'. They urged their readers to vote for ratification of the Lisbon Treaty in June 2008 and gave them good reasons—though the *Irish Times* made a bad mistake by carrying an editorial which asked 'are we out of our minds?' when it appeared that the vote might be lost, as indeed it was. That was a gross error of tone.

The *Irish Times* and *Irish Independent* both covered the early stages of the Iraq conflict very well indeed, though in strikingly different ways. The *Irish Times*, like RTÉ, sent its own reporters. The *Independent* relied on the services supplied by major British newspapers. The *Irish Times* has been praised for giving 'an Irish perspective'. This is at best overblown. The *Independent* carried the reports of Robert Fisk—whom I have described as probably the best reporter in the world, and who has strong Irish connections. One can take this 'Irish perspective' stuff too far. In my opinion, the *Irish Times* made a mistake by describing Conor O'Clery as its 'Asia correspondent'. Asia is a big place. It makes better sense to call someone the China correspondent, but one journalist, no matter how good, could not dream of reporting with any authority on a country as vast, and as secretive, as China. Were I to have the job, I might have to follow the example of a London *Times* Paris correspondent of an earlier age, who would stick his head round the kitchen door and ask his French wife, '*qu'est-ce qu'on pense?*' (what are people thinking?). But I believe the residents of Beijing are less voluble than the Parisians.

To my way of thinking, Irish newspapers are more at fault for failing to examine the Celtic Tiger boom thoroughly and failing to put it sufficiently in context in two respects, the spectacular development of the economy and the political and administrative blunders which have diminished its benefits and contributed to the catastrophe of 2008.

From this criticism I exempt many excellent business and economic writers and the editors who have employed them. Authoritative coverage in this area began in the 1960s with the appointment of Nicholas Leonard as business editor of the *Irish Times*. It may have reached its zenith when the dashing young Matt Cooper took financial coverage to new heights in the *Irish Independent*. At present, the economic correspondent of the *Irish Independent*, Brendan Keenan, has a sensitive ear for politics as well as finance.

But in their general coverage of the boom the newspapers mainly went with the flow. They did too little to explain to their readers the origins of the Celtic Tiger or the fundamentals of the developments that have occurred since 1993, and they did not sufficiently challenge the mistaken consensus that Irish governments between 1993 and 2007 practised the right economic and fiscal policies, even when the crisis loomed.

Ireland ceased to be 'an agricultural country' long ago. The Lemass–Whitaker initiatives, education reforms, entry to the European Economic Community and the drive for foreign investment transformed the country. We attracted multinational companies by offering a favourable tax regime and a well-educated and highly-skilled workforce. With time, the skills levels grew higher and higher. We began to invest, albeit tentatively, in research and development, and we created a new breed of young hi-tech entrepreneurs. The latter took a bad hit in the 'dotcom meltdown' of the year 2000, but we will recover. Meanwhile we made magnificent progress in similar areas, like exports of financial and legal services. In time, and not much time, we will rely on these more than on industrial exports. And loudly as our farmers may protest at what happens in world trade talks, globalisation has been good for us. All told, a model of how to turn a backward country into a modern (post-modern?) economy in a generation or two.

But the progress here has not been accompanied by improvements in the political system or the administration. On the contrary, both have grown markedly and dangerously worse. Our parliament has almost no real means of holding a government to account. Inefficient and unaccountable quangoes proliferate at such a rate that the government itself cannot say how many there are. The health and transport systems are in chaos. At least one-third of our water supplies are polluted. The crazy decentralisation project has made a rational environmental or regional policy impossible—not that there was ever much hope of either.

Decentralisation was the brainchild of Charlie McCreevy, who announced the plan shortly before Bertie Ahern sent him to Brussels as a European commissioner: Ahern wanted him out of the way while he gave his government a 'softer face'. McCreevy was adored by the business community as a tax-cutter and is constantly lauded as our best finance minister ever. To call him the worst would be closer to the mark. He said he would spend money while he had it and not otherwise. He cut back only when we encountered a little local difficulty (it was a world-wide difficulty too) in 2000–2002. He cannot be blamed for the excessively low interest rates which have prevailed since we entered the European common currency, but he did not pursue fiscal policies which would have compensated to some extent. In the end, we found ourselves wrapped in a massive property and housing bubble, which like all bubbles has burst.

Yet the upheavals which have occurred in all the three main Dublin newspaper groups were directly related to economic developments in only one instance, and in that instance other factors were at play.

————

The Irish Press group collapsed in 1995. The circumstances are described in a first-class book by a former news editor, Ray Burke (not to be confused with the onetime foreign minister of the same name) and I will not dwell on them here. Enough to say that although the print unions should take a share of the blame, the core problem was bad management. At one time the *Evening Press* and *Sunday Press* had been market leaders in their fields, and to the very end the morning paper struggled to maintain standards. Editorially as well as commercially, its situation was hapless.

Half the country would never dream of buying it because of its support for Fianna Fáil, while Fianna Fáil for their part considered that it lacked enthusiasm for the party. But whatever anyone may think of the group, editorially or politically, the loss for Irish journalism was tragic.

The later upheavals in the *Irish Times* were almost equally sensational but obscure by comparison with the stark events on Burgh Quay. John Martin provides more information and explanation in his book than Dermot James in *From The Margins to The Centre*, but it remains unclear to me how the victims included T.B. McDowell as well as the other two top people in the organisation, Louis O'Neill and Conor Brady. It turned out that the terms of the trust had not, after all, made McDowell invulnerable.

These events coincided with, and were partly related to, the country's minor economic troubles in the period 2000–2002. Like the government, the company had spent money recklessly during the boom, and Brady's departure in 2002 was widely attributed to the massive editorial over-spending. But there had been enormous over-spending on the commercial side as well, and the proximate cause of the company's temporary financial troubles was the decision to pay a supposed IR£60 million to build the new printing works at Citywest out of reserves instead of borrowing the money in the normal way. Many thought Brady had been scapegoated, and I largely agree.

However, it is clear that in the editorial department enormous amounts of money were wasted. Seamus Martin in *Good Times and Bad* describes the proliferation of overpaid and redundant executives, mocked by other members of the staff as 'floor walkers', who supervised persons who themselves were employed to supervise, and a culture of management by committee instead of leadership.

Over the years, Brady had had difficulties with commercial executives and with McDowell. I do not know the details of the first, but the second is public knowledge. McDowell shocked Brady when he told him that he intended to give one of the top jobs in the company to his daughter Karen Erwin. It was immediately assumed, by Brady and it would seem by everybody else in the *Irish Times*, that this was meant as a preliminary to the ultimate transfer to her by her father of the exceptional power he himself wielded. The term 'the Protestant succession' came back into fashion. The theory was that McDowell, unable to prevent a Catholic from becoming editor, meant at least to ensure Protestant control—and family succession—in the boardroom. If so, the move failed. McDowell was deposed and given the title 'president for life', a powerless honour, and a new regime began. I cannot say whether there is any significance in the fact that Gageby never received any honours like this or like the title of 'editor emeritus' conferred on Brady.

The NUJ chapel saw their opportunity to demand transparency and an improved style of 'corporate governance' from the new regime. They got promises, but no transparency.

Their own tactics were not wise. They spent too much of their time trying to discover the terms of Brady's financial settlement. Had I been in his shoes, I would have considered it none of their business.

When Geraldine Kennedy was appointed editor, the journalists were divided on something else that in normal circumstances would have been none of their business. She insisted on getting the same terms on salary, pension and so forth as the chief executive, Maeve Donovan, reputedly worth about €500,000 a year. Her salary in 2007, not counting perks and pension rights, was €380,000. In my opinion that is far too much, but Maeve Donovan's remuneration was probably the going rate for the chief executive of a company the size of the *Irish Times* and Geraldine Kennedy was quite right to insist that she herself should not accept less. That would have made it appear that she occupied a lower place in the pecking order. Nobody could believe that she was motivated by greed. In the recent crisis-that-never-was she had suggested that 'maybe some of us should give up our company cars.' The *Irish Times* journalists who publicly objected to the size of her 'package' showed very poor judgment.

I took an intense interest in the procedures for the appointment. I feared a repetition of the chaos of 1986. I was delighted to find that my fears were groundless; so far as I could see, everything was done by the book. Moreover, the job went to the candidate I privately favoured; and the new Irish Times Trust is a decided improvement on the old one. It has members of a better quality, and it has no McDowell for a puppet master.

However, over the last few years I have come to wonder about the extent of the influence wielded by the chairman, Professor David McConnell, or any other member. Power in the *Irish Times*, as everywhere else, is chiefly in the hands of the executive directors. The system there has the advantage that it protects the company from a takeover bid. But that might not remain the case if the company found itself embroiled in a real financial crisis. And even under the reformed regime I doubt if there is sufficient protection for editorial independence. The hopes of the journalists for transparent corporate governance have not been fulfilled; and we still have not seen a complete and objective history of the newspaper. Dermot James's book is useful (and beautifully produced) but it sheds insufficient light on the Gageby-McDowell dynamic. By contrast, John Martin's *The Irish Times: Past and Present*, while undoubtedly much more challenging and informative, concentrates too much on a thesis derived in large part from one incident, and tells us little in the way of detail about the relationship between Gageby and McDowell.

His thesis, to put it in a nutshell, is that McDowell's influence lives on. Although he argues it well, I believe that it is a profoundly mistaken view. Gageby killed off the Anglo-Irish, or West British, or unionist—call it what you will—culture once and for all; and not only in relation to the Northern question. One thing that he, like Garret FitzGerald, understood was that our total participation in the European unity project would take us out of the shadow of British influence.

Nevertheless, there are a great many things that we still need to know, especially about the relationship between Gageby and McDowell but also the relationship between the trust and Gageby's successors. John Martin makes some interesting points about editorial independence. Are there any documents still extant which might enlighten us? Have any of the participants' families got papers stowed away in the attic? If so, I do not expect to live to read them. Indeed, I am not certain that they exist. The trust once commissioned Tony Gray to write a history of the *Irish Times*. Not only was the end-product suppressed, he was paid handsomely to destroy all the copies of the typescript. But for the sake of our children and grandchildren, I urge any who may possess papers of interest to make them public—and I commend the search for information to academics as well as journalists.

———

Meanwhile, the Irish Independent group stayed on the north side of the Liffey but moved from Abbey Street to Talbot Street. It continued to make enormous amounts of money, but from early in the twenty-first century it underwent its own upheavals.

Much of these was connected with, or prompted by, the decision of the *Daily Mail* to mount an onslaught on the Irish market. It began by launching an early-morning free sheet, *Metro*. Independent News and Media felt it had to respond by producing its own free sheet, *Herald* AM. Over the quality of these publications I will draw a decent veil of silence.

The issue here was not and is not quality but finance. The publishers of *Metro* and *Herald* AM will never make much money out of them. The advantage lies with the *Mail*, which appears to have bottomless resources.

That applies with greater force to the advent of the very much costlier (in terms of investment) and cheaper (in terms of cover price) *Irish Daily Mail*. Its proprietors seem to be willing to venture enormous sums of money, in the tens or scores of millions, to get a foothold in the market. Evidently they have taken Scotland as their model. There, they spent huge sums and ultimately succeeded.

But there is a big difference between the two markets. In Scotland two famous dailies, the *Scotsman* (Edinburgh) and the *Herald* (Glasgow), are struggling to maintain circulation. They do not compare with our two powerful brands, the *Irish Independent* and the *Irish Times*—to which may be added the *Examiner*, which, though not truly a national newspaper, maintains high standards and earns big profits. The war may last a very long time, but it has to ensue in a victory, or at worst a draw, for the Irish papers.

Of these, the *Mail*'s main target from the beginning was obviously the *Irish Independent*, like itself a middle-market publication. After the first year or two, however, it became clear that the *Independent* had suffered little and that the *Mail*'s Irish circulation of about 50,000 daily had been gained elsewhere. It was clear, too, that the *Mail* was having difficulty in trying to transport its 'ethos' across the Irish Sea.

The ethos is not easy to describe. In the first place, it consists of doing whatever the *Mail* does superbly well. The paper pays admirable attention to detail, from the serious news and features all the way down to the horoscopes. It has its finger on the pulse of its Middle England readership (which does not necessarily resemble a Middle Ireland readership as closely as it may think). The Sunday version carries articles of stupefying length on strangely old-fashioned themes, like the activities of wartime spies and the antics of aristocratic English settlers in Happy Valley in Kenya. These have no attraction for the likes of myself, but the *Mail* knows what its readers want.

Its politics is notoriously right-wing, and pervades the entire paper. A former editorial executive chuckled as he described to me some of the methods in which it is expressed and in which the staff are indoctrinated. He said that they leave the political bias out of the first paragraph of a news story and save it for the second or third paragraph. This, while entertaining, is not entirely accurate, as the following illustrates: On

21 May 2008 the lead headline read: DAY OF SHAME FOR THE HSE. The story began: 'On a disastrous day for the HSE, the Taoiseach was yesterday forced to apologise ...' Second paragraph: 'Brian Cowen's apology came as another family spoke of the agony' (caused by another health scandal). Third paragraph: 'And to cap the misery, the Impact trade union outlined details of a work-to-rule ...'

The scandals and troubles were all too real, but none of them came anywhere near the worst failings of the Health Service Executive. Nor did the handling of the story reach the venomous tone of the paper's campaign against Cowen's predecessor, Bertie Ahern, who had lately been forced out of office.

This campaign had long caused puzzlement among Irish journalists who watched with interest the political line taken by the *Mail*. Why would an English newspaper train its guns on an Irish government and Taoiseach? Others had taken the directly opposite line, especially Rupert Murdoch's News International, whose *Sunday Times* has scored a notable success with its Irish circulation. The Murdoch papers, and Murdoch himself, had 'cosied up' to Bertie Ahern and Fianna Fáil. As so often, the simplest explanation is probably the best: the *Mail* had seen its chance to flex its muscles in Ireland, and to drive a Taoiseach out of office would be a sensational *coup*. In the event, it deserved and got no credit, and it may have alienated Irish readers who might not like Bertie Ahern but have no liking for abusive journalism. It is my turn to chuckle when I picture to myself its puzzlement over the smooth manoeuvrings, by Ahern and key members of his cabinet, which preceded his departure.

Both the *Mail* and the Murdoch newspapers are vehemently anti-Europe. They campaigned against a Yes vote in the 2008 referendum on the Lisbon Treaty. It is impossible to tell whether they have influenced their Irish readers on this issue or whether the readers resent dictation from English newspapers.

With time, however, the *Mail* may become, like the *Sunday Times*, more sophisticated and more in tune with its Irish readership. The *Irish Independent* can never rest easy while it faces this formidable competitor in its own sector of the market.

Before the *Irish Daily Mail* arrived on the scene, the *Irish Independent* had already made a profound change. It followed the example of its London sister paper and produced a tabloid or 'compact' edition as well as a broadsheet edition. However, even after the compact version's sales exceeded those of the broadsheet by two to one, it did not follow the

London *Independent* to the extent of switching to the tabloid form exclusively. Producing, in effect, two papers every night caused acute production difficulties, but there are two arguments in favour of retaining the broadsheet version. First, our rural readers are conservative and might not take to the change. Secondly, there is some advantage in retaining the 'broadsheet' tag because it suggests quality. I have some doubts about both of these arguments. There are many middle-market and indeed upmarket tabloids, of which perhaps the most famous example is *Le Monde*. I also consider the design of the *Independent* compact version superior to that of the broadsheet. And tabloids are easier for the reader to handle.

After the move to Talbot Street, much of the sub-editing (along with much of the commercial operations) was 'outsourced' and my best friend on the paper, Michael Wolsey, took charge of the company which has since carried out most of the sub-editing. I had already said goodbye to another colleague whom I had come to admire. Vinny Doyle, long past retirement age, completed his two-decade reign by presiding over the change to the compact form. Unlike Douglas Gageby, he retained his grip on coverage and editorial policy to the end. Gerry O'Regan, the man who had first invited me to write for the paper, succeeded him.

At O'Regan's first editorial conference, he delivered what he called 'random rants' but which I have no doubt were carefully prepared. His chief message was that there would be no 'dumbing down'. Some thought this conflicted with another message, that he wanted to see no lead headlines referring to the 'debt-GNP ratio', but I saw no conflict: debt-GNP compares with my old bugbear EEC fish limits as a headline guaranteed to turn the readers off. *Phoenix* magazine thought that Brendan Keenan objected to the debt-GNP ban. Not so: Keenan, like myself, approved.

When O'Regan finished speaking, nobody offered any comments. He turned to me and said: 'Mr Downey, you're seldom short of an opinion and you told me before that you've seen a lot of "those fuckers" off. I suppose you meant Brady.' I remembered the conversation, but I assumed my most innocent expression and replied: 'Gerry, I don't know what you mean. All I can say is that I like the tabloid version.'

He proceeded to make radical staff changes, some overnight. We got a new news editor and a new back desk—and an almost entirely new political staff. We lost our correspondents in Belfast, London and Brussels. The political editor, Gene McKenna, left to work for Bertie Ahern. Miriam Lord, queen of colour writers, accepted a tempting offer from Geraldine Kennedy. I was sorry to see them go, and sorry to see the departure of other friends like Michael Hilliard, Gerry Mulligan and Bernard Purcell, who in London had been a good friend in bad times.

Earlier, I had sent O'Regan a note of congratulation on his appointment. In it, I said that I hoped he would wish to retain my services in some capacity, but if not, that too was perfectly all right with me. When we met, he said that he wanted me to carry on exactly as before. As it turned out, he would give me an even better deal, but of that, more in a moment.

Chapter 13 ❧

2003: ROUGH AND SMOOTH

In September 2003 I gave a party for a hundred guests in the Burlington Hotel to celebrate my half-century in journalism. The timing was slightly wrong in two respects, and entirely wrong in a third. My guests, who included Vinny Doyle and Geraldine Kennedy, mostly assumed that it coincided with my seventieth birthday and my retirement. In fact, the fifty years had already passed, my birthday had not yet arrived, and I had no intention of retiring.

I had planned a quiet affair, but my daughters vetoed that and insisted that there must be speeches. As the main speaker, they nominated my dear friend Dermot Gallagher, by then secretary general of the Department of Foreign Affairs. His speech dwelt at great length on my achievements; he did not mention his own, though these exceeded anything to the credit of other men from Leitrim. A few minutes later the former Fine Gael deputy from Longford, Louis Belton, took me aside and said: 'The third greatest Leitrim man is standing by the door.' He meant his colleague Gerry Reynolds, who might have been a cabinet minister if Fine Gael, contrary to their usual form, had succeeded in winning a general election. Sadly, Gerry Reynolds soon left politics; and Leitrim, more sadly still, was badly carved up in the next review of constituency boundaries with the result that it no longer has even one deputy, much less a minister.

Gerry Mulligan took the podium for long enough to say that Vinny Doyle was 'the best editor the *Irish Independent* ever had' and I was 'the best editor the *Irish Times* never had.' He then presented me with a caricature by Ken Lee, showing me surrounded by such impedimenta as a book on socialism, a Crystal Palace Football Club scarf, and a cricket bat. This last, I fear, may suggest more proficiency at the game than I had ever attained.

I did not know that the best was yet to come. I did know that I must suffer the losses inseparable from advancing age. Long before, I had lost invaluable friends like Donal Foley, Peter Froestrup and Stephen Hilliard, who left the *Irish Times* to become a Church of Ireland rector and was stabbed to death by an intruder in his rectory in Wicklow. Now the forest of deaths grew thicker.

At Mary Holland's funeral, I met some of the surviving founders of the SDLP: Gerry Fitt and Paddy Devlin had gone before. There were hugs. There may have been some tears. There were few words: there was little need for words. None of them needed to dwell on what they had gone through or how much veteran journalists like Mary Holland and myself had shared with them. The game they had played so bravely and nobly had started, not with the eruption of 1969 or the foundation of the party in 1970 but with the civil rights movement and the first shots fired in Malvern Street, off the Shankill Road, in 1966. A solemn thought, that the conflict had dominated all our adult lives. And another solemn thought, that the SDLP would end on the sidelines.

The Northern Ireland peace process had as its chief objective the bringing in of Sinn Féin and the IRA from the political cold and turning the 'republican movement' into a peaceful, constitutional organisation. Some such process had been inevitable for years, even decades. Since the 1970s it had been impossible to defeat the IRA, and after the H-Blocks crisis it had been impossible to marginalise them. At all times, even through the worst of the violence and despair, the British government had maintained some degree of contact with the IRA; and shortly before his resignation as Taoiseach Charles J. Haughey had opened secret communications with them. The story is too well known to need much elaboration here. Albert Reynolds built on Haughey's work, but did not have time to complete it. Simultaneously the Hume-Adams talks were held and became the subject of bitter controversy. Hume was denigrated as a lover of terrorists: outrageously, by people who must have known him as a lifelong worker for peace. At a more serious level, his role was deliberately played down because Reynolds and John Major were negotiating the outline of a settlement and they could not risk the perception that it had 'Adams's fingerprints' on it.

The Sinn Féin–IRA relationship with both governments deteriorated after Reynolds lost office in 1994 and John Bruton became the leader of the rainbow coalition government. The British played a stalling game, largely because Major's House of Commons majority was at constant risk. His party was hopelessly divided on the issue of Europe and he needed unionist votes in the division lobbies. There is no doubt that the strategy of delay was deliberate: two of his ministers boasted of it.

At home, the IRA hoped for the advent of a more compliant Taoiseach. Bruton's interest in the North did not match that of Reynolds or his successor Bertie Ahern. He once told a radio interviewer that he was tired of having to talk about the peace process. But in any case it is extremely doubtful that the breakthrough Reynolds had sought could have been achieved by any Taoiseach before 1997.

Not long into Bruton's premiership, one of his closest advisers told me that the chances of a permanent IRA ceasefire were at best 40 to 60. Soon his words were borne out in the grimmest manner, when a bomb at Canary Wharf in London killed two people and caused enormous damage. There have always been arguments about whether the IRA timed their terrorist moves to coincide with, and influence, political developments. I believe that in general terms that was not so—they did not have sufficient political sophistication or sure-footedness—but I also believe that the Canary Wharf atrocity was planned for a specific political purpose, though not the one frequently attributed to the IRA. Critics of the peace process have claimed that it was a warning of a renewed terrorist campaign in Britain and that the British government would bend every effort to prevent that. In reality, the IRA's ability to mount such a campaign was extremely limited, mainly due to improved police methods and a flood of useful information to the security services from within the IRA; in later years it would emerge that the organisation was riddled from top to bottom with MI5 agents. The atrocity was planned chiefly to demonstrate impatience with the slow pace of talks which would bring Sinn Féin into government in the North, and was aimed both at the British government and at Bruton—who, whether the IRA knew this or not, was himself frustrated with the way the Major government was dragging its feet. Major's ministers for their part were not motivated by any dislike of the content of the talks but by their dependence on unionist votes in the House of Commons, comparable to the situation of the Callaghan government two decades earlier.

When Ahern became Taoiseach, he effectively restarted the process in tandem with the new British Prime Minister, Tony Blair. He scored a massive success with the Good Friday Agreement of 1998. But it would take another nine years to make peace permanent, to persuade the IRA to decommission their armaments and support the reformed police force, and to bring on board the extreme unionists led by Paisley, whose demagoguery had contributed so much to the beginning of the Troubles but who had given me a hint of his long-term thinking a quarter of a century earlier on the terrace at Westminster. One after another, the Ulster Unionist Party leaders had tumbled and at long last Paisley, as forecast by Haughey so long before, towered over the scene. On the other side, Sinn Féin overtook the SDLP as the main nationalist party.

In 2007 an executive was formed with Paisley as First Minister and Martin McGuinness as Deputy First Minister. For years, the two governments had concentrated on the DUP and Sinn Féin to the virtual exclusion, and the distress, of the SDLP and the UUP. Seamus Mallon, former deputy leader of the SDLP, protested to Blair's close adviser (and author of one of the best books on the subject) Jonathan Powell. Powell replied with a question: 'Your point …?' It was politics in the raw. It was necessary. But it was not nice.

There were many casualties in addition to the three and a half thousand killed and the scores of thousands injured. Hume's reputation will recover—has to some extent already recovered. History, if not his own UUP, may look with some kindness on David Trimble, who was briefly First Minister but was destroyed by Sinn Féin's cunning and withholding of co-operation.

Trimble genuinely wanted peace and power-sharing, but he was an awkward partner, notorious for his red-faced rages, often over trifles. Almost nobody could handle him except Ahern, who had a virtually unique knack of putting him in a good mood—and even Ahern, according to Powell, once had to walk out of a room for fear he might hit Trimble. One day I found the UUP leader unusually jolly and sociable when he came to speak at a lunch given by the Association of European Journalists, of whose Irish section I was then the president. He had had a fruitful meeting with—of course—Bertie Ahern. On the way into the dining room, he was buttonholed by one of our members, Enzo Farinelli, who asked him for an interview afterwards with Vatican Radio. He graciously consented. I remarked: 'By the way, David, Enzo is a cousin of Gaetano Alibrandi.' To my amazement, Trimble had never heard of Alibrandi, who had been a long-serving and extremely controversial papal nuncio in Dublin.

At lunch, he was seated between me and Seosaimhín ní Bheaglaoigh, who like himself was knowledgable about music. As an ice-breaker, I asked him about an interview he had given, in which he refused to answer a question about Wagner, brusquely noting shortage of time. I said jokingly: 'That's the kind of thing people say who don't want to admit that they like

Wagner.' He was neither amused nor offended, but launched into a prolonged dissertation on his actual musical tastes, which featured composers I had never heard of and operas by Richard Strauss which are performed only once in fifty years or so. A pity that he did not know as much about our public affairs as he did about opera.

But he got his Nobel Peace Prize, jointly with Hume, for the right reasons, which had nothing to do with obscure operas. He too was essential to the process. However, the two men who deserve the most credit, apart from Hume, are unquestionably Ahern and Blair. Ahern displayed enormous fortitude in the face of years of setbacks, and an extraordinary capacity for working on his briefs in between frantic vote-getting tours of the country and exhausting foreign travel. No other British prime minister would ever have devoted so much time and commitment to Ireland as Blair did. I will never forgive him for Iraq, and I am severely critical of Ahern's premiership, but I cannot withhold praise for their work on Northern Ireland.

In addition, Ahern deserves credit for frustrating one of Sinn Féin's ruthlessly though often clumsily pursued ambitions, to share in government in both parts of Ireland. At the general election of 2007 they looked likely to double their Dáil representation and bid, if the configuration of parties favoured them, for a place in a coalition government. Fianna Fáil fought back to such effect that Sinn Féin did not win a single one of their target seats and, surprisingly, lost one they already held. One of the messages of the election was that the North was indeed 'another country', where the same political rules did not apply as in the Republic. But we knew that already. The dreams of Wolfe Tone and Thomas Davis—the dreams, for that matter, of twentieth-century politicians as distinct as John Redmond and Éamon de Valera—had faded. We had no wish to engage in an island-wide civil war of Catholic against Protestant. And we had been disgusted and alienated by the bombings, the shootings, the torture, the destruction, the lies. We wanted peace, but we also wanted the removal of the Northern incubus and we would not call it back to obscene life by giving Sinn Féin a significant part in our own politics.

———

Ahern had been a political operator since his schooldays. Others tolerate the grind of constituency work. He relished it. Even as Taoiseach he spent his spare hours knocking on doors, reminding voters of his existence between, as well as during, election campaigns. He cultivated an image of himself as a bonhomous 'man of the people', at bottom a simple soul, fond of a pint of Bass with his cronies, apt to get his finances and his private affairs in a tangle, and with the imperfect grasp of the English language which has given birth to so many Bertieisms, like his warning against 'upsetting the apple tart' and his claim, when the Celtic Tiger's roar had become a little muted, that 'the boom times are getting even boomer.' Even now it is impossible to say to what extent these were simply gaffes or part of his genius for using language to conceal instead of communicate. It is certain, however, that his outstanding characteristic was exceptional cunning, combined with an ability to note the fall of every sparrow in his constituency and his capacity for arduous work, on briefs and in negotiations. His officials, and his interlocutors, admired him for this; and that he could handle David Trimble testifies to his personal skills.

Early in his career, he hitched his wagon to Haughey's star and was invaluable to Haughey throughout the 'heaves' of the early eighties. Nevertheless, Reynolds spared him in the 'St Valentine's Week Massacre' and kept him on as Finance Minister. He retained this office through the interregnum of 1992–93 during the negotiations with Labour which followed the collapse of the Fianna Fáil–Progressive Democrat coalition and the failed talks between Fine Gael and Labour.

Throughout that autumn and early winter, the currency crisis which I have mentioned earlier had raged along with the political crisis. For Ireland, it could be solved only by devaluing the Irish pound within the ERM, but it was impossible to devalue until we had a new government in place. As soon as the Fianna Fáil–Labour coalition was formed, we devalued. It was precisely the spur the economy needed. Reynolds and Ahern therefore must have some part of the glory for acting as midwives to the Celtic Tiger. Not a particularly large part, however, for two reasons. The recovery had already started, though it had not yet been fully reflected in the statistics; and no Irish government would have had any choice but to devalue at the beginning of 1993. The resolution of the currency crisis was followed by a flood of cheap and easy credit which turned a modest recovery into an unbelievable boom.

After the resignation of Reynolds in November 1994, Ahern succeeded him smoothly as party leader. Not only was he the obvious choice, he was also reckoned the best to come to terms with Labour. He himself would have preferred a coalition with Labour to any other option, and when Spring forsook him and instead entered a partnership with Bruton he was, uncharacteristically, plunged into gloom. But he quickly pulled himself together and set about uniting his fractious party. After the 1997 general election he set out with typical fortitude to achieve what seemed an improbable ambition, to make a minority Fianna Fáil–PD coalition, dependent on the support of several independent deputies, last a full five-year Dáil term. He not only succeeded but repeated the exercise, albeit in more comfortable circumstances, between 2002 and 2007.

But what did he do with all his power and skill? The conventional wisdom holds (or held until 2008) that he ran a wonderful government and that he had in Charlie McCreevy a wonderful Finance Minister. I disagree.

Certainly the country prospered. For the first time ever, we had full employment. Immigration (on a huge scale, probably at least 200,000 in total) replaced emigration. Houses and office blocks grew like mushrooms. Irish tycoons invested billions abroad, and scores of thousands of humbler folk bought villas and apartments in sunnier countries. Sales of consumer goods soared. Expensive restaurants did a roaring trade. The two-house, two-car, two-holiday family became an aspiration frequently fulfilled.

At the same time, however, the public services grew worse instead of better. The two-tier health system is the most notorious example, but our spectacular failures in transport and, lately, in education are more ominous from the economic viewpoint. Public transport is in chaos. The motorway programme is still only half-completed. The government promised 'fourth-level education' to bring us to the next stage of our economic progress, which means replacing manufacturing industry with financial and legal services and repairing our backwardness in the most important element of all, innovation. It has not delivered.

The government's policies turned out to mean the waste of billions upon billions on ill-planned and largely unsupervised projects. This went hand in hand with the importation into Ireland of the daftest kind of American 'neo-conservative' theories, based on the proposition that all history could be overturned, the boom could go on for ever, and bank regulation was unnecessary. When that ludicrous proposition was belatedly disproved in 2007, the shock was intense and we were left in poor shape to face the harder times.

In his last budget before Ahern sent him into exile as a European

Commissioner, McCreevy announced a batty scheme for the decentralisation of whole government departments to various locations, some grotesquely unsuitable, around the country. The attempts to implement this manifestly unworkable plan have been almost a complete failure. That matters very little in itself, but it matters a great deal in its consequences, the undermining of public service morale and the prevention of any sensible regional policy. The ultimate cost, if it ever can be estimated, will amount to many billions and we will live with a deplorable legacy for a generation.

During all this time, various judicial tribunals inquired into several scandals, from institutional sex abuse to gross Garda misconduct in Donegal. The longest-running are the inquiries into planning corruption and into the financial affairs of Haughey and Michael Lowry.

In the course of its proceedings, the Mahon Tribunal inquired into an alleged payment to Ahern from a property developer. This led on to a broader trawl of Ahern's financial dealings, some of which turned out to have been highly unorthodox.

The hearings into these were held in private, but in September 2006 the *Irish Times* got hold of a leaked document and published its contents. It could have come from any one of a multitude of possible sources, since documents were circulated not only to the lawyers involved but to witnesses and potential witnesses.

From the journalistic viewpoint, Bertiegate One was a thundering scoop. From Geraldine Kennedy's personal viewpoint, it set the seal on a career which had already been marked by the publication of a story that had prevented the formation of one government and now a second which bade fair to bring down another. From the political viewpoint, it was undeniably a crisis: for Ahern, for Fianna Fáil, and in a special way for his coalition partners, the Progressive Democrats. Would the PDs insist that Ahern must go, as the previous generation of PDs had insisted that Haughey must go? If they did not, what had become of their high moral ground? If they did, would they be wiped out at the ensuing general election?

They engaged in ferocious internal conflict on the issue, and would repeat the exercise during Bertiegate Two in May 2007. Ahern called a general election almost at the last moment before his second term of office was due to expire. His decision coincided with a spate of stories about his finances, most of them based on his own appearances at the Mahon Tribunal to give evidence in public.

This time the bitter PD internal disputes immediately became public knowledge. The outcome was foreordained. They had a choice of evils. Whether or not they forsook the perilous moral high ground, they faced certain humiliation at the polls. They could not force Ahern's resignation. They could walk out of cabinet, but a party that breaks up a government in the course of a general election has no chance of success, little of survival; a party openly and fiercely divided at such a time is doomed both to failure and to humiliation. Whatever choice they made was certain to be the wrong one. In the event, they lost both the moral high ground and their political standing at the same time. On polling day, the Progressive Democrats were almost wiped out. Ahern formed a coalition supported by their two surviving deputies and the Greens and with outside support from a handful of independent deputies. The party leader, Michael McDowell, lost his Dáil seat.

During the first half of the election campaign, Ahern was visibly rattled and dejected and reluctant to speak to journalists. Among the Fianna Fáil activists, morale plunged. Workers at the party election headquarters in Dublin dubbed the building 'Meltdown Manor'. Then the Finance Minister, Brian Cowen, single-handedly turned it round by reminding the voters of the good times they had enjoyed under the Ahern regime and making them fearful of changing horses. Finally Ahern recovered and won the customary set-piece television debate with the Fine Gael leader, Enda Kenny.

But his days were numbered. In early 2008 he suffered blow after blow, many self-inflicted. His own evidence to the tribunal was confusing and contradictory, sometimes all but incomprehensible, but the worst blow of all was delivered, reluctantly, by another witness. He had said that none of his dealings were in sterling. A building society manager contradicted his statement. Then a former constituency secretary, Gráinne Carruth, was called. She confirmed that she had made lodgments in sterling for Ahern. She wept and murmured 'I want to go home', and Ahern brazenly blamed the tribunal for reminding her of the penalties risked by an untruthful witness. Few accepted his claim that she had been bullied. The general view was that she had been 'hung out to dry' by himself.

With very few exceptions, the Fianna Fáil infantry faced the anger and embarrassment in silence. But the time had come for the heavy cavalry to move. A small group of ministers conveyed to their leader the message he knew was inevitable. He resigned, but completed the 'lap of honour' due to him for his Northern triumph. He addressed the joint Houses of Congress in Washington and met Ian Paisley on the site of the Battle of the

Boyne. But men worship the rising, not the setting sun. As soon as Ahern placed his resignation in the hands of President Mary McAleese, he was history. Cowen took over the leadership without a contest.

Meanwhile, Geraldine Kennedy and the reporter who had written the sensational story, Colm Keena, were ordered by the High Court to disclose the source of their information. They refused to do so, and refused to hand over the document on which the story was based because scrutiny of it might have revealed its source.

They could not have handed it over even if they had so wished, because it no longer existed. The editor had ordered it to be destroyed.

Here she made, in my opinion, her only mistake. On first seeing it, she should have had it copied and then had it destroyed without waiting for an order to produce it. In all other respects she deserves praise for standing firmly by the principle which holds that a journalist must protect his or her sources even if that carries with it a risk of imprisonment.

I am surprised that she should not seem to have reflected on the dilemma of another editor, Peter Preston of the *Guardian*, who many years earlier had found himself in a similar situation. Faced with an order from a London court, he handed over a document leaked by a civil servant. An examination enabled the court to determine the source. The official, a young woman, went to prison. It would be unfair to blame Preston, who continued to agonise over the incident year after year. Had he defied the court, he would have risked not only imprisonment but fines on the paper so crushing that it might have gone out of business. As I have just said, my own solution to such a dilemma is the early destruction of the evidence. That of course may not save us from punishment if we know the source regardless of the documentary evidence and refuse to disclose it, but it can help us to uphold the principle of protecting our sources.

Journalists are not entitled to any exemptions from the laws that apply to all citizens and, much as I admire the liberalism of the United States system, I have doubts about the extent of the freedoms enjoyed, and often abused, by American journalists. I strongly approve of codes to prevent intrusions into privacy and similar malpractices. But although most of my work has taken me out of the streets and into the palaces of the mighty, I remain at heart an old-time 'foot-in-the-door' reporter who would do anything compatible with decency and legality for a scoop. If on rare occasions the best principles and practices of journalism bring us into (non-violent!) conflict with the law, we must stand by them and bear the consequences.

Towards the end of 2006, Gerry O'Regan invited me to write a weekly political column, to appear on the 'op-ed' page—the right-hand page opposite the one that carries the editorials. I would be under no constraint as to the subjects discussed or the opinions expressed. He insisted that it should start on the first Saturday in 2007.

I accepted his offer instantly. Short of editing a national newspaper, it is hard to think of anything more desirable for a journalist than occupying the most enviable slot in the top-selling paper on the best day of the week for readership.

In middle age, after my devastating *Irish Times* disappointment and my *New Nation* over-optimism, I had, largely thanks to Vinny Doyle, carved out a new career for myself. I hardly know whether to regard the weekly column as merely an extension of that or as yet another career, embarked upon in old age. At any rate, I have seldom relished anything so much in my life.

To be sure, old age is not all it's cracked up to be. When people talk about wisdom, they usually mean no more than sad experience, not to say resignation or fatalism. One learns too much, too late. I have spent a lifetime learning, not how much I know but how little I know, and most of what I do know is not very palatable. I have learned a lot about human nature, especially its worst aspects. I have lived in very comfortable times in very comfortable societies, but none of us can avoid knowing the sleeveens, the liars, the mean-minded, the bootlickers who swarm everywhere. None of us, in the television age, can avoid the daily sight of the horrors that afflict most of humanity. And no student of history and politics can ignore the lesson: that the powerful never learn the lessons, and that they carry on making the same stupid mistakes for the same stupid reasons—greed, folly and sheer love of cruelty—down the ages.

When I was young and foolish, I believed in peaceful revolution. I no longer believe in that. I believe in institutions, and I believe that institutions can be improved. The United States, a splendid model— flawed, but all institutions need constant reform—has survived George Bush. The European Union is even better. In my childhood I lived, unknowingly, in some of the worst times ever known to the human race, especially in Europe. In almost all my middle and later life, I have lived in very good times.

In the spring of 2007, I was very ill and underwent several operations.

Nurses in St Vincent's Hospital teased me, attributing my troubles to too much rich food and wine. The doctors encouraged me to continue working even while I was in hospital, and let me out to write about the general election campaign in between operations. But I managed only one little tour outside Dublin before pain and weakness forced me back into hospital again. This was to dear old Leitrim (no longer poor old Leitrim, since no county had benefited more from the Celtic Tiger boom). I interviewed the only North Leitrim candidate, Michael Comiskey of Fine Gael. He deserved to be elected. He was not. At the same time, South Leitrim lost its only deputy, John Ellis of Fianna Fáil.

But the new prosperity more than compensates for the lack of Dáil representation. I don't know how much of it will survive the collapse of the boom in 2008 with the world financial crisis and the crash of the Irish construction industry and property market, which has all but destroyed the banking system, but while it lasted I rejoiced to see the prosperity extending into every corner of the country. Regional disparities of wealth are remarkably low.

This, however, is not true of disparities of wealth measured by class and individuals. These have increased spectacularly, as have class distinctions and class consciousness. Perhaps that was inevitable in such a prolonged boom, and the same phenomenon is even more salient in the United States and other countries. But I fret about the growth of the underclass, whose children are excluded from the amenities, and above all from the opportunities, enjoyed by the rest of the population and whose communities are plagued by gang crime, drugs and suicide. I worry, too, about the ostentatious displays of great wealth all around us, and even more about the way that during the boom so many people took them as normal and indeed commendable.

And I am not entirely happy about the future of Irish journalism. In my time, most of us were no doubt under-educated, but we knew grammar, syntax, spelling and punctuation. We cared about facts and knew how to dig them out. What goes on in those journalism schools which turn out graduates who aspire to become instant stars but who write 'pair' for 'pear' and cannot punctuate a sentence of more than one clause? Once, they could rely on sub-editors to repair their deficiencies. In the age of text messages and Internet blogs, the standard of literacy among sub-editors too has taken a dive.

But I console myself with the reflection that before even my time Morrison Milne did not know the meaning of the word 'incommunicado'.

Some of the Irish journalism of the present reaches or excels the high points of the past. And for all the threats from the new technologies with which the Irish media have been too slow to come to terms, for all the fears for the survival of newspapers consequent on the economic and financial crash of 2008 and on the fearful threat from the Internet to revenues of the print media everywhere in the English-speaking world, for all the concern that someone like myself must feel for the growth in Northern or foreign ownership of Irish provincial papers and radio stations, for all the nastiness and stupidity of 'tabloid television', the three main newspaper groups, and RTÉ, stay afloat and can survive.

For myself, I have had a wonderful time. I have known the best things in life, love and literature and sunshine (and it is true that the best things in life are free, for anyone can be loved and anyone can borrow a book from a library and the sun will shine on our descendants as long as the human race refrains from destroying the only planet we've got). I have revelled in good music and good wine and good conversation and the love of my family. I have had marvellous friends and still have, though too many of them have gone, some full of years and honour, some before their time. I have been a close witness of great events and occasionally almost a participant—though not fully a participant, for the journalist who gains entry to the palace should always keep one foot in the street, figuratively speaking. If my climb to the very top of my profession was frustrated when I had stepped on to the second last rung, I have had unique opportunities to reach mass readerships and elite readerships, notably, but not only, through the *Irish Independent,* the *Irish Times,* and *Business and Finance* magazine. I hope I have given them some enlightenment. I am fairly sure I have given them some pleasure, though not as much pleasure as I have derived for myself.

Journalism should be fun. I have had a lot of fun.

INDEX